Getting Started in

FINDING A FINANCIAL ADVISOR

Books in the *Getting Started In* Series

Getting Started in

FINDING A FINANCIAL ADVISOR

Chuck Jaffe

WILEY

John Wiley & Sons, Inc.

Published by John Wiley & Sons, Inc., Hoboken, New Jersey.
Published simultaneously in Canada.

For general information on our other products and services or for technical support, please contact our Customer Care Department within the United States at (800) 762-2974, outside the United States at (317) 572-3993 or fax (317) 572-4002.

Wiley also publishes its books in a variety of electronic formats. Some content that appears in print may not be available in electronic books. For more information about Wiley products, visit our web site at www.wiley.com.

Library of Congress Cataloging-in-Publication Data:
Jaffe, Charles A.
  Getting started in finding a financial advisor / Charles A. Jaffe.
    p. cm. — (Getting started in series)
  Includes index.
  ISBN 978-0-470-53878-4 (pbk.)
  1. Financial planners. 2. Investment advisors. 3. Finance, Personal. 4. Financial planning industry.
  I. Title.
  HG179.5.J338 2010
  332.024—dc22

                                        2009049439

Printed in the United States of America

10 9 8 7 6 5 4 3 2 1

For my girls—Susan, Thomson, and Whitney—who inspire me every day, and for my biggest fans, Herb and Evelyn Jaffe.

Contents

Chapter 7

Chapter 8

Chapter 9

Chapter 10

Chapter 11

Chapter 12

Chapter 13

Chapter 14

Chapter 15

Acknowledgments

A s in any project of this nature, there are people whom it could not have been done without. My list is a bit different from the people behind those other projects.

The people "responsible" for this book are the kind of folks I hope you never encounter in your own lives. On the big-picture level, crooks like Bernie Madoff and Robert Allen Stanford made it abundantly clear that sometimes people who invite a money manager into their lives are actually inviting trouble.

Before those recent headlines, there was Brad Bleidt, a financial advisor who actually owned the radio station I worked for in 2003–2004, who it turned out was running a Ponzi scheme for the better part of 15 years. His saga got me thinking that a book like this might be necessary.

Because I was working for Brad's station—and refused to quote anyone affiliated with the station in my columns—I never did a background check on Brad and was as shocked as anyone when his horrible story came to light. In reporting on his downfall, it became clear to me that many of his customers might have known something was amiss if they had just been armed with a bit more protective information. You may never have heard of his investment fraud, but the people he stole from were every bit as devastated as the victims of a high-profile guy like Madoff.

Then there was Gregg Rennie, who was a major sponsor of the radio show I did in 2007–2008. Because I would periodically have him appear on-air with me, I did a complete background check on Gregg before ever working with him, looking into every form and figure I could find to make sure there was nothing amiss. He passed every test. A few months into the show, I knew that Gregg was facing some financial issues on some real estate investments; the stock and real estate markets were cratering and he mentioned his issues privately when telling me that he was going to scale back his involvement in the show.

What happened next, however, shocked me. The guy with the clean background and no signs of trouble—who talked the right talk and seemed to have his priorities in order—wound up facing Securities & Exchange Commission charges over selling fraudulent investments, stuff he allegedly just "made up." He was caught before his actions ever had the chance to grow into a full-blown Ponzi scheme, but the few people he hurt were every bit as devastated as anyone else losing money.

That experience convinced me it was time to write this book. I know it can't prevent someone from being in the wrong place when an advisor, like Gregg Rennie, goes bad, but it can help people sidestep most of the bad actors in the financial services industry.

I wish it hadn't taken those bad actors to motivate me to make this book happen; I'm not really thanking them, but I have to acknowledge that if it weren't for rogues, scoundrels, and idiots, I could have spent my time playing with my dog on the beach, rather than locked in my office trying to make my deadlines.

Speaking of deadlines, I need to thank Debra Englander and Kelly O'Connor at Wiley for being just a bit flexible with mine and for giving me the guidance necessary to get this done. Their focus and structure makes this book much more readable than anything I could have come up with on my own.

Years ago, I wrote my first book, also about choosing financial advisors. It was published by The MIT Press, and I need to acknowledge that those folks there helped to give me a good framework for this book, even while they were publishing a bad book themselves. I wish that book had been more focused and less fluffy. I probably should apologize to the people who read that book; this book—the structure, design, and content—is the book I really wished I had published first. I thank Wiley for knowing about the other effort, giving me a chance to get it right, and then helping me deliver up to my own expectations.

My colleagues at MarketWatch are always instrumental in my success, if only because they give me the flexibility to do my work there and take on projects like this one at the same time. I am blessed every day to work with editors like Dave Callaway, Steve Kerch, and Jonathan Burton; I am sure they will be pleased with this book, not because it has their names in it here or because they love the content, but because I'm more likely to submit my columns on time now that it's over with.

Over the months when this book was taking shape, my daughters Thomson and Whitney steadfastly refused my offers of money to come down into my office and just write random chapters or pieces of the book. Thomson said she'd only do it if she could write about unicorns—there is a reference to them somewhere in the book—and Whitney said she would only do it if she could mention playing lacrosse (there's no mention of that). Ultimately, they reminded me with a smile that I needed to get this done, if only so I could go back to having more time with them; they proved wise beyond their years.

Finally, none of this happens without my wife Susan. For years now, whenever I have included her in one of my columns, I have introduced her as "my wife Susan, the most patient and understanding woman in America." In fact, I do that in a few places in the book too. It's not hyperbole. Anybody who can put up with me for more than a quarter century—and who can put up with me while I go through the personal misery and torture of writing a book on top of everything else I do—comes close to sainthood. I am truly blessed.

Introduction

The safest way to double your money is to fold it over once and put it in your pocket.

—Kin Hubbard

There has never been a time when people needed more help with their finances, nor a time when they were more scared about hiring an advisor.

As the stock market was reaching the depths of its biggest downturn in our lifetimes, Bernie Madoff's $50 billion deception of rich, brilliant investors was coming to light. And while the world's largest investment fraud scheme captured the big headlines and the big investors, there were dozens of smaller schemes perpetrated on average folks by rogue brokers and financial planners.

Chances are good that you never heard about Earl Blondeau, the Raleigh, North Carolina, investment advisor who used his job to gain access to funds being held in trust for the benefit of a client, or of Dallas advisor Cliff Robertson, who not only duped investors of their life savings and tapped their bank accounts, but stole his clients' identities too. While the Madoff case caught the headlines, the smaller cases—and I picked those two at random from a file filled with hundreds of advisor arrests and guilty pleas from the last two years—were far more common and devastating.

Beyond the victims who were directly affected by these frauds, the damage included the public perception that hiring an advisor could, indeed, be asking for trouble more than finding a solution. While that kind of knee-jerk over-reaction is not rational, it's hard to overcome, especially during financial times when the market makes many of the best advisors look like they are unable to help.

Moreover, fear actually makes many consumers more susceptible to the bad guys. Not knowing whom to trust, they wind up at a cocktail party or on the sidelines of the soccer field chatting with someone who happens to be an advisor and thinking, "Providence has brought me someone I can trust, at just the right time in my life." Invariably, every bad guy was similarly trusted by

1

people who let those personal connections override the standard due diligence necessary to separate the quality advisors from the boobs, idiots, frauds, and charlatans.

This book will walk you through that process, and no advisor deserves to be working for you if he or she can't pass muster. It's a self-help book for finding people who can help you.

It's important to recognize two key facts when it comes to hiring financial advisors:

1. The vast majority of them are honest, scrupulous, trustworthy, hard-working folks with good intentions.
2. You can do almost all of these jobs yourself.

It's equally important to recognize the corollaries to those facts:

1. It doesn't help you that there are so many good advisors if you pick an incompetent, lazy, or crooked one.
2. You can butcher your finances as well or better than anyone else if you don't know what you're doing.

Think of financial advisors the same way you think of carpenters, plumbers, electricians, and auto mechanics. In each of those cases, you can do the job yourself—there are books and how-to articles, dedicated specialty magazines, and television shows dedicated to showing you the way—but you're better off hiring a pro if you lack the time, ability, know-how, and willingness to finish the task properly and without incident.

Having picked up this book, you are on the verge of making one of the biggest financial decisions of your life, one that will have more impact on your financial well-being than simply picking a good stock or mutual fund. That's precisely why it's important to go through this process the right way.

You don't need to read every page to find great advisors. Decide what you need from this book and use it to your advantage, whether you get the soup-to-nuts education on selecting advisors of every stripe, or use it as a guide for grilling the candidates, questioning their references, and doing background checks.

Either way, it should help quell your fears on both sides of the current fright-mare affecting consumers. It will help you decide if you need an advisor to get through these tough times and will then enable you to hire one who won't be in tomorrow's headlines.

Part 1

A Soup-to-Nuts Guide to Selecting Your Advisor

You Need Financial Help. Now What?

The only way not to think about money is to have a great deal of it.
—Edith Wharton

Most people know when they need help to solve one of life's problems. Oh, they might pull out a plunger when the toilet backs up, or pop the hood and look at the engine when the car breaks down, or take a store-bought remedy or cook up chicken soup to try to heal themselves, but if they lack the skill to make a quick fix, they're going to find someone to lend a hand.

And that makes sense with your plumbing or your car, because a bad repair job could damage or ruin one of your biggest assets. Likewise, your good health is irreplaceable.

Yet, when it comes to finances—which hopefully will be the biggest asset of your lifetime—people are skittish, scared, and reluctant to seek out help.

Talking about money is still one of the biggest taboos in modern society, so people learn their lessons from parents, friends, and co-workers, at the barber shop or on the sidelines of the kids' soccer games. They'll watch television shows or listen to radio hosts, read articles, and try to cook up a portfolio or an investment strategy with help from all of those sources. A 2009 study by Sun Life Financial showed that one third of Americans cited online or television news as a place where they turn for financial advice; that's nearly the same percentage of people who cited financial advisors.

But finances and money are not like food, where failure to follow a recipe or simply using bad ingredients can leave a bad taste in your mouth. You can throw out a bad dish and forget about it by the time your next meal arrives, but bad financial mistakes will be with you for years, possibly as long as the rest of your life.

In the end, there comes a point—typically when someone has amassed enough money that he can see the cost of mismanaging it—when most people acknowledge that they could use some help, the kind of insight that will make them comfortable that their biggest decisions will turn out right.

That's when one of two things happens: They jump on board with the first possible helper they find, or they put off looking for help, believing that it's easier to find a mythical creature like a unicorn than it is to find someone who is smart, savvy, and worth the cost of their advisory fees.

Either they believe that the easiest way to amass a small fortune is to start with a big one and let a financial planner, insurance agent, banker, or broker lose it down, or they don't believe anyone could turn their meager holdings into that small fortune.

Both sides are wrong, because the expectations are wrong.

Go back to the basic need for help, the necessary fix to the plumbing or car. You want things fixed and running right, safe and protected, so that you can live your everyday life without worrying about a messy problem or a personal catastrophe. You don't expect an auto mechanic to change your car from an American-made sedan into a Porsche or Lamborghini, you simply expect them to help you keep the car running properly so that you can reach your destination and make the journey to wherever you want to go.

That's precisely why you should hire financial advisors, to help you make the journey from where you are to where you want to go.

At the very least, over the course of a lifetime, you will need to manage investments, amass college and retirement savings, secure and work out loans, buy or sell property, insure that home and your other possessions, protect your family and home against catastrophic losses, develop a plan to pass your life's work to your heirs, and pay taxes on the whole thing.

Say hello to a broker or financial planner, banker, real estate agent, insurance agent, lawyer and/or estate planner, and a tax preparer or accountant.

Finding someone trustworthy who can do any or all of these jobs is not as hard as searching for a unicorn, but it's also not as easy as handing your money to the next person you meet who purports to know something. That's why you want to go about hiring financial advisors the right way, no matter which job they'll do for you.

I'm always amazed that people spend more time researching a new flat-screen television or home computer than they spend checking into the background of the person who will determine a big chunk of their financial future. Presumably, no one fears offending the television by asking tough questions about it, whereas they are uncomfortable asking personal, prying questions to people they don't know.

By reading this book, you are distinguishing yourself from that crowd and showing that you want to do the research and ask these types of questions. Good for you.

You're about to learn that hiring good advisors is not an impossible task. You'll be able to do a lot of research from home, on your computer, and the rest you can do by simply taking your time to get questions answered.

With that in mind, you should remember throughout the process of looking for advisors that you (and, hopefully your spouse or life partner) are the only person you trust implicitly to have your best interests at heart. Everyone else must earn your trust, starting from scratch; no one gets a pass, no matter how much you love or trust the person who gave you a recommendation. If they can't live up to the rigorous selection process described here, you either can't trust them or they don't deserve to work with your hard-earned money.

Start your search for any type of financial advisor by asking yourself a few simple questions.

Smart Investor Tip

If they can't live up to the rigorous selection process described here, you either can't trust them or they don't deserve to work with your hard-earned money.

What Kind of Assistance Do I Need?

Need is a critical factor in most of your other purchases, and it plays a direct role in your choice of advisors. If you just don't want to deal with the hassle of filing your tax return, but you are a basic two-income family with a plain-vanilla earnings picture, you have a lot of choices, but if you are an entrepreneur with head-of-household status, supporting children and parents and wanting to make sure you take advantage of all available tax credits, you'll need someone who has worked on cases like yours before.

The more advanced your needs, the more you will tilt your decision-making process to getting additional services and paying the full ticket price.

That's why you start the process with a needs assessment, a self-examination of what you are trying to accomplish, what type of advisor is best suited to help, and what you want in an advisory relationship from that service provider.

This is particularly important in financial services, in which so many products are "sold," rather than purchased based on the consumer's knowledge. No one wakes up one morning and says, "Today, I need to go to the grocery store, fill the tank with gas, and buy a variable life insurance policy." She *might* be thinking it's time to increase her coverage safety net and, perhaps, save some more, but it's the insurance advisor who pushes the policies. And because variable life policies are not right for everyone, it's only years later when the person wakes up and starts second-guessing her decisions.

The process is not that dissimilar from when a consumer buys some new technological gadget or doodad, and is pushed into all sorts of features that he doesn't really know about or need. You don't want to "pay up" to get features and abilities you don't need; that's a waste of money that ultimately will play into how satisfied you are with the advisor.

Knowing your needs and being able to explain them to an advisor will go a long way toward ensuring that you hire people who can remain good advisors for the rest of your lifetime.

The Ideal Advisor–Client Relationship

There are some advisors you date, and others you marry.

If what you need is a quick fix—you want to write a simple will, you are looking for a one-time portfolio review, you are selling your house and moving away, or you need to answer an unexpected notice from the Internal Revenue Service—you may want to engage an advisor on a one-time gig, getting the job done without much regard for the future.

But if you need help and can see yourself requiring assistance and hand-holding again in the future, then you should look for an advisor you can have the "ideal relationship" with. The ideal relationship between client and advisor ends under one of two circumstances: You die or he or she retires.

Being a serial employer of advisors—where you move from one to the next—is asking for trouble; it gives you more chances to encounter a rogue, and each new counselor may try to prove his or her worth by changing up what you did before, and a constantly changing strategy is the same as having no strategy for reaching your goals.

So while you might be looking for help because of something that is happening "right now" in your life, try to view potential advisors as someone you'd like to call on whenever you need help for the rest of your life.

What's It Going to Cost Me?

Price is always a key consideration. No one, no matter how wealthy, has the ability to say "cost is no object" when it comes to his or her financial affairs; that is how large fortunes unravel in lurid tales of greed, fraud, or ineptitude.

Just as you eyeball grocery prices before making a selection or get an estimate before hiring a contractor to do some home repairs, you need to ask financial counselors how they bill for their services. You may worry that they will burst into an "If you have to ask me, you can't afford me!" rage, but that hotheaded reaction would actually be a good thing, because it would let you know you're talking to the wrong advisor.

Smart financial advisors of all stripes are happy to explain their charges and justify the reasons behind their rates; it is up to you to decide if you want to pay the freight.

A price check also is important because fees and payment structures can vary tremendously from one advisor to the next. I have seen two financial planners in the same town, both providing similar sample plans and advice, charge rates that varied by hundreds of dollars per hour. The higher charges could go to pay for the fancier office, the years of experience, and the professional designations earned, or it might just be that one provider believes he can get away with charging more.

Smart Investor Tip
Smart financial advisors of all stripes are happy to explain their charges and justify the reasons behind their rates; it is up to you to decide if you want to pay the freight.

We'd all love to get free advice, but you may be hiring a planner or broker because the free "counsel" you have gotten from friends and loved ones has been worth every penny you have paid for it, and now you want a better grade of assistance. That said, seek out a price point and pricing structure that you feel good about, because that will encourage you to use the advisor's services regularly and build the relationship.

What Do I Get for My Money?

If you haven't worked with an advisor before, you don't truly know what to expect. Sure, you've seen financial planners and brokers on television shows, but you're doing your own reality program here. Even if you think you know what to expect from an advisor, learn about everything available.

One key place where consumers make a mistake is that they focus entirely on the bottom line, without recognizing that what matters with an advisor is the journey to reach that end point. Consumers focus in on "How much money have you made other clients by picking mutual funds?" rather than on "How do you determine what mutual funds are right for me?"

What most people want from a financial advisor—particularly financial planners and people who manage money—is "emotional discipline," the ability to put together a sensible plan and then stick with that program through thick and thin. The advisor doesn't just determine the strategy or pick the investments, she provides the hand-holding necessary to see the plan through tough economic and market times.

Smart Investor Tip

Your needs and desires must be a match for what the advisor is offering, or you'll never be satisfied.

Just as you would want a refrigerator salesman to explain the different ways the removable shelves can improve your life and allow you to decide whether it is worth paying for a second "crisper," so can you talk to a prospective financial advisor about what the relationship is going to be like and what you can expect. Will it be regular phone calls and the ability to chat without receiving a bill every time you need a consultation because you anticipate a major event in your life? Will the broker accept your calls whenever the market makes you nervous? Does the accountant or financial advisor offer a regular newsletter to customers, and is that publication merely a pass-along from a national office or does it reflect the advisor's feelings about the market, economy, law changes, investment strategies, and more? How much of your contact with the advisor will be person-to-person, and how much will be you getting blast-mail tweets because your counselor uses Twitter to soothe clients?

Your needs and desires must be a match for what the advisor is offering, or you'll never be satisfied.

Can One Size Fit All?

Bankers can sell you investments, many insurance agents do financial and estate planning, accountants and tax preparers offer investment advice, stockbrokers now offer planning services, and financial planners offer just about everything.

These hazy definitions and boundaries make it so that advisors frequently cross the line from one specialty to the next, hoping to sell you another product or to capture more of your assets under their management.

It's tempting to let an advisor cross the line into a different arena, because you already enjoy working with him, he understands your situation and has earned your trust. One-stop shopping is a convenience many people desire.

But a good accountant isn't necessarily an outstanding financial planner, or vice versa. Advanced credentials are no guarantee; the fact that a counselor studied for a certificate in another specialty does not make him good at that job, especially if it is no more than a sideline business. While it may be common practice for an advisor to wear two hats, it is malpractice if he can't do each job equally well.

Over your lifetime, you are building a team of financial advisors, and you don't want a team of "utility infielders," players who are qualified to fill many vacant positions, but not good enough to star at any one job.

Each job an advisor is going to do for you requires starting your search from scratch, asking new questions and determining whether you can be as happy with her counsel in the second area as you are in the job you first hired her for. You don't want to be her guinea pig. Without the same expert credentials as a full-time practitioner, you should stick to one advisor for each need.

And while consumers value convenience, think of the potential inconvenience, too. If the advisor fails in his second job on your team, you actually lose counsel in two areas, as your primary relationship is likely to be impaired when you fire him from his secondary role. Financial services is not a one-size-fits-all business; if an advisor's play to get a bigger role feels forced or the least bit uncomfortable, don't let it happen.

Can I Afford It?

You've already looked at the cost, but affordability is a different issue. Some of the priciest financial planners in the world charge thousands of dollars for the same services that their clients could get for 90 percent less.

There is financial assistance at virtually every price point, from ultra-discount to through-the-nose chic. On the low end, it might be free advice offered by a public agency such as the Internal Revenue Service or a consultation with your own mutual fund company or using their discounted advisory services; the upper end of the scale includes top planners, who charge hundreds of dollars just for an initial interview—regardless of whether you hire them to work for you—and money managers who take a big slice of the assets they run for you each year.

A lot of people who could not actually afford to work with upper-crust private money managers snuck and chiseled their way into becoming clients of convicted fraud Bernie Madoff. They were stretching their finances for something they could not afford—and lowering their defenses at the same time, because they could never get a personal consultation or meeting with Madoff—all because they assumed that a rich, wealthy advisor with a long record just had to be terrific and safe and worth the risk of putting all of their eggs in one basket. They might have been right, had they not selected a crook.

Smart Investor Tip

The Madoff case is proof that it is not enough to simply look at what you are being charged; you must see how it fits into your budget.

The Madoff case is proof that it is not enough to simply look at what you are being charged, you must see how it fits into your budget. If you want ongoing financial planning services but cannot afford a $300-an-hour planner, then you will have two shopping choices: Change your expectations about how often you actually work with this advisor or set your sights on a lower-priced advisor who can meet your quality expectations and still deliver the service you need.

The Right Time to Hire an Advisor

If you knew trouble was coming, you'd get out of the way or fix the problems long before they get out of hand. With your finances, it is best to assume that there is trouble ahead and to go for assistance that will help you avoid it.

If you wait until you have trouble before hiring an advisor, the process becomes much harder to do properly. You'll go with a gut feeling or forego background checks or simply lower your standards to get out of the pinch.

But there's a big difference between "waiting too long" and having real trouble. If the IRS is beating down your door demanding money, you need help right now. If you just inherited $1 million and want to put it to work securing your future, you can set it aside in an interest-bearing account and take your time finding the right advisor.

No one ever got to retirement age and said, "Shoot, I can't quit now because I missed a day [or week or month] in the market." Plenty of people have rushed into bad financial advisory relationships and arrived at retirement age years later to wonder where their money had gone.

It's best to hire advisors when you don't need them. If you can't do that, at least understand that most financial concerns are not so pressing that you should settle for an advisor without putting him or her through a full and thorough review.

Can I Do It Myself?

Financial planners like to compare what they do to doctors, as if managing money is somehow akin to brain surgery.

It's not.

For years, advisors have hated me for comparing them to plumbers and auto mechanics, but that's a much better comparison than a doctor. While you might be able to diagnose your own physical condition, you could not operate on yourself, no matter how many books and articles you read or courses you sit through.

But you can learn how to do auto repairs, fix plumbing, or make home improvements by reading books, watching television, and taking classes.

You can also learn how to manage your money and buy financial products on your own. You can even use software products or websites to help with your legal needs, your taxes, and more.

But this is a case where you need to "go strong or don't go at all." Being partially competent to help yourself means you are mostly incompetent; you will not get away without financial help forever, you will just put it off to a point where your own shortcomings become such a problem that you can't overlook them anymore. The problem for most people is that, by the time they reach that point, they have already hurt their finances and have probably done a lot more damage than could have been done by a mediocre advisor with complete training.

Just because you can do these things yourself doesn't mean you should. So if you need someone to fix your financial plumbing or to put a new engine into your investment portfolio to improve its get-up-and-go, take control of the process by finding the right person for the job and by recognizing that the right person might not be you.

Key Points

- If the issues that are pushing you to seek out assistance can't be fixed quickly by some single action, then you are looking for solutions that can last as long as your lifetime. If that's the case, you should be looking for an advisor you can trust for the rest of your life.

- Every job and every task done by every financial advisor of every stripe can be done on your own, without help. But "go strong or go get help." Admit that you know what you are doing, or that you haven't got a clue. The last thing you want is a half-hearted or half-baked effort, especially from yourself.

- The right time to start your search for an advisor is the minute you are certain you need help; the right time to hire an advisor is when you are certain he or she is the best person available to help you.

You Get What You Pay for, and Pay for What You Get

So far, I haven't heard of anybody who wants to stop living on account of the cost.

—Kin Hubbard

Nobody likes paying for something he believes he can do himself. Nobody likes paying for something if she can never be sure if she is getting her money's worth.

Nobody likes paying for something when he can't see exactly what the provider has done to earn so much.

And, thus, nobody likes paying for financial advice.

But unless you are sufficiently qualified and dedicated to do this yourself, you will have to pay someone to assist you in reaching your financial goals. I've heard plenty of people brag about how much money they save doing key financial chores on their own—and I am all in favor of getting things cheaply and paying no more than is necessary—but I have seldom heard those same people boast about the results.

Indeed, for most consumers, the ideal financial plan (or insurance, tax, or estate plan) has three qualities: It is cheap, easy, and successful. You can get all of those things in your financial relationships, but almost never more than two of them at any one time. And make no mistake about it, costs matter; investment returns are never guaranteed, but your laying out money to pay for help—no matter what return you actually get—is a foregone conclusion.

That being the case, costs—and the ways you pay—will always be a central issue in your relationship with an advisor.

There's nothing inherently wrong with paying for financial help— advisors of all stripes need to eat too—so long as you know what you are getting, how you are paying, and can be confident that those charges are reasonable for the services you are receiving.

If you are hoping I'd give you a dollar amount, forget it; it's just not that easy. Some advice is too costly, at any price. Somewhere between managing money on the cheap and paying through the nose lies the ideal payment structure for the average consumer. Moreover, the range of costs can be huge, depending on everything from an advisor's experience and credentials to the region where you live.

Smart Investor Tip

There's nothing inherently wrong with paying for financial help so long as you know what you are getting, how you are paying, and can be confident that those charges are reasonable for the service you are receiving.

There are several ways to pay for financial help. Bankers typically are not paid directly for their efforts but have their pay built into loans and other basic services. Bank advisors, however, may work on a commission basis if they are dispensing more sophisticated advice. Tax preparers, by comparison, work almost entirely on a fee-for-service basis, getting paid either for time spent preparing a return or by the form, by which each completed piece of paperwork is worth a set price.

Most real estate agents work entirely on commission, while brokers, financial planners, and insurance agents can be paid in several ways, from commissions to a fee based on a percentage of the money they manage for you, to a flat hourly fee. Some hybrid payment structures, such as "fee offset," combine flat payments with commissions.

And some fee structures are hidden, making it feel like you are getting the services of the advisor for free when, in fact, you are paying for his or her services through higher ongoing investment expenses, such as the heightened costs from owning C-class shares of a mutual fund or the insurance premiums that go largely to an advisor during the first few years of some policy contracts.

One way or the other, you are paying the freight here; that being the case, you must know how and what you are being charged. Many financial services customers are afraid to ask up front, because they fear the "If you have to ask, you can't afford me" attitude.

To heck with that: If the advisor isn't willing to discuss his compensation with you up front, the relationship is doomed before it starts, so fire away with your questions and listen closely to the answers. Remember, cost concerns are one of the key reasons why customers wind up disappointed by their advisor, so making sure it won't be a problem for you is critical to having a successful advisory relationship.

Don't Be Fooled by an Advisor's Minimum

One of the biggest misconceptions in the advisory world is that the counselors who work with big-money clients must be good. I can't tell you the number of people who have used an advisor's minimum asset requirements as a selling point, as in "He only works with clients who have a million dollars, so he must be good."

Ironically, these same people often feel honored that the advisor has waived the minimum for them, which actually proves that the advisor does not limit the practice only to top-dollar clients.

Account minimums—the smallest amount of assets a consumer needs to work with an advisor—are not so much a badge of honor or some type of accomplishment as they are a way of valuing time. There's not a great advisor alive today who started with a million-dollar minimum. In fact, top advisors will regale you with stories of hustling for clients and scraping along trying to get almost anyone interested, and how they have customers who joined them at the beginning of their practice who—like their practice itself—have grown from no assets to be wealthy over time.

Account minimums are actually about the advisor's available time. Say a good advisor can service 250 clients and truly provide the kind of service she thinks will benefit her customers. It takes nearly as much time to service a client with $50,000 or $100,000 as someone with $1 million, but they are making one-tenth or one-twentieth the asset-management fees or commissions.

Thus, there comes a point where it is only worth the advisor's time if his next client can be expected to deliver a certain minimum amount in fees. If he charges 1 percent of assets under management and he has a $250,000 account minimum, he is saying that he does not want to take on clients who will fail to generate at least $2,500 in revenues for the practice. The more successful the advisor becomes, the more valuable his or her time, the more the minimum rises.

High minimums are a misdirection play, getting you to take your eye off the ball, which is the advisor's ability to help you reach their financial goals. There are plenty of advisors with million-dollar or $5 million account requirements simply because they have been around for a long time, not because they are great stock pickers, money managers, or investment strategists.

What's more, if you are the smallest client of a big advisor, how can you expect to get the best that the counselor has to offer? It's a fair question; if you had a client whose business brings in $10,000 minimum per year (1 percent of a $1 million under management) and another who brings in $2,500, who do you think would command more attention?

That's why you shouldn't be impressed by an advisor's high-net-worth customers, nor should you feel blessed that someone is letting you into her exclusive club, even if you don't really have the assets to belong; that kind of thinking is precisely what swayed many people to let their guard down and give money to Bernie Madoff.

Remember, the next great advisor is out there looking for a client like you, and she will treasure your money and not treat it like an afterthought to her thriving practice.

Avoiding Sins of Commission

Many people go into their search for financial help convinced that the one thing they know for sure is that they do not ever want to pay commissions, where the advisor gets a cut of the action, because that encourages the broker (typically) to make moves that generate fees. As a result of that public backlash at commissions, the financial services industry has moved toward flat fees, which it pitches as a safe, conflict-free way to do business.

Wrong.

The most important thing to remember about paying for advice is: No matter the fee structure, there are potential conflicts of interest in virtually every type of advisory relationship.

While there is no question that commissions encourage an advisor to be a pushy salesman, the issue is right out in the open, easy for you to recognize and understand. If your advisor buys you a portfolio of mutual funds and earns a commission on the purchases, but comes to you a month later saying it's time for a change, selling one fund to buy a new one—a transaction that generates a fresh commission—your guard goes right up. After all, if the fund was worth buying a month ago, and you weren't timing the market, something strange or bad must have happened to justify the change so quickly. If you sense that the problem is less about the mutual funds and more that the guy has a car payment coming due, you'll quickly take steps to stop the problem.

Smart Investor Tip

No matter the fee structure, there are potential conflicts of interest in virtually every type of advisory relationship.

Investors worry about "churning," trades made more to generate commissions than for real strategic reasons, but the attention paid to the issue and the step-ups in disclosure requirements over the years have made churning a much less significant concern.

According to the latest statistics from the National Association of Securities Dealers, churning is a problem in roughly 2 percent of the complaints filed against advisors. By comparison, breach of fiduciary duty—where an advisor fails to put your best interests ahead of his own—is involved in roughly one of every four complaints. That problem can arise no matter how you pay an advisor (there's much more on fiduciary responsibility in Chapter 4).

How Advisors Are Paid

Let's examine the most common ways you will pay an advisor, and the plusses and minuses to each method of payment.

Method: Fee-Only Advice/Service

How it works: Your annual fee is a flat percentage of the money that the advisor is responsible for, typically somewhere between 0.75 and 1.25 percent. Many advisors use a sliding scale, so that the percentage drops as your assets grow, or the amount charged declines after certain breakpoints. The advisor is paid only by you; there are no commissions, either from you or from a third-party, for providing you with counsel.

Plusses: The advisor's interests are aligned with yours; if you get great results, so does she, because your success means a great pool of assets to charge that fee on. No sales charges; all of your money goes to work and the fee is earned over time.

Minuses: If you don't have much money to work with, you'll have a hard time finding fee-only advisors who want to take you on as a client. Most advisors want to get all of your available resources under management—which may entail selling investments you have now—rather than only handling some of your money. And critics say that a fee-only advisor can become disinterested over time, because he gets paid regardless of whether you act upon his advice.

Possible conflicts: The advisor's focus will be on getting assets in the door, and their advice may skew in that direction. Say you receive an inheritance and want to know if you should pay down the mortgage or invest the proceeds; the advisor's pay goes up if you invest the money and stays flat if you pay off the debt. There may also be times when the advisor makes moves not because he believes the portfolio needs to be changed, but because he knows it's frustrating to pay a fee to an advisor who is not "doing something."

A Conflict over "Nothing"

While paying a fee for assets under management does diminish conflicts of interest, it creates an interesting problem, where an advisor may sometimes make moves in order to justify his or her ongoing worth.

Say the advisor puts together a portfolio. It gives you roughly the return you expect, you go in for your annual review and the advisor says "change nothing." She collects her fee, and the next year the market is not so kind to your portfolio. Nothing horrible, mind you, but you're getting nervous come annual review time, when the advisor again tells you, "Don't change a thing." The third year, the advisor knows you are not particularly happy with the results; the market has been tough, and the portfolio has been in line with expectations, but you're frustrated.

Fearing that you may want to pull the plug on the whole thing if you hear another "Don't change a thing," the advisor advocates changes, not because they are the best long-term moves—in fact, studies show that changing a portfolio for the sake of making a change tends to do worse than going the buy-and-hold route—but because she needs to justify the fee.

It won't result in more fees for the advisor, but it's hard to say the advisor has your best interests at heart. Situations like this are why there is no such thing as conflict-free financial planning.

Method: Commission or Fee-Based Commission

How it works: You pay a fee—or your advisor gets a fee from a third party—on every move you make. In some cases, as with some mutual funds, you might only pay something that's labeled a "sales charge" when you buy or if you sell after a short holding period, but a payment to the advisor from the fund company is built into the investment structure, and you could be buying an investment that is more expensive for life in order to pay that fee. Likewise, with insurance agents, commissions frequently are buried in initial premium payments, so that it's not quite as clear as "make this investment, pay the advisor X percent off the top." Make no mistake about it, however, whether it is a front-end load, a back-end sales charge, surrender fees, or 12b-1 fees for mutual funds, it's a "commission" if you are paying extra, and the advisor gets that money, either directly from you or from the company managing the investment.

Plusses: Commission sales typically are available to all consumers, no matter how little money you have to work with. If what you want or need is someone to process your transactions, you can focus on paying the fee—possibly even negotiating it down—and getting the investment.

Minuses: Because the advisor only gets paid when you act on his advice, you may be getting a salesman more than a long-term advisor. The brokerage firms, for example, are filled with young bucks anxious to make their bones, but the rate at which these newbies wash out of the business is high. Even if the advisor sticks around, he only has an incentive to work with you when he senses a sale coming on. You may talk to an advisor today, come up with a decision on an investment or a portfolio to buy, and then may not be able to get much ongoing counsel if the seller doesn't sense that he can make another sale and capture another commission.

12b-1 Fee

Named for the regulation that allows it, a 12b-1 fee is a "sales and marketing fee" paid on top of the management fee of a mutual fund. In most cases, at least some of this fee acts like a "trailing commission," paying the advisor who sells the fund for his or her continuing efforts to keep your account open and in place. These fees add 0.25 to 1.0 percent to the cost of a fund and tend to be highest in cases where the fund is set up to avoid front- or back-end sales charges and make it feel like the customer is not paying for advice.

Possible conflicts: The basic problem here is that the advisor's best interest is served only when selling you something or getting you to make a move. The bulk of your financial life, you are holding and building, not buying. Moreover, many commissions are buried inside of financial products like insurance policies; the advisor will talk about the benefits to you of buying a certain financial product, without necessarily disclosing properly the way or the amount she gets paid. Finally, a commission salesperson may get an incentive or a heightened commission to sell products from specific companies, like the house mutual funds or issues that simply carry a bigger front-end sales charge; those higher payouts may unduly influence the advisor's thinking.

The Costs of Alphabet Soup for Mutual Funds

In mutual funds, share classes represent different ways of paying a financial advisor.

For Class A shares, think "all at once," because this is the traditional, up-front sales load. These days, that sales charge will take anywhere from 3 to 5.75 percent off the top of your investment.

For Class B shares, think "back-end costs," because the front-end load is gone, but you will pay a back-end fee if you sell the fund during the first few years. During the period when the surrender charge is in place—typically four to six years—you'll pay higher expenses than in an A share, with the difference basically being the compensation for your advisor. Once the back-end load phases out—it typically starts at 4 to 6 percent and drops by roughly one point per year—B shares typically convert into lower-cost A shares.

With Class C shares, think "costs, costs, and more costs." There is no load on the front or back end of your purchases, but the ongoing costs of holding the fund are higher forever. This is a good way to hold a fund for a short time, but it tends to be the most expensive over time. Sadly, many consumers miss that and are attracted to C shares—and pushed toward them by advisors—because it "feels" like there are no sales charges attached whatsoever.

While no one likes paying up-front sales charges, Class A shares are typically cheapest for a long-term shareholder and are the only ones with "breakpoints," discounts in the sales charge for investing more money. As you pass breakpoints—which can start at anywhere from $25,000 to $100,000 depending on the firm and the fund—an advisor who keeps selling you B shares is artificially inflating their payout.

Some fund firms have other share classes, often for retirement-plan investors or for their own payment plan with broker-dealers. Be sure you understand how it works and what it costs you.

Finally, many advisors put their clients in no-load funds, meaning shares with no sales charge whatsoever. Don't be fooled into thinking those advisors do not get their cut; they may not get paid directly from the fund company, but they're paid a percentage of the assets they manage for you.

Thus, if a financial planner charges 1 percent of assets under management and puts $10,000 of your money into Fund X, you may not be paying any direct sales charges for owning the fund, but the "true cost" of your fund ownership—the expenses of the fund plus any and all advisory fees, sales charges, and commissions—will be the fund's expense ratio *plus* the advisor's 1 percent. If the fund has an expense ratio equal to the average stock fund (1.4 percent), and its performance stays roughly flat, your true cost of ownership in the fund will be $240, the 1.4 percent of $10,000 that the fund takes to cover costs plus the $100 you paid the advisor to have that $10,000 under management.

Method: Flat Fee/Hourly Rate

How it works: You pay either a flat fee for service or an hourly wage based on the amount of time the advisor works with you or works on the services she provides you.

Plusses: You pay only for what you need, and you know upfront how your costs will be calculated and what they are likely to be.

Minuses: There are not many financial advisors who work on an hourly basis. Those that do typically give you the basics but let you implement the program itself; that's not good if you need help to turn an "action plan" into real action. The hourly fees are often jacked up—expressly because an advisor would prefer to have an ongoing relationship—so that the perceived cost benefit of paying this way disappears and paying a fee for assets under management becomes the most efficient means of getting advice.

Possible conflicts: There are plenty of ways to pile on the hours, and there are unnecessary costs that can be built into a flat fee. Overall, however, paying a flat fee or an hourly wage has the fewest potential conflicts of interest.

Method: Fee-Offset

How it works: The advisor accepts commissions and fees from third parties in addition to fees charged against your assets. When you make a move that generates a third-party commission, you get a rebate for some or all of the monies the advisor receives. Industry-wide, this arrangement is not all that common.

Plusses: Ideally, you get the best of both worlds here. You pay for unbiased advice—as in a fee-only arrangement—but if the move generates monies, your asset-management fee is reduced. It keeps the advisor interested in you both when she is selling you something and when she is simply giving you advice.

Minuses: The fees are sometimes a bit higher than in a fee-only arrangement, because the advisor may have costs—order processing, sales quotas, and more—as a result of working with those commission-generating third parties. Some advisors do not give the customer a 100 percent rebate on the commissions they receive.

Possible conflicts: If the advisor keeps some of the commissions, how can you be sure that the original advice was unbiased? You can't, and that removes much of the advantage you signed up for when you decided to go this route.

Key Points

- For most people, the way you pay sales charges and commissions is less important than how much you pay. If you pay 1 percent of assets under management, and it winds up costing more than a transaction-based fee, then perhaps you need to accept that a commission set-up is better suited for you.

- No matter how an advisor is compensated, there are always going to be potential conflicts of interest. Be aware of them, look for them, avoid them.

- Paying more than you have to for advice is bad, but so is paying anything for bad advice. A good advisor who helps you reach your goals will be worth what you pay him or her; a bad advisor is a bad advisor at any price and in any fee structure.

The Seven Big Mistakes People Make When Hiring Advisors

Learn from the mistakes of others; you can never live long enough to make them all yourself.

—John Luther

I have given countless talks over the last 15 years to groups of people interested in hiring financial advisors or working better with the helpers they have, and I typically poll my audience to learn about their experiences.

I ask that people who are working with an advisor—or who have had one they stopped using—raise their hands. Then I ask them to keep them up if they hired the first financial advisor they met with or if they hired someone recommended by family or friends. Virtually all hands stay up.

Next, I ask them to keep their hands up if they did a background check on the advisor—and talked to an independent reference—before they agreed to work together. I have never had a single hand stay in the air.

Plenty of people do everything wrong in the hiring process and still wind up happy with the outcome, but if you're reading this book, you want to avoid these common mistakes. If you do, your chances of living happily ever after—or at least until the advisor retires and you have to hire a replacement—are infinitely higher than if you skip these items and leave it up to fate to bring you someone you can work with.

Big Mistake 1: Interviewing Just One Candidate

In all of the speeches I have given, before thousands of investors, I have had less than two handfuls of people say they had actually done two or more interviews before hiring a financial planner. Everyone in my audiences except those few determined souls was an easy mark for a rogue or incompetent.

You have come to a point in your life where you know you need help. Emotionally, that makes you like a man dying of thirst, unable to tell a mirage from reality and willing to drink sand if he can be convinced it will quench his thirst.

The first advisor you meet could be a complete idiot, but almost certainly will sound great to you. That's because his spiel makes it sound like he can solve your problems, and you lack the know-how to tell if he can't and the comparison to any other advisor to establish how you truly feel about him. You have no clue if he is selling you a bill of goods, a one-size-fits-all plan that maximizes his take and minimizes your service, or if he truly is a cut above the other helpers in your area.

There are reasons why some investors lower their guard this way, not the least of which is that many financial planners, wealth advisors, and estate and tax counselors will charge a fee for the first meeting, even if it is meant to be a howdy-do. They're not giving away their time to meet you, although they will give you credit for that initial payment if you sign on as a customer.

Not wanting to lose their meeting fee—and feeling like the first guy seems qualified—the consumer becomes a customer in one fell swoop.

You can solve that problem by arranging interviews with several advisors and arranging to meet any who charge a meeting fee last, if at all.

Another reason why investors drop their guard and hire the first person they meet is that they got the advisor's name from a friend or relative whom they trust. That colors their judgment, because of the way they feel about the person making the referral, or the way they envision this advisor helping them live the lifestyle they see their friend or relative enjoying.

Unless you know that your friend or relation put the advisor through the kind of rigorous process espoused in this book, you're relying on someone who picked her helper badly, even if the outcome has been good. Moreover, if your neighbor is a doctor and you are a teacher, the financial advisor she works with may just not be right for you.

Years ago, a leading financial planner in Boston told me her life was so busy with books and her radio show that she had stopped taking on new clients, and that when people inquired about her services she gave them the names of two young "up-and-coming financial planners" in the area. Alas, she had never worked with these men, had done no background checks, and had simply picked them because they were "bright, energetic, and asked good questions at the [Certified Financial Planners] group meetings." I'm sure the people she referred to them took her word as gospel; four years later, one of those advisors was under indictment for fraud.

Smart Investor Tip

Unless you know that your friend or relation put the advisor through the kind of rigorous process espoused in this book, you're relying on someone who picked her helper badly, even if the outcome has been good.

Ideally, a consumer—especially someone who has never hired a financial counselor before—will interview at least three candidates before making any decision on who to work with, and at least one of those interviews will be with a candidate whose name came from an independent referral, like an industry association or a local trade group.

Put a "Control Group" into Your Search

Think of the hiring process like a science experiment. When you did those exercises in high school or college, you typically wanted to have a "control group" or a "control set" of data, an untreated subject that becomes your test benchmark.

For advisors, your control subject is an advisor who comes without the baggage of being your neighbor's advisor, the person who made arrangements for your parents, or someone who works with a co-worker.

Those advisors have the plus of working with someone you know and trust, but the negative of the emotional baggage that comes from what you know of your trusted friend. If your neighbor drives a Porsche or Jaguar, your sub-conscious will think that his advisor can lead you to the point where you can buy a sports car. Since people talk so little about their specific financial circumstances—maybe the money to buy that fancy car came from an inheritance—you can't truly judge how similar or different your finances are.

Removing the emotions from one advisor allows you to see everyone you interview more clearly.

Find control advisors by approaching the industry associations and trade groups, local organizations, or use the Yellow Pages, if necessary. Contact information for those groups is in the chapters on interviewing each individual type of advisor.

Big Mistake 2: No Background or Reference Check

"He's got a fancy office, drives a nice car, and has a lot of rich clients," is not a background check, it's a fitting description of almost every financial advisor charged with fraud in the United States over the last two decades.

Your retirement nest egg, college savings, and more are the biggest, most important assets you will ever accumulate and try to grow, and yet most people spend more time trying to figure out which vacuum cleaner or microwave oven is the best value for their money than they do trying to determine if an advisor is safe to work with.

Moreover, they rely on shallow logic as a reason to avoid a few phone calls or a search online. The advisor is on the radio, so he must be good. He's been quoted in the newspaper by that columnist I like, so he's qualified. He works with someone I know, and she has a nice house.

Now I'll let you in on a few secrets that may change your opinion of the advisors you see in the media.

For starters, most journalists will call anyone to be a source when they are on deadline. I'm a past president of the Society of American Business Editors and Writers, and I've long talked to my peers about the need to do background checks on sources. I have always been told there is no time, so that the reporter or columnist relies on the same people again and again because he thinks that person is "safe." To the best of my knowledge, I am the only personal finance journalist who does background checks on brokers and planners before quoting them.

I came to that habit the hard way. In 1994, when I joined the *Boston Globe* as personal finance columnist, I was given my predecessor's contact list;

getting what amounted to a copy of the man's Rolodex was a huge gift, because it gave me names and numbers of his local sources.

My editor noted that the last columnist relied very heavily on a few financial advisors, and that one woman was definitely his favorite. Sure enough, in time, I called her; she was articulate and funny and seemed smart, and I dropped a quote from her into my column. The day after it appeared, I got a call from a reader who was upset that I had quoted this advisor, because she had been through a horrible experience with her. The reader—who was still trying to recoup losses in investments she was told were "safe"—had lived with my predecessor's constant quoting of this woman, but was afraid I would now start quoting her regularly, when she was not deserving of the attention.

I followed up that phone call by doing a background check on the advisor and found a raft of complaints with the Massachusetts Securities Division, far too many problems to have a great opinion of the advisor. I never quoted that financial planner again; since then, I have always done a complete background check on advisors before I will let them act as an expert in my column.

The radio fallacy is another good one. Most of the financial advisors who are on the radio have paid for the time, meaning they bought their own show to use as a personal advertising vehicle. Oh, they may rent out some of that time to friends and associates, making the show easier to do and making it sound more legitimate, but they're doing an on-air marketing pitch. The information they give may be fine and dandy, but the radio station didn't vet their credentials or make sure they're solid advisors; it simply cashed their check and gave them access to the airwaves. (Perhaps this is why so many advisor/radio hosts make headlines for getting in trouble with the law; at the radio station that has been my off-and-on home since 2003, two prominent "personalities" have been indicted or convicted of fraud.)

Background checks can't protect you completely. In 2007, I ran an advisor named Gregg Rennie of Quincy, Massachusetts, through the full test and found everything on the up-and-up; Rennie was becoming a primary sponsor for my radio show, and I wanted to know if he was bad news. Alas, at some point over the next few months, Rennie's personal financial picture changed, and he wound up selling fraudulent investments, basically starting down the road of a Ponzi scheme in order to stay afloat himself, according to the Securities and Exchange Commission.

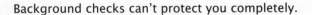

Smart Investor Tip

Background checks can't protect you completely.

No background check will help you if the advisor has a clean history but "goes bad" while you are a client, but most background checks will eliminate anyone who has previously been a bad actor, and many of the advisors behind the nation's most notorious financial frauds would have been found out by a simple phone call or Web check to the state securities administrator or insurance commissioner.

Contact information for the groups that can provide your background checks is included in the chapters on interviewing each type of advisor.

Big Mistake 3: Focusing the Search on Cost or Payment Style

Cost is an object, but it's not THE object.

The same goes for payment style, the various methods of working and compensating an advisor discussed in the last chapter.

Cheap advice is, well, cheaper, but not necessarily better, appropriate, or the elusive "right for you." If you save a few hundred dollars in fees to the advisor, but wind up with someone who is incompetent and whose decisions cost you thousands of dollars down the line, you did not get a bargain. Likewise, if you go for more expensive counsel but can't get the quality of service you desire, you'll be unhappy no matter how respected the advisor and how sound his advice.

You need to look at what you are getting for your money and determine a reasonable balance between services, costs, and method of compensation.

If all you are looking to do is add a mutual fund or two that you can throw some money into every month and hold for years, you shouldn't be paying a big fat fee for an overall asset-allocation plan. You can get the information you want yourself with a $19 piece of software, a $40 online research service, or maybe a free posting on an online bulletin board. But if you require a needs analysis and a plan of action to get you from where you are now to your financial goals, you don't necessarily want to make your lifetime decision based on "I hate paying commissions" or "This planner charges less by the hour."

Smart Investor Tip

Cost is an object, but it's not THE object.

What will be most important to your satisfaction long-term is how much you trust and respect the advisor, how comfortable you are taking her advice, how she communicates with you, and whether she can help you reach your goals. If she enables you to reach your financial goals comfortably, she is worth what you are paying her, in whatever fashion you compensate her.

By focusing in on costs and payment style as the primary selection criteria, you're taking your eye off the ball. Instead of finding that person who can give you the "emotional discipline" necessary to reach your goals, you've found the person who makes you feel like "I can afford this."

It's kind of like picking your next car on the basis of the mileage the car gets on the highway. That's an important factor, but you will find that comfort, style, ownership costs (especially charges related to repairs to keep your car rolling and moving forward), city gas mileage, and your driving habits will all combine to determine just how happy you are with the vehicle.

If your selection priorities for an advisor get out of order—and the cost or payment structure has become more important than competency and comfort—you are setting yourself up to a fall. It's not surprising that when customers who make this mistake come to their senses, they need to go out and find a "better" advisor.

Big Mistake 4: Expecting Professional Credentials and Designations to Make an Advisor "Good"

As you will see in Chapter 5, there are so many professional credentials and designations out there for financial advisors that you could drown in a sea of alphabet soup.

That said, every credential is different. Some are worthwhile, some are bogus. Within every credential, there are advisors who are good, and others who stink.

The real question about credentials boils down to "Does this advisor have the expertise I need?"

Credentials help to answer that, but, on their own, they say nothing about the individual's personality, manner, disposition, or ability to instill the "emotional discipline" this book talks about so much. Too often, a consumer decides he needs to work with a certified financial planner—or a certified public accountant on his taxes—and uses the credential as one more reason to hire the first person he interviews. The advisor has the right credential, so he must be right.

I will allow, for a moment, a comparison between financial advisors and doctors (because, if you read Chapter 1, you know I prefer to compare them to plumbers and auto mechanics), but only because it allows me to make a reference to the movie *Patch Adams,* a not-so-great Robin Williams flick based on a true story, in which Williams plays a doctor with great skills but even greater personality. Throughout the movie, the people who have the most say over his ability to become a doctor—who will bestow upon him the professional credential he needs to practice medicine—are trying to teach a system that makes someone technically proficient, but emotionally detached.

Ultimately, the most brilliant student at the school, a doctor named Mitch (played by Philip Seymour Hoffman) approaches Patch Adams for help, not because he believes Adams is a better doctor, but because the guy with the unique style knows all of the things about patient relationships and dealing with people that aren't being taught in the hospital or at the school.

Your search for advisors is about finding "the right person," not "the person with the right credential," and there is a big difference. In this case, you don't just want a skilled doctor, you want one with the right bedside manner.

I know plenty of Certified Financial Planners whose personal style is so strange, different, or off-putting that the only way I could work with them personally is if I was in a coma. They've got the credential, but they'd be the wrong fit for me (and I can say the same thing about people with virtually every credential out there).

Hire a person, not a credential; when times get tough, it's going to be the human being—and not the letters after her name—that you rely on.

Smart Investor Tip

Rogue advisors can throw a lot of letters after their name to make themselves look impressive; they only get caught when someone checks with the credentialing agency and finds out that they're a fraud. Don't repeat Big Mistake 2 and skip the background check on an advisor's credentials, especially if his or her designations and expertise are a factor in your decision. Make sure that the group that oversees the credential you care so much about has a record of your advisor, that there have been no problems, and that the advisor has done everything necessary to remain in good standing with the organization.

The professional designations database at www.finra.org includes definitions of each credential and typically has links that will allow you to check an advisor's status online.

Big Mistake 5: Setting Expectations and Viewing Results Based Entirely on Returns

People hire advisors because they need help and want to get their finances in order. They fire advisors because they don't earn a "big enough" return.

It's a recipe for disaster.

If you are an average investor, you're looking for a partner, someone who will help you develop strategies that enable you to reach your long-term goals. In most cases, achieving that success requires participating in stock market gains during good times without losing your shirt when the market sours. For most consumers, it's more about avoiding surprises and losses than it is about getting rich quick.

And yet, when push comes to shove, advisors get dumped because they "failed to beat the market" each and every year.

For starters, the best way to consistently beat the market on the short term is to make focused, concentrated bets that pay off handsomely when you are right . . . and then be right all the time. Of course, when you are wrong, those bets backfire big-time, which is precisely why advisors push diversification, asset allocation, and long-term thinking.

It's possible to reach your desired goals without every year being a banner year. Look at the mutual fund performance charts, for example, and you tend to find that the issues with the best long-term records are funds that are consistently above-average, without ever reaching the top—or falling to the bottom —of their peer group in any year.

That's what most people want from their advisor, the kind of long-term performance that allows them to ride the market rollercoaster and get off at the end with a big smile on their face.

Alas, too many financial-services customers want to jump off mid ride. Despite what they said when they signed up to work with an advisor, they want to change the criteria for judging their counselor mid-stream, typically at just the wrong moment.

The phenomenon is best illustrated by a story told to me by Roy Diliberto of RTD Financial Advisors in Philadelphia, a former president of the Financial Planning Association. Early in 2009, one of Diliberto's clients came into the office, unable to take it anymore. The market had been in a raging decline for months, and he wanted out. When Diliberto suggested that would be a mistake, the client explained that either Diliberto move him all to cash or lose the seven-figure account.

Mind you, the diversification Diliberto practiced had made the man's losses much *less* than the bloodletting that was happening on Wall Street. Every step the advisor had taken had protected the client; despite the downturn, the customer was in no jeopardy of falling short of any of the financial goals he had laid out when first hiring Diliberto.

Ultimately, Diliberto talked the client in off the ledge, a move that proved itself savvy in short order, as the market reached bottom in March 2009 and then started a strong recovery. Had the customer followed his own devices, he would have gotten out of the market at the worst possible time and would have fired Diliberto for "poor results" when the advisor had done precisely what he had been instructed to do from the get-go.

"Your financial planner can control many things, but the stock market isn't one of them," Diliberto said. "If he does the job, and you fire him because the market is bad or you think you can get a better result somewhere else, you're making a long-term decision based on a short-term feeling. If that guy had fired me, and then gone off to find someone else, he eventually would have fired that person for bad performance, too, because there will always be one more time when the market goes down and you go with it, or the market goes up and you don't feel like you got every possible dollar out of it."

Big Mistake 6: Letting the Advisor Control Everything

You may be looking for hired guns to help with your finances, but there is one key phrase to remember in all this: *"It's my money."*

Advisors are partners in your financial success, but you have the most at stake and, therefore, you run the show. With that in mind, you are entitled from the very beginning of the relationship to ask about anything you want, from why a recommendation was made to why something cost more than you expected.

You need to be treated like "the boss," too. Some advisors treat customers shabbily when the client doesn't take their advice or make a suggested move. That reaction is an instant warning sign that the advisor respects his position more than yours and may have put his interests first.

The fact that the advisor is "smarter" about financial matters—or that he specializes in this stuff, while you don't—is a non-starter. You're the one who lives with the consequences, good or bad, of implementing the suggested strategy.

Smart Investor Tip
You need to be treated like "the boss," too.

Try not to sign away control of your assets to anyone, except in the event that you are incapacitated. We've all heard stories of the sports legend or movie star who turned a large fortune into a small one by letting an agent or financial planner "handle the money." The Bernie Madoff case, of course, included numerous victims whose advisor had the discretion to manage their money, and who bet it all on Madoff; that's the kind of all-in strategy that should not be followed without your approval, and certainly not with an investment strategy that, like Madoff's, was so complicated on the surface—so as to bamboozle the public—that most advisors could not have explained it to customers.

Delegating authority is great; surrendering it isn't. You want advisors to believe they must do a reasonable job of representing your interests in order to keep you as a customer; advisors who know that decisions must be run by you—and that you are involved and actively review your interaction—are less likely to take actions that could jeopardize the relationship.

Remember, too, that you have a basic responsibility to know what's going on in your portfolio. Acknowledge your smarts and your shortcomings; make advisors talk to your level of sophistication and tell them when you have reservations and your gut tells you not to follow a suggestion. If an advisor does not respect those feelings and your judgment—if she treats your cash like it's *her* money—reconsider the relationship.

Big Mistake 7: Hiring Friends and Relatives

In the mid-1980s, my wife Susan—the most patient and understanding woman in America—was convinced by a friend that we needed some financial planning help. The friend just happened to be a new financial advisor, and she wanted to be the one to advise us, fresh out of college and newly married, as we started building our lives together.

I didn't think we needed help, but Susan sold me on the idea that Sandra, her friend, could help us find better financing options for our first new car. Sandra also could provide a second opinion to my judgment on mutual funds and asset allocation.

Best of all—and Sandra gave us this in writing—it was a money-back deal. If we weren't satisfied or Sandra did not provide us with ideas and information we didn't have on our own, we could get our money back.

So I signed the contract.

Obviously, the selection process was all wrong. No references, no other planners, no background check, pretty much every mistake in the book (or at least this chapter).

The results were, sadly, predictable. Sandra's mutual fund selections were mediocre at best; I already had a portfolio of better funds, so there was no reason to pay a commission for her choices. The bulk of her advice consisted of trying to help us improve our cash flow so that we could purchase insurance products that, at the time, we had no need for and no real way to afford. Sandra's counsel on the car boiled down to suggesting we pursue a great loan deal that I had found on my own.

Obviously, we were owed our money back.

We're still waiting.

Susan couldn't bring herself to push for it; she didn't want to lose a friend or have me come off looking like a jerk. Sandra ran in the small circle of friends we had at the time; although talking to friends about our professional relationship would have been a breach of ethics, we feared that kind of gossip. In short, we were young and didn't put up much of a fight.

Despite telling Sandra that I was disappointed, I never got—nor did I pursue—my money back. With the financial relationship going nowhere, Susan and Sandra grew distant; both women surely must have known that get-togethers would lead to shop talk.

So we lost a friend and $250. I'm bothered more by the lost money than the lost friendship, because I came to realize that Sandra valued the friendship differently than I did, or she never would have jeopardized it with a business proposition. (By the way, Sandra is still a financial advisor. She said hello after a speech I gave to an advisory group in 2002; the subject of her bad advice or my $250 refund never came up.)

My experience with Sandra all those years ago is common for many investors. For years, industry surveys have found that more than 40 percent of all people take financial advice from friends, family, and business associates, and an AARP Financial study from 2009 confirmed that more than half rely on people with close ties when they're going through a life crisis.

For most people, doing business with a friend or family member spells trouble for one big reason: You let your guard down.

There is an assumption that friends and family get special treatment, a little extra hand-holding, an insider's edge on hot information, or some extra level of dependability. In addition, the crucial element of trust—the cornerstone of your search for any advisor—tends to be in place with both your kin and your playmates. Clearly, unless he is a complete fraud, you can assume your friend or family member wants both the personal and professional relationships to prosper.

But good intentions don't always deliver the goods. The nephew with the ink still fresh on a real estate license, for example, may not have enough experience to get you the best deal on the sale of your home.

And let's not forget that plenty of rogue advisors have no qualms about ripping off friends and relations. In the well-publicized case of Brad Bleidt, a Boston advisor/radio host who was busted in 2004 for running a long-standing Ponzi scheme, the victims included his mother and grandmother. Bleidt had sworn an oath that he would not "wrong, cheat, or defraud" his brother Masons or the lodge when he joined the Masons (ironically named Golden Fleece Lodge); it was there that he started shearing his "brothers" of their life savings.

Likewise, many of Bernie Madoff's victims were folks he met at his country club, on the golf course, at charity functions, or through some personal affinity; he counted on those ties raising trust and lowering resistance.

Smart Investor Tip

If you must consider doing business with friends or family, try to stick to the selection process you use with a complete stranger.

Working with friends adds emotions on all sides. Ask your best childhood friend to provide a written history of his business experience and credentials, and he may take offense; fail to ask a full set of questions, and you can't be sure you have the right expert for your needs.

If you must consider doing business with friends or family, try to stick to the selection process you use with a complete stranger. It will increase your odds for success. If you interview several prospective insurance agents and come away feeling your brother-in-law is not a good advisor, you avoid the unpleasantness of having to sever the business relationship later when it falls short of your expectations. On the other hand, if he truly is the best option, you will never second-guess whether the relationship colored your selection.

And if you ultimately decide to cross the line and work with friends or family, try to make it clear up front what you can do to keep the business side of your relationship from spilling over into the personal side and potentially creating problems.

Remember, there is more than money at stake when you do business with friends and family. Factor the extra value of your friendship into your decision making; you'll lose a lot more than just money if a financial relationship with a friend or relative goes bad.

Key Points

- Trust, but verify. You can think that an advisor looks and sounds great, but until you have done a background check and talked to at least one more candidate for the job, you can't really verify your gut feeling.

- If your financial matters don't end up quite as you planned, chances are you'll blame the advisor. If you made one of these seven obvious errors, you will deserve a lot of the blame yourself.

- You're always better protected when you don't let your guard down. The victims in most financial frauds will tell you they could never have seen the bad outcomes as a remote possibility; just because you can't see trouble coming doesn't mean it's not out there right around the corner.

Chapter 4

Why You May Be the Only One You Can Trust

Doing what's right isn't the problem. It's knowing what's right.
——Lyndon B. Johnson

When frauds like Bernie Madoff and Sir Robert Allen Stanford make headlines, the follow-up stories always talk about how advisors need to be "fiduciaries."

It's a $10 word that doesn't ordinarily come into conversation, so it's not worth two cents to the majority of people who don't understand it. Oh, they may hear a phrase like "fiduciary duty" and know it applies somehow to their finances, but they don't truly know what it means. It's a term that politicians are throwing around, thinking it solves problems; alas, it will not protect investors from guys like Madoff, Stanford, or the local broker-turned-rogue.

As this book goes to press, President Barack Obama has proposed a regulatory overhaul that would hold brokers to a "fiduciary standard;" in plain English, that means the brokers would be forced to place their client's interest ahead of their own.

That may sound odd, because most people assume that the broker or financial intermediary they work with has their best interests at heart. Truth be told, however, most of the people who want to give or sell you advice about your money need only to live up to a standard of "suitability," meaning they can't put a client into inappropriate investments, such as speculative penny stocks for an 80-year-old widow. They must reasonably believe that the investment and insurance products they want you to buy are appropriate for your situation.

Read that again. The standard is "appropriate" for you, not "best" for you. Ouch.

That's one of the dirty little secrets of the financial world.

Who Is on Your Side?

Here's the quick-and-dirty guide to who lives by which standard: Someone who sells advice is, in all likelihood, a fiduciary, while someone selling investment products is not.

You may have a tough time telling the difference. A lot of consumers think they are being sold advice, when they are being pitched products. The financial services industry has created that situation, largely because so many people did not want to act as fiduciaries and do what was best for the customer if it meant doing something that was not ideal for the service provider.

The fact that customers don't necessarily know the difference between the two standards is one thing. Requiring a fiduciary standard for everyone is something altogether different, because the goal would be to eliminate the confusion and give the customer the standard of care he or she currently expects, even if it's not what he or she is getting under the letter of the law.

Smart Investor Tip
Someone who sells advice is, in all likelihood, a fiduciary, while someone selling investment products is not.

Requiring brokers to operate under a fiduciary standard could force them to offer products that are less costly and more tax-efficient. They would have to disclose potential conflicts of interest, such as any fees or payments received for favoring one product over another. That could mean clients will be offered fewer proprietary products if the broker can find a lower-cost option elsewhere.

For example, a broker couldn't put you in a mutual fund with higher fees— or one he gets a bigger commission for selling—if he could get a comparable fund with lower fees elsewhere.

The Dollar Difference between "Suitable" and "Best"

Financial services pros say that the difference between the suitability standard and a fiduciary responsibility is semantics. They couldn't be more wrong, because once you put those words into actions, the costs can add up in a big, fat hurry.

For proof, here's an example using easy, round numbers:

Say you are 35, plan to retire at age 65 and have $10,000 a year to save for retirement. Your broker has a plan for netting a 6 percent return annualized over the next three decades. It will turn your money into an $800,000 nest egg when you plan to call it quits. Not bad.

What you're not necessarily aware of is that the broker earned a big fat commission for selling you on the plan, and that the higher expenses charged by his financial firm—which runs the funds you bought—also took a cut off the top.

Had the broker directed you into a portfolio of low-cost mutual funds, your same money might have netted an 8 percent return. Over 30 years, that would have left you with a retirement war chest of $1.1 million.

The high-cost, high-commission investment might qualify as "suitable," because it meets your need to amass a retirement nest egg. Despite leaving you dramatically poorer, it passes the regulatory sniff test.

Meanwhile, had the advisor put your best interests first, you would have paid less commission and purchased the lower-cost fund, and you might be $300,000 richer for it.

While situations can be drawn up to show nearly any possible outcome, better or worse than this one, the key to remember is that the dollars at stake between "appropriate" and "best" are very real. And they're yours.

For years, investment advisors have been held by regulators to a fiduciary standard. Brokers, however, were excluded from the definition of "investment advisors," so long as they didn't get paid special compensation for their advice. If the advice was "solely incidental" to their brokerage services, they merely had to uphold the suitability standard.

Over time, however, many brokers held themselves out as financial planners but lived by the more lenient standards. Some brokers also became registered both ways, operating under the suitability standard when they sell product, but operating as a fiduciary when they sell their advice. Ultimately, the SEC held that an advisor can play both roles.

The bills winding their way through Congress as this book goes to press include provisions that would allow this kind of "hat switching" to continue.

In fact, they parse this dilemma by insisting that fiduciary applies only when someone acts like a broker, and suitability applies when they work as a broker. That means that the advice must be in your best interest when they give it to you, but that the investments must merely be "suitable" when you actually buy them. That's legalese that only a defense lawyer could love, and it's why this kind of confusion will continue.

And that's before you get to brokers who give themselves flowery titles—like fee-based consultant—to create an air of "we're on your side" without actually having to live up to a fiduciary responsibility.

In addition, money managers—who frequently deal with the investments but who may have no direct contact with the customer—live by a different fiduciary standard. They need to run their portfolio in a way that they believe is in the investor's best interest, but since they have no personal interface with the customer, they can't necessarily make client-specific judgments. A hedge fund manager, for example, can make sure that her newest customer is an "accredited investor," meaning he or she meets certain standards for having a high net worth, but will have no clue when that investor's college tuition check is due or when retirement kicks in.

The consumer is caught in the middle of this confusion, between the partners—the ones who want to profit *with* you—and the salespeople, the ones who want to profit *from* you.

The financial-services firms know that customers want objective advice, but they're not willing to abandon the commission-based sales model that the business was built upon.

Who Is a Fiduciary?

Do you know which advisors must put your interests first, and which are merely held to a standard of suitability? In many cases, advisors make it harder to figure out, because they operate under different titles; a "wealth manager" or "financial consultant" could be either a broker or a financial planner, but it's mostly a title the advisor applies to him- or herself. What determines whether these counselors are fiduciaries is not what they call themselves, but what they do for you.

Under the law, there are two kinds of financial advisors, those whose primary business is selling you products, and those whose main business is advising you in exchange for a fee. The ones who provide advice and ongoing investment management are typically fiduciaries; the ones selling you a product or providing you a service are not, or may function as fiduciaries only in certain parts of their business.

Know, too, that many advisors wear more than one hat, which can further blur the lines. When in doubt, ask if the advisor functions as a fiduciary, but here's a guide—based on the rules as this book went to press—to the status of the most common advisors:

Professional title	Fiduciary?
Attorney	Yes
Certified financial planner (CFP)	Maybe
Certified public accountant (CPA)	Yes
Financial planner	Maybe
Insurance agent	No
Real estate agent	Yes
Registered investment advisor (RIA)	Yes
Registered representative	No
Stock broker	No

Know Where You Stand

In interviewing a financial advisor, you will always need to ask if she is legally obligated to act in your best interests at all times. If so, she should put that in writing.

If an advisor claims to be a fiduciary but is not willing to put that on paper—which would force him or her to stand behind their word in court—run away. An advisor who acts like a weasel before he has your money to work with is sure to turn into a rodent once he gets your cash.

That said, you may still be interested in working with advisors who are not fiduciaries. If, for example, you have an existing relationship with a stockbroker, and he or she has done good work on your behalf, you may be completely comfortable taking his or her advice going forward.

There's nothing inherently wrong with an advisor who does not agree to live up to the fiduciary standard; it's just that you need to be aware of the potential conflicts and be on guard at all times when working with that person. "On guard" does not mean you'll lose sleep every night wondering whether he is about to rip you off; it's more like reminding yourself, every time he gives you a recommendation, to make sure that he has kept his interests aligned with yours, so that his vision of "appropriate" equals your version of "best."

Fiduciary Is No Guarantee

The politicians and proponents of a full-time fiduciary standard want to believe that once the advisor is required to put your interests first, you're home free, and you can say goodbye to rogues, crooks, and bad guys.

Bzzzzzzt. Wrong answer.

No matter what supporters say, the fiduciary standard is no guarantee of competency, nor is it an ironclad promise that the advisor's ethics and morals will never waver. Congress will never be able to mandate an ethical standard that keeps an advisor out of personal financial troubles and stops him from becoming so desperate that he dips into client funds or cooks up a scheme to surreptitiously "borrow" client money to get through a rough patch.

Smart Investor Tip

. . . the fiduciary standard is no guarantee of competency, nor is it an ironclad promise that the advisor's ethics and morals will never waver.

In fact, in the most recent statistics from arbitration cases conducted by the National Association of Securities Dealers, "breach of fiduciary duty" was cited as a problem in nearly one-quarter of all arbitration cases. Most of those alleged breaches were conflicts of interest, rather than theft or fraud, but the point is the same; just because someone has a fiduciary duty doesn't mean he'll actually do it. (Interestingly, "unsuitability" of investments was cited in about half as many cases as breached fiduciary responsibilities.)

The high bar set by assuming a fiduciary role makes a client's job easier—because it should stand out to you pretty quickly if your advisor's actions are not in your best interest—but if your advisor "goes bad," the standard itself won't protect you, nor will it get your money back.

Fiduciary or not, there will never be a substitute for your own due diligence in making sure that your interests are properly served by every advisor you work with.

Key Points

- Most advisors live by a suitability standard, meaning they must provide advice that's appropriate. You want what's best. There's real dollars in the difference.

- No matter the advisor's standard, your standard should be that no one gets your trust just because he has a title and an office. Fiduciary standard or not, if he can't prove to you that he is on your side and has your best interests at heart, he's not likely to be an advisor you can work with for a lifetime.

- If the government requires a fiduciary standard, that will make it clear where an advisor's interests are supposed to be, but it's no guarantee of how he will actually treat you. Moreover, don't expect the government to get this issue right; the bill proposals have enough loopholes that "increased protection" might be more lip service than reality.

Chapter

Swimming through Alphabet Soup

Back where I come from, we have universities, seats of great learning, where men go to become great thinkers. And when they come out, they think deep thoughts, and with no more brains than you have. But they have one thing you haven't got. A diploma.
—The Wizard of Oz (said to the Scarecrow)

Say you're nearing retirement age, and you want to improve your portfolio to make sure it lasts a lifetime and helps meet your personal goal of putting the grandkids through college someday. You also need to help your grown daughter as she goes through a divorce, and you have a desperate need for estate planning—as well as ongoing tax counsel—plus a needs evaluation on long-term care insurance, and you've heard about annuity products that could help you lock in an income stream for you and your spouse for the rest of your lives.

Theoretically, that means you are looking for a financial advisor who is a CFP, CCPS, CDP, EA, CIC, CEP, or CAS. Or perhaps you'd settle for a CPA/PFS who also holds the AEP, BCA, CDFA, CAA, CASL credentials, although there's definitely a chance you won't get enough advice on the grandchildren's college savings that way.

Confused?

You should be. There are more than 100 professional designations and credentials for financial advisors, and that doesn't count some of the flimsy, half-hearted, or just plain silly things that some advisors latch on to as a way to impress you. Every few months, there seems to be another new designation, as if consumers or the financial-services industry need them.

Advisors use financial licenses and designations to market themselves to you. Oh, they'll say that they got the credential in order to be more qualified to handle a specific financial task or job—and there may be some truth to that—but they know that the more credentials they have, the more they can impress potential customers, and the more services they can offer their clients.

If credentials are truly important to you, and you have the needs laid out in the hypothetical above, you'd hire a Certified Financial Planner (CFP) who is also a Certified College Planning Specialist (CCPS), a Certified Divorce Planner (CDP), an Enrolled Agent (EA, for your tax needs), a Chartered Investment Counselor (CIC), a Certified Estate Planner (CEP), and a Certified Annuity Specialist (CAS).

Or, if you went the other way, you'd have a Certified Public Accountant/Personal Financial Specialist (CPA/PFS), with a whole raft of other credentials to cover the rest of your needs.

Yet the truth is that an ordinary financial planner with a customer base that is mostly people of your age and assets and concerns could probably do the job, without having a single advanced credential. You may feel more comfortable with someone who has additional training to meet your needs, but you can also overvalue that additional training and pick an advisor more on his or her credentials than his or her true worth as a counselor.

Don't sell experience short and give too much credit to letters after the advisor's name. Some titles and designations have valuable significance; but others are misleading, or worse. As a consumer, you should know that titles and credentials can misrepresent an advisor's ability to give you appropriate, knowledgeable advice.

Smart Investor Tip

Don't sell experience short and give too much credit to letters after the advisor's name.

Credential confusion can leave consumers vulnerable to unsuitable recommendations and costly investments; state and federal regulators have reported a huge increase in deceptive practice cases, particularly involving senior citizens, who swallow the alphabet soup as if it's truly meaningful. They believe that advisors with a credential that makes them some type of expert on the finances of senior citizens makes for the perfect helper; however, it may also open the door to rogues and scoundrels. As a result, some states have implemented new regulations that limit the use or mention of credentials by certain types of advisors.

Credentials Are Misleading

Even if you know what a CFP is, you probably don't know what an advisor does to earn the designation. And CFP is a common credential, unlike most of the 100-plus designations that most consumers have never heard of.

In general, legitimate credentials prove that an advisor is furthering his or her education; with the rules and regulations of finance changing nearly every day, current information and knowledge is crucial.

But having credentials doesn't make someone worthy of being your advisor, a conclusion I draw from personal experience. In June 1995, I was one of five journalists who took the two-day, 10-hour exam for becoming a Certified Financial Planner. It was a media ploy by the folks who administer the CFP standard; even if we had passed the test, we would not have qualified as CFPs.

I did not study for the test and did not expect to pass, nor did I want to; I would have lost all respect for both the test and the group if I could ace the exam without formal training. None of the journalists passed.

What I learned was not how tough the test was, but rather that the mark of CFP—a standard I have tremendous respect for—does not make someone a great financial planner. It proves technical proficiency, the ability to analyze a portfolio and make appropriate suggestions, but it gives no insight into the advisor's "relationship skills."

An advisor could pass the CFP exam largely by boning up on some financial formulas and rules, but could be lacking the basic human skills necessary to build a comfortable relationship with you. Since a successful relationship with an advisor depends on developing a working partnership, credentials alone can't make someone a good advisor.

Don't get me wrong. Technical expertise is critical, especially when it comes to the legal, insurance, and tax arenas in which a mistake could have severe costs.

But I do not know of a single financial planner—and I have asked hundreds of them in the years since I took the test—who ever had a client come in and ask for the calculation of the Sharpe Index of Performance on a mutual fund. In fact, only one or two of the planners I've queried could actually calculate the Sharpe Index without the formula in front of them. (The Sharpe is sufficiently esoteric that most planners can't adequately explain it and I'm not even going to attempt it here.)

Yet the Sharpe Index was on the CFP exam that I took.

Meanwhile, subjective decision making about how someone can cut spending to improve savings or reduce debt was not anywhere on the CFP exam. And the same planners who have never been asked by clients to calculate a Sharpe Index have dozens of clients who need help changing their spending habits.

Until I saw what the test measured, I never understood how the CFP Board of Standards had bestowed its precious mark on some of the very best and very worst planners I know; the answer is that the exam is an incomplete gauge of an advisor's skills. I like or dislike the CFP designees I know because of their demeanor, ability to communicate complex information, and the investment approaches they espouse, not because they are technically proficient at the esoteric points of personal finance.

That's why credentials are a starting point and not the Good Housekeeping Seal of Approval.

What All Those Letters Stand For

With over 100 credentials and designations, ranging from the ordinary to the ridiculous, and more being created every day, it's impossible to cover every credential here. Clearly, the most respected designations are those that require the most knowledge and preparation, that espouse the highest ethical standards, and that are given by top-flight educational institutions or industry organizations. Not all of the most-common designations actually meet that standard.

Here, in alphabetical order, is a list of the 20 marks and designations you are most likely to run into during your search for financial advisors:

- **AEP:** The Accredited Estate Planner designation requires the recipient to have five years of estate planning experience. The person must be an attorney or financial planner with appropriate credentials in that field. Given by the National Association of Estate Planners & Councils, the credential requires just two graduate level courses, but then needs 30 hours of coursework every two years to stay in good standing.

- **ATA** or **ATP:** An "Accredited Tax Advisor" or "Accredited Tax Preparer" has completed the College for Financial Planning's Accredited Tax Preparer Program and passed an exam administered by the Accreditation Council for Accountancy on Taxation.

- **CAA:** A Certified Annuity Advisor must be a lawyer, insurance agent, or financial planner, who then completes classwork (either self-study or in a classroom) developed by Advisor Certification Services.

- **CAS:** The Certified Annuity Specialist designation competes with the CAA. It requires a bachelor's degree or one year of experience in financial services and completion of a self-study course and passing an examination administered by the Institute of Business & Finance.

- **CDP** or **CDFA:** One growing sub-specialty among financial advisors is dealing with divorce cases. A Certified Divorce Planner is an experienced advisor who has completed coursework from The Institute for Certified Divorce Planners, while a Certified Divorce Financial Analyst is an experienced advisor who chose instead to study with the Institute for Divorce Financial Analysts.

- **CFA:** Chartered Financial Analysts pass a rigorous, three-level test on investment analysis, economics, portfolio theory, accounting, corporate finance, and more, administered by the CFA Institute (formerly the Association for Investment Management and Research). CFAs also must demonstrate expertise in a specialized area of investments.

- **CFP:** Certified Financial Planners must meet experience and education requirements and pass a 10-hour exam given by the Certified Financial Planner Board of Standards. To remain in good standing, they must take at least 30 hours of continuing education classes every two years.

- **CFS:** Certified Fund Specialists need only have a bachelor's degree or one year of experience in financial services to take the self-study course and pass an examination administered by the Institute of Business & Finance.

- **ChFC:** Chartered Financial Consultants are typically insurance agents with several years of experience, who have passed courses in financial planning from The American College. It is a credential for an insurance agent who wants to branch into other types of financial planning; many agents get this in conjunction with the CLU credential, since some of the academic requirements are the same.

- **CIMA:** The Investment Management Consultants Association (IMCA)—a trade group for advisors who specialize in high net-worth clients and institutional investors—gives the Certified Investment Management Analyst credential to experienced consultants who complete a five-month study program at the University of Pennsylvania, the University of Chicago, or the University of California-Berkeley. Candidates cannot have any history of criminal or regulatory violations, civil judicial actions, or warranted customer complaints. IMCA has also started awarding the Certified Private Wealth Advisor (**CPWA**) credential for expertise in "the life cycle of wealth."

- **CLTC:** The "Certified in Long-Term Care" program is run by the CLTC Board of Standards and is one of the few standards that look at the vexing issue of long-term care insurance. That said, the credential has no prerequisites or required experience; it is given for the completion of a correspondence course or a 2-day in-person class, plus an exam.

- **CLU:** Chartered Life Underwriter is generally considered the highest professional designation for life insurance agents, who must meet extensive experience and education requirements, with the courses coming from The American College.

- **CMFC:** Chartered Mutual Fund Consultants have completed a 72-hour self-study course on mutual funds. The program is administered by the College for Financial Planning and overseen by the Investment Company Institute, which is the trade association for the mutual fund industry.

- **CPA:** Certified Public Accountants are tax specialists who must have a college degree, pass a strict national exam, and keep current on changes in tax law.

- **CRPC, CRC, CRFA, or CRP:** These are four separate-but-similar designations for advisors who want a credential that shows their ability to assist retirees and pre-retirees. Chartered Retirement Planning Counselor, given by the College for Financial Planning, seems to be most popular, but not significantly different from a Certified Retirement Counselor (bestowed by the International Foundation for Retirement Education), a Certified Retirement Financial Advisor (given by the Society of Certified Retirement Financial Advisors), or a Certified Retirement Planner (from Retirement Planners LLC). There is also a **PRPS**—Personal Retirement Planning Specialist—credential, given mostly to insurance professionals looking to broaden their expertise, especially as it comes to selling annuity/lifetime income products.

- **CSA or CSC or CSFP:** Certified Senior Advisors have taken classes on working with senior citizens that go beyond the finances to help them understand the health, insurance, and other issues that could come into play. The same applies to the Certified Senior Consultant and Chartered Senior Financial Planner credentials.

- **CWM:** Chartered Wealth Managers have at least three years' experience and typically have an advanced degree. They complete coursework with the American Academy of Financial Management. A similar, competing credential is the CWC, or Certified Wealth Consultant, run by The Heritage Institute.

- **EA:** Enrolled Agents are tax preparers who either worked for the IRS for at least five years or passed a test on federal tax law.

- **JD:** The Juris Doctor is a law degree, not an actual financial-planning credential. That said, there are plenty of lawyers who wind up in financial planning and services, whether that is through estate planning, tax law, or getting an additional financial-planning credential. When that happens, you can expect that the JD mark will be prominent among their credentials.

- **PFS:** Personal Financial Specialists are CPAs who have met education and experience requirements and passed a comprehensive exam on financial planning. Because this credential is always linked to the CPA—designees typically list it as CPA/PFS—the person who has it is typically qualified to help a client with both investment and tax issues. That said, many PFS advisors no longer do tax work and focus more on tax-efficient financial planning.

- **RIA:** Not really a credential at all; when someone tells you he's a "registered investment advisor," it simply means that he has registered with the U.S. Securities & Exchange Commission and has paid a registration fee.

Designations Don't Make You "Professional"

All of these letters are supposed to be "professional designations," which is a misnomer because—with the exception of lawyers—none of the members of your financial team truly is a "professional."

Most dictionaries define "profession" as a vocation or occupation that *requires* advanced training either in sciences or the liberal arts. You do *not* need an advanced degree to practice as a financial planner, insurance agent, real estate agent, stockbroker, tax preparer, or accountant. Standards vary for each role, with state or federal law dictating whether practitioners must even be registered or licensed. Even then, "registration" is more about putting your name on file than it is about having achieved a minimum standard of education and academic excellence.

In other words, you can be a "financial planner" without having the "Certified Financial Planner," "Personal Financial Specialist," or any credential.

Titles Can Be as Confusing as Credentials

Legally, you're not a "doctor" without the degree to back it up. That doesn't happen with most financial specialties, where an advisor typically can pick the title for himself, no degree required.

As a result, advisors who use the titles of financial planner, financial advisor, financial analyst, financial consultant, investment counselor, wealth advisor, wealth manager, personal finance specialist, tax preparer, and more may be true specialists with lengthy, detailed educations, or they may be some guy who thinks he's good at this stuff.

As with credentials, it's important not to let the titles confuse you. What an advisor is called—and what designations she has—is less important than what services she provides and your belief that she can help you reach your goals.

That doesn't demean the designations; there's no denying that an advisor who goes through training and education to get them is set up to be a better, more skilled, more competent advisor.

Moreover, there are a number of cases where the governing bodies that designate the criteria for a particular standard are warring with competing organizations touting a different standard. For example, an advisor looking to become more knowledgeable on the use of mutual funds could pursue the Chartered Mutual Fund Counselor (CMFC) designation, or the Certified Fund Specialist (CFS) standard. Or she could decide that the continuing education she gets on mutual funds just from being a Certified Financial Planner is sufficient. Truth be told, if you took three advisors, and each took one of the paths described here, you'd have a hard time telling the difference.

That's precisely why your decision will come down to more personal factors and be less about credentials.

What Credentials Mean for You

As a general rule, credentials underscore two things for a client:

1. The advisor has done some beyond-the-basics study in an area where you need expertise.
2. The advisor can charge you more money.

That's why it's important to make sure that an advisor's designations are meaningful to you and your needs, because you will almost certainly be paying up for the expertise and credibility these marks bestow on an advisor.

It's impressive when you find a financial planner who has done the work to earn the "Chartered Financial Analyst" designation; the CFA is one of the most demanding and respected marks in the business, and it is held primarily by stock analysts and institutional money managers. A financial planner who gets one will tell you that it makes him better at selecting stocks and mutual funds.

Smart Investor Tip

Make sure that an advisor's designations are meaningful to you and your needs, because you will almost certainly be paying up for the expertise and credibility these marks bestow on an advisor.

That may all be true, but if you just want a basic mutual fund portfolio, the CFA means that the planner is way overqualified for the job. There's nothing wrong for that, unless you are paying the freight for all of this expertise that you aren't using and don't expect to need. In that case, someone with less invested in getting credentials (perhaps with the much easier to attain Chartered Mutual Fund Counselor mark) can provide qualified assistance at a lower cost.

You also need to decide if an advisor has "too many" credentials. While someone with the many marks described in the situation at the start of this chapter could handle the various situations of the client described at the top, your situation may be much simpler. You may just be looking for solid financial planning advice for someone who has your career track, say a nurse, teacher, or factory worker.

All of those professional marks are nice, but there is no substitute for the experience of someone who has a client base just like you, where instead of trying to be all things to all clients, she specializes in the needs of a small group of like-minded, financially homogenous people.

When I need experts to help me work on my columns, I have generalists and specialists. If I am writing about saving for college, certain advisors will get the call, and it will be a different group of advisors if I am looking at estate-planning concerns, and so on. And then there are some generalists whom I can call on almost any question, although they sometimes have to acknowledge that being certified as a jack of all trades is not the same as being the master of all of those skills.

> ### A Credential Gives You Someone to Complain to . . . Maybe
>
> The best credentials are given by groups that keep a close watch over their marks. They don't want to support a rogue advisor any more than you would want to hire one, which is why they have an investor complaint process that you can go if you have trouble with someone using their designation.
>
> This is another way that the quality of credentials can be differentiated. If the credential gives you another avenue to pursue if you are wronged—another bit of leverage to persuade an advisor to do the right thing and set things straight—it is more valuable to you. When you check out the advisor's credentials, take notice of whether the group has a way for you to lodge complaints should you need to in the future.

Ask These Four Questions about an Advisor's Credentials

When an advisor makes his or her credentials part of the presentation—a presumed reason why you would want to hire him or her—ask these four questions:

1. What did you have to do to earn this mark, and why did you consider it important to achieve this distinction?

Some credentials require experience, knowledge, continuing education, and the ability to pass a test, while others are online open-book study. Some advisors use their membership in a trade group, like the Financial Planning Association, as if it was a meaningful credential. Maintaining certain designations requires adhering to an ethics policy; other times, all that's necessary to remain in good standing is to pay dues. And some marks seem to be little more than a show.

Aside from knowing what goes into earning the designation, find out why the advisor went to all the effort of getting the credential. You may learn a lot about the advisor's experience and clientele that way; if he pursued an annuity designation or estate-planning credential because clients were aging and asking about those specialties, you'll get a better idea of whether you fit in with the advisor's "typical client."

2. Are there continuing education requirements? If so, what must you do to meet them?

Ask about the courses your prospective advisor must take to stay current on the credential, and ask how that education might help him in his work with you.

Continuing education courses run the gamut from nuts-and-bolts practice-management classes to specific ideas for helping clients get more from their money.

You want an advisor who is building expertise as it relates to you (rather than learning how to get more profits from each client, which some organizations consider suitable continuing education). Rules and laws governing money management change so quickly that anyone who stays out of the loop for over a year may never get back into it.

3. Can you give me the contacts for the sanctioning body?

No advisor should be afraid of your contacting the group that issues the credentials to make sure everything is on the up-and-up. While you can get the contact details on your own—check the professional designations database at www.finra.org, the website of the Financial Industry Regulatory Authority—play dumb here because you want to see if the advisor will make it easy for you.

Most consumers don't do their homework and make appropriate background checks, which has allowed crooks who pretend to have credentials to stay in business. In addition, most sanctioning groups will kick out members who run afoul of bylaws or codes of ethics, so someone who has a credential up on his office wall may not necessarily be entitled to continue using it.

If an advisor believes you will follow up with the sanctioning body—which could result in very real trouble if the credentials are fake or expired—you'll get a half-hearted answer that probably leaves you on your own for doing the search. That said, not every credentialing agency has a public disciplinary process that allows you to see if an advisor has gotten in trouble with the group; luckily, most advisors don't actually know if their credentialing agency makes disciplinary information public.

An advisor who really works with the sanctioning group will have the phone number or Web address handy and should have no fear of your checking out the credential.

4. Does the designation mean anything unique in the service?

With tax preparers, for example, an enrolled agent can represent you in an audit; the return-preparer at the corner fast-food tax joint can't.

An accountant who also has a law degree, meanwhile, may be adept at trust and estate planning work. The same could be said for a financial planner with a law degree. Plenty of advisors use credentials to cross over from one specialty to the next, which is good if your financial needs spill from one area to the next.

I once had a reader ask if I had ever heard of a financial planner with a "CPhD," a pompous-sounding designation that was new to me (and to every regulator I asked about it). It turned out to mean the planner was "Certified in Philanthropic Development" by a national philanthropy group, something that might have been terrific if the reader had been looking to create a big foundation as part of his estate planning, but that had no real bearing on the basic day-to-day financial guidance the customer wanted.

Assume that the letters after an advisor's name mean something in terms of the price you will pay, as in "the more credentials, the bigger the bill." That's not always true, but that kind of thinking will help you find someone who is "properly qualified" to work with you, rather than being over- or underqualified.

Don't pay for expertise you don't need. You may decide you don't need a certified public accountant to do an ordinary tax return, for example. At the same time, you might prefer hiring a lawyer who has taken specialized classes in elder law. And you probably won't care if your financial planner has a "CPhD."

By making the advisor spell out the benefits you get from his expertise, you go a long way toward defining what to expect from the relationship.

Key Points

You need to separate valid designations that will help an advisor serve you from credentials that deceptively imply that someone is qualified to advise you. Look at:

- **Qualifications:** What did the advisor do to qualify for the title? Does the title require the advisor to live by a strictly applied code of ethics?

- **Training:** Was it a quick one- or two-day class followed by a test? An online, open-book, at-home study course? Or was it classroom work, seminars, and sanctioned meetings? Does the credential require a minimum amount of practice experience, or can anyone get it? Does the training for this designation or title, along with other qualifications, truly signify that this person has adequate knowledge and expertise to advise clients in the subjects it applies to?

- **Legitimacy:** You want credentials that are respected and acknowledged by the rest of the financial industry, including regulators. Lacking that respect, the designation may be nothing more than marketing spin from a salesperson trying to look more qualified than he really is.

Part

II

Selecting, Interviewing, and Getting Rid of Your Advisor

Chapter 6

Your First Meeting with an Advisor

A meeting is an event where minutes are taken and hours wasted.
—Captain James T. Kirk

Years ago, a colleague of mine told me about problems he was having with his financial planner. He was disappointed with the level of service and attention he was getting, he felt the advisor was not responsive to his questions and concerns, and he was unhappy with the sales charges and fees he was paying.

It was a story I had heard many times before, typically from people who jump into a relationship with a financial advisor without doing much homework.

But my friend protested my assessment, saying he had been "meticulous" in the selection process. He had done a background check, he interviewed two candidates (hiring the second person he met), he interviewed references, and he had done precisely what the advisor wanted during the initial meeting to get things moving when he signed on.

"Well," I asked, "did this woman lie to you? Did she tell you how you would pay her and then do something different? Did she tell you how she'd work with you, and then not live up to it?"

Sheepishly, my friend said that he had not been lied to.

"We never really got to those things," he admitted. "I didn't have a full understanding of how she works with clients and how she charges people."

The wrong time to find out that you have a problem with the way an advisor works is after he's been hired.

My friend let the planner take charge of the initial interview. Instead of a wide-ranging feel-each-other-out chat, the planner asked a raft of questions, all designed to determine how much money was involved and my friend's goals and objectives. He got caught up in the process and stopped asking the questions he had prepared. When the advisor asked if she should go ahead and prepare a basic financial plan, he liked how excited she was to do the work and liked her energy, so he gave the go-ahead.

He was told to expect the plan in three weeks.

A month later, he received by mail exactly what had been promised, an action plan for how to reach his goals. The plan suggested an asset allocation, and recommended certain mutual funds to do the job; all of those funds had sales charges or commissions. The plan lacked specific advice on how and where to cut spending to improve cash flow and reduce debt.

And the bill for this service was more expensive than expected, if only because implementing the plan would involve buying loaded mutual funds and paying a sales charge on each transaction.

The customer wanted more feedback and interaction, better explanations for charges, and help with implementation. He wanted to receive the plan in person, or at least to open it and go through it with the advisor on the phone.

The planner—widely considered one of the nation's elite advisors, by the way—clearly thought she was being hired to do a one-time periodic review, to keep front-end costs down, and to make it that the client could implement the advice on his own—picking no-load mutual funds that would allow him to follow the proscribed asset-allocation plan—or following up with the advisor and paying for whatever additional services were needed.

The miscommunication was cleared up to everyone's satisfaction after I prodded him to request a second meeting to express both his displeasure and what he expected from the relationship.

But the problem occurred because the first interview went from being a "How do you do?" to being "You're on the job." That should never happen.

Is It Worth It to Pay for a First Interview?

Before scheduling an initial meeting, find out if you will be charged for it. Some advisors are always on the clock, even for a first-time sit-down, while others charge a fee, but then rebate the initial consultation fee if you become a client. And some advisors take the meeting for free and hope it delivers business down the road.

Charging for a how-do-you-do is a privilege advisors earn when they are successful; time is their currency, precious enough that they don't want to waste it on unproductive interviews. Still, their fee actually puts pressure on you to choose them, so that your money doesn't go to waste.

Avoid initial consultation fees when possible, and never pay a consultation fee to an advisor who stands to make big money from you on contingency (upon the sale of your home, a win in your court case, etc.). If you must pay fees, schedule the advisors who charge to be the last ones you talk to—so you can cancel the interview if you find a great advisor during one of your free consultations—and be sure to do all of your background checks on those advisors in advance. You don't want to pay for a sit-down only to find out that the advisor's disciplinary history or record of legal problems makes her someone you won't hire.

You Called the Meeting—You're in Charge

The initial meeting with any advisor is a physical and mental handshake, an exercise in sizing someone up. The advisor wants to earn your business, and you want to choose the best possible helper. Your first interaction and impression will go a long way to determining if a long, rewarding financial relationship is in the cards.

Many times, advisors dominate the interview. They need to get information to know if they can help you, and they have these meetings all the time, so they know the ground that should be covered and can direct you toward what they consider most important.

Don't be bashful. Get every bit of information you need, whether the advisor thinks it's important or not. If the advisor is not willing to accommodate you when she does not have your business, how will she treat you if you become a client?

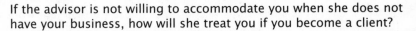

Smart Investor Tip
If the advisor is not willing to accommodate you when she does not have your business, how will she treat you if you become a client?

The advisor's experience often leads her to jump ahead and assume she'll get your business, because that's what happens with most people. It should never be a foregone conclusion that your first meeting will lead to working together, particularly since you should interview several candidates before making a decision. Unless you simply need someone to facilitate a transaction—so that you need someone to process your stock trades or punch out your tax return in a flash—you should plan to do three to five meetings before settling on an advisor.

You need those go-sees to find the right balance between art and science. The science part of any financial relationship is how well someone does with "procedures." Just about any lawyer can draft a will, and you will seldom meet a tax preparer or accountant who backs down from a challenging tax return. Brokers and financial planners can come up with investment ideas for anyone.

What distinguishes one advisor in your mind will be how he or she finesses the science and blends it with art. It's about how confident the advisor can make you feel about their ability to handle the chores, and how comfortable the advisor can make you overall.

Smart Investor Tip

First interviews are about how confident the advisor can make you feel about her ability to handle the chores and how comfortable the advisor can make you overall.

Don't End the Interview with "You're Hired"

The first advisor you talk with always sounds good; he will be able to answer your questions and handle the concerns that drove you to seek help in the first place. You are likely to spend the most time with the first advisor because the discussion will be new territory for you.

Most advisors I talk with say that they don't think that the bulk of their clients ever met with someone else. They were hired by the end of the get-acquainted meeting and assume they have gotten the brush-off when a prospective client has to "think it over." All have had the occasional client washout, when either the advisor or the consumer did not do enough work to make a good match and the relationship dissolved down the road.

No matter what kind of advisor you are looking for, the search and initial meeting should follow a similar pattern. In the chapters discussing how to select each specialty, you'll find specific questions to ask during an initial interview, covering the unique circumstances of each specialty.

Here, however, are the key elements to be done before, during, and after a first date to plant the seeds for a longer relationship.

Prepare in Advance

You don't want to waste an advisor's time—or your own—so do some legwork, either by phone, on the advisor's website or with his or her assistants, to try to make sure you have the potential for a good match.

For example, ask about costs and account minimums up front; it's silly to interview a financial planner with a $500,000 account minimum when you have $50,000 in assets.

You also want to get the basics on whether you fit with the profile of the advisor's average client. If you're scheduling meetings with financial planners about making estate plans or helping you make the most out of the sale of your small business, for example, make sure prospective advisors actually handle those matters regularly. Many financial planners specialize in money management and may not be focused on the need that has driven you to seek assistance.

Whenever possible, talk directly with the advisor, rather than an assistant. While most advisors will not turn away potential business unless they are too busy to handle new accounts, what you hear in their voices will go a long way toward helping make your decision. Obviously, as you lay out the basics of what you are looking for—and the size and scope of the job—you should be listening for interest and energy.

Smart Investor Tip

Talk directly with the advisor, rather than an assistant.

Once you are certain you want to meet with an advisor, set up an initial meeting 10 days to two weeks into the future, so that you have time to prepare thoroughly. It may take a few days to properly check on an advisor's background; unless you have checked on his or her regulatory history before ever calling to chat, you will want to have that work done before you get acquainted.

In addition, many advisors send prospective clients advance materials to streamline the interview process. Leave enough time to read everything, complete any paperwork they send, and gather necessary documents and records.

Include Your Spouse or Partner in the Selection Process

If you are married, your spouse should look everything over and should be included in the initial meeting, even if he or she is not the primary decision maker on these matters. Remember you are purchasing trust, so you want to make sure your partner knows what is going on and has faith and confidence in the advisor.

A good advisor will want to hear from both of you; if one partner sits in the room silently, a high-quality counselor will try to draw him or her out. Equally important, you want your partner to concur on your goals for this advisory relationship and to be comfortable turning to this counselor in the event anything happens to you.

If you like the advisor, but your significant other dislikes the advisor's clothing, dress, manner, or anything, you may need to keep looking. While it may seem silly to get rid of a potential financial helper because of a bad haircut, anything that makes your partner uncomfortable—and less likely to call on the advisor in a real time of need—is a valid reason to keep looking. For all of the information this book will help you get from an advisor, there's no denying that an advisor's gender, age, personality, and the convenient location of his or her office will have a lot to do with who you ultimately hire. No matter how much detail and science you apply to choosing helpers, "gut feeling" will always be a key determinant of whom you actually hire.

If you are hiring an advisor to help with an estate plan, consider bringing along a family member who will be involved in disposing of your estate, preferably your chosen executor. Remember, once the plan is in place, it will be your family—and not you—who deals with the advisor; that person needs to be as comfortable and confident in the advisor as you are.

Do Your Background Checks

Over time, many financial counselors have disagreements with clients, often no more than simple misunderstandings. In today's litigious society, that means there are a lot of good advisors out there with one or two black marks on their record.

Before your first sit-down, you want to arm yourself with information about those incidents. You can do this either when you are first sorting out advisors—doing the work on your short list of candidates before the initial interviews—or immediately after your phone conversation, when you have decided to set up an interview.

If the advisor is sending you any paperwork to prepare you for the meeting, ask for any regulatory or background information, such as a Form ADV for financial planners. (You'll get more on these types of forms in the chapters on picking advisors.)

You want the background data in hand before your initial interview so you can ask about any black marks or red flags and get an explanation of what happened and how problems were resolved. Clients may have had unrealistic expectations; the advisor may have created that kind of problem. Whatever the situation is, you want the advisor's side of the story, and you want to make sure you can avoid a similar fate to the person filing the complaint.

If the advisor balks at owning up to the past, or the answers sound hollow, you won't be hiring him or her. Far better to confront the person with what you know in the first meeting than having to call back or arrange for a second meeting *before* you hire them.

If an advisor's disciplinary or regulatory history comes back with enough black marks to scare you, cancel the initial interview immediately.

Do Your Homework and Reveal Your Faults

Before an initial sit-down, prepare a written statement of what you want from this relationship, and the specific reasons why you are seeking help now. This ensures that the interview will cover your most pressing current needs and your long-term expectations.

Make a list of your interview questions—or highlight them in this book and plan to bring the book along—so that you don't forget to ask everything you consider important. And if the advisor sends you advance paperwork about your assets and intentions, complete it.

Smart Investor Tip

Make a list of your interview questions—or highlight them in this book and plan to bring the book along—so that you don't forget to ask everything you consider important.

Don't hide your financial blemishes and mistakes. Most of us don't like discussing money, especially when it covers what we've done right and wrong with it. Our money foibles are often our most intimate secrets.

You need to trust that any advisor will care for those secrets and treat them like the sensitive information they are. You can't worry about what this advisor will think of you or your past decision making. Advisors understand the need for confidentiality—anyone with an advanced professional credential probably has a code of ethics to live by—but you need to understand the need to be completely honest. You must disclose all relevant information so your advisors can make informed decisions; no advisor can meet your expectations and help you reach your goals without a complete and truthful picture of your situation.

Many advisors say that clients frequently fudge debt problems during initial meetings, trying to make their finances look better than they really are. Then, when the advisor takes them on as a client and finds out the truth, it nullifies a lot of work that has been done; instead of plowing ahead with investments and financial plans, the advisor is now working to reduce the debt, a situation that is particularly likely to anger an advisor who was counting on money being put to work in order to generate a paycheck. Lying about your finances or overlooking your faults gets the entire relationship off on the wrong foot.

In preparing your interview questions, be sure to think about your personal habits and circumstances. If you are the kind of client who intends to call every week or every time the market hiccups, you need to tell the advisor; if your personal quirks would drive an advisor crazy, then he or she is not the right person for you. Reveal any unusual life circumstances that might affect the advisor's work. If you have a child with special needs who requires a lifetime of support, for example, the advisor needs to know that up front, because it impacts every move they suggest. Likewise, a gay individual or a couple in a nontraditional relationship may be reluctant to share this information right away, but there are special rules and strategies that come into play in these situations, and not every advisor has the technical expertise to handle them.

Ideally, you want an advisor to "hire" you as a client every bit as much as you want to have them help with your finances. The best way to know if you are the kind of client he or she would enjoy working with is to give them the whole picture.

Get "Samples," but Don't Expect Something for Nothing

The advisor is selling you a service; he or she should be able to show you what it looks like. An insurance agent can show you a needs analysis, a real estate agent can show you houses she has sold and the listings and ads she writes, and a financial planner can give you a sample plan.

A sample lets you see what you ultimately will be paying for. Many financial advisors have taken real plans and changed the names to Prince Charming and Cinderella or to John and Jane Doe; others give you real plans, but black out the names and addresses.

You should also come away with an advisor's regulatory paperwork, anything he or she needs to give you by law or should give you to understand the scope of his or her practice. Many will send this to you in advance, but don't be afraid to ask for the documents (the chapters on interviewing each type of advisor tell you what documents to ask for).

When you do your multiple interviews, you will be able to compare these samples side by side and see who is talking your language and whose work is over your head. You can see sample investment choices and the logic behind certain decisions. Be sure you know what the services exemplified by the sample would cost in real life.

If you think that an advisor will solve all your problems in the initial meeting (and at no charge)—or that you can apply the sample advice to your specific situation—you will be disappointed. You may get some free counsel—most advisors can't help themselves—but you shouldn't expect fast, free help.

The initial meeting is not supposed to leave you with answers to everything, it is only supposed to help you answer one question: "Is this advisor the right one for me?"

If You Have Concerns, Spill Your Guts

If something is said—or not said—that raises your concerns during a first interview, tell the advisor. Maybe you want clarification about how you could get your money back if you are not satisfied. It might be the discussion of the red flags uncovered in the background check or anything that makes you nervous at all, but try to get a better explanation before leaving the office. If you are looking to switch advisors, it could be as simple as not hearing enough to be convinced that a new relationship will be improved and different from what you have now.

Smart Investor Tip

If something is said—or not said—that raises your concerns during a first interview, tell the advisor.

If the advisor cannot adequately address your concerns, hire someone else. But try not to leave the first interview with questions that you failed to ask.

Get References

Some advisors consider "I have to go home and think about it" to be the brushoff. (Show them this book and tell them you are using it to help in the selection process if you feel compelled to reassure them of your sincerity.) You want and need that time, not only to do other interviews but to check references.

There is a potential problem here in that some firms do not provide references or give out only the names of people to whom they give professional referrals, such as a financial planner using the lawyer to whom he refers estate work as a reference.

Explain, as politely as possible, that client references will allow you to ask about the character of a relationship. You're not going to ask about the specifics of the other person's finances, and you expect them to be sweet on the advisor (after all, they are current clients); what you want to know that only a reference can provide is the tone and tenor of the relationship, things like "How does this advisor work with you, how does he respond when you don't take his advice?" (The questions to ask references are laid out in Chapter 14.)

Smart Investor Tip

If an advisor balks at references, ask for the name of the client who walked in just before you, or the one who had your appointment time yesterday, or who will have it tomorrow. The advisor always has a reason to call the people who just had an appointment, and since he is meeting with an established client tomorrow, he will be sitting down with someone he can tell about your request for a reference.

If your advisor is unwilling to give you the names of references (especially clients, rather than professionals, with whom there might be a business or monetary tie coloring the reference), he may not be worth keeping on your short list.

That's a tough call. References are an additional check and balance, but an advisor who uses confidentiality and convenience as an excuse to withhold names has not necessarily killed the deal, particularly if the advisor has addressed your reservations and if you found him through a referral from a friend or other financial counselor.

Having completed a detailed interview, armed with references, a sample plan and more, you can leave the office, go home, make comparisons, and discuss and mull over your advisor choice with your loved ones. Having repeated the interview process with at least one other advisor—preferably two or more—you should be comfortable making a decision that will pay off for years to come.

Key Points

- Your initial meeting with an advisor is the time to get everything on the table and to gather as much information as possible, so that you can ultimately compare your candidates on a side-by-side basis.
- Do background checks before meeting an advisor for the first time. If you find trouble, save yourself the interview time, or get a good explanation from the advisor as to what went wrong and why it won't happen to you.
- An initial interview is not the last step in the process. You're not ready to hire someone until after these interviews are over and you have had time to evaluate what you have learned.

Chapter

7

Interviewing a Financial Planner

Plans are nothing. Planning is everything.

—Dwight D. Eisenhower

You need help, plain and simple. Between making the money and living your life, your financial chores are never completely done right. You might be brilliant at managing cash flow and savings, but not so good at investing. You've got the big-salary job, but you're worried about losing it and are unprepared for what could happen next in this economy. You're a fabulous investor, but you'd face a struggle to pay for an emergency car repair. You've done everything right, but you just can't tell if you need and can afford long-term care insurance. You're afraid that Uncle Sam will get everything you spent your lifetime earning, or you're terrified that what you leave behind could tear up your family. You know that you are set for life, but want to make sure your spouse or partner can live out their days in comfort.

Whatever your situation, there's a reason why you need financial help, and it has gotten pressing enough that you are now ready to go out and hire somebody to give you a hand.

Those reasons should not include "I need to beat the market."

A financial planner's job is to look at your entire picture and to come up with a program you can follow for the rest of your days that will take you to your financial goals. It is to do battle with the market, so that a downturn, bear market, or lousy economy doesn't crush your dreams; the stock market doesn't know when your next tuition payment is due, when you need cash to replace a car or pay for a wedding, or when you will finally pay off the mortgage.

"Beating the market" is about having enough money to do what you want, not about having a return that tops an arbitrary, not-tied-to-your-life benchmark every year. If the market "beats you," it means your plans left you short of achieving your hopes and dreams; that is the outcome most consumers want to avoid when they seek financial help.

What Are You Looking For?

Before you start your search for a financial planner, you should have an idea of what you are looking for. There's a very good chance that someone whose primary job is that of a broker or money manager can market what he or she does as a form of financial planning. For the purposes of this book, however, you want a financial planner if you are looking for an advisor who will look at and evaluate your entire financial picture. You want a broker if you are looking for someone to help you invest, without regard to the rest of your financial situation, and you want a money manager if you prefer to have an expert invest for you—without your direct involvement or day-to-day oversight.

What this truly means is that titles matter less than services. If someone says she is a "wealth manager" or an "investment counselor," she could fall under any of the three titles—planner, broker, money manager—as her primary business. It is your job to articulate what you want from an advisor and to make sure your final choice can meet your needs the way you want them met.

I recently saw a question posted on an online message board about someone who was ". . . mostly looking for the *money manager* [emphasis added] to actively manage a portfolio for me. As well as manage my personal finances, how much I should be spending everywhere etc., based on what I'm making, etc. . . . How much of my assets to invest in certain ideas, final judgment on going through with certain ideas, making sure I don't do anything stupid or fall for any scams, etc."

As you will see if you are interested in hiring money managers and read the chapter on interviewing them, this guy wasn't really interested in hiring a "money manager" at all. He didn't want someone to come in and take over a big chunk of his portfolio, he wanted someone to review his personal finances and investments and help him develop a strategy for the future. He wanted, in short, a financial planner, even though he was saying something different.

Remember, too, that when you hire a financial planner, you may be getting one who can perform many advisory functions, including that of a money manager, an insurance agent, and even an accountant/tax preparer. Or you might be getting someone who simply does the financial basics and leaves execution and specialization to other experts.

Can I Do This on My Own?

Most people only turn to a financial planner when they have already found something they don't do well on their own.

Truth be told, there is nothing that a financial advisor can do for you that you can't do on your own, or with the help of some good books, computer programs, or online services. The problem is that most people don't rely on those resources, and instead try to make do, until they have problems or enough money that they fear creating problems.

That said, if you have a hard time settling on a financial advisor, you may decide you want to step up and do the job yourself. But go strong or don't go at all; after all, you decided to seek help to avoid trouble, so you must be sure that you have the ability to sidestep it on your own.

Finding Candidates for the Job

Just as your friends and relatives have different tastes in restaurants, books, clothing, and vacations, so might they have a different approach to working with an advisor than you have. And while you might think you know co-workers and neighbors, the truth is that most people say very little about the inner workings of their finances; that co-worker could have paid off the kids' college with an inheritance rather than a college savings plan, or she might have a raging debt problem that you don't know about (face it, somebody makes up those statistics).

Smart Investor Tip

You will have to check out the advisor for yourself to know if he or she can be good for you and your personal circumstances.

As such, they can be a great referral, but not much more than that. You will have to check out the advisor for yourself to know if he or she can be good for you and your personal circumstances.

Moreover, you will want your search to include at least one planner whose inclusion on your list is not colored by what you think of the person who suggested you go. Consider the advisors who come independent of word of mouth to be your "control group," a kind of test for the word-of-mouth planners, to see just how much your judgment may be clouded by friendship.

Many people who have tried this at my suggestion have found that the advisor with whom they had no connection came off as most knowledgeable and helpful; a big reason for the difference is that their loved one picked a financial planner by serendipity, rather than science.

Here are several organizations that can supply names of financial planners in your area:

- The Certified Financial Planner Board of Standards will allow you to look for advisors by name, city, state, or zip code, and it will let you know if the advisor's certification status is current, and whether there is any disciplinary history to worry about, allowing you to find a planner candidate and do the first background check all at once. See www .cfp.net, and look for the "Find a CFP Professional" link.

- The Financial Planning Association's search feature will tell you if a planner will give you a free consultation. All listed members have at least a CFP credential, but be aware that the fanciest listings—and the ones at the top of the list—are typically from advisors who paid a fee to be on the referral service, rather than accepting a free, basic listing that is available to all members of the group. Look for the "Find a Planner" link on www.fpanet.org.

- If you know that you would prefer to work with a fee-only advisor, you might search the National Association of Personal Financial Advisors, whose members must be fee-only planners. Click the "Find an Advisor" link at www.napfa.org. Remember, however, that there are fee-only advisors who never join NAPFA; if you can't find a member in your region, the candidates you get from the other groups may still be available on a fee-only basis.

- Some people believe that a planner who has an accounting background can be a particularly effective quarterback for a financial team, because their credential basically ensures they know the investment, tax, and estate-planning angles to be covered. The American Institute of Certified Public Accountants oversees the Personal Financial Specialist designation for CPAs who complete a rigorous curriculum in financial planning. You can find a CPA/PFS in your area by hitting the "Find a PFS" key on pfp.aicpa.org.

- The Investment Management Consultants Association—a trade group for advisors who specialize in high net-worth clients and institutional investors—will give you contact details for members who have the Certified Investment Management Analyst (CIMA) credential or its new Certified Private Wealth Advisor (CPWA) designation. There are links to the "Find a CIMA" and "Find a CPWA" databases at www.imca.org.

Checking Them Out

If you took a referral from an association, you should have checked credentials, if possible, while there. That said, unless the referral database is simply a listing of members in good standing—or like the CFP Board of Standards's site, volunteers disciplinary history—you will need to go farther to get to safety.

A financial advisor that is considered to be a "registered representative" (read: account executive at a brokerage firm) is regulated by the Financial Industry Regulatory Authority (FINRA). FINRA's BrokerCheck service will give you a lot of details if you plug in an advisor's name, including previous firms he or she has worked for, any disciplinary actions and customer disputes filed against him or her, states he or she is licensed to do business in, industry exams he or she has passed, outside business affiliations (which may show conflicts of interest).

The service is free and takes just minutes. If your advisor has a common name, however, you will want the Central Registration Depository (CRD) number, which goes a long way to making sure you have the right guy. When the system first debuted and I wanted to check it out, I ran my friend Sean Duffy through the database and found out he was one of 12 guys with that name working in the brokerage business.

To use BrokerCheck, go to www.finra.org.

If you are dealing with a registered investment advisor (RIA) instead of a registered rep, you'll need to check with the Securities and Exchange Commission, your state securities administrator, or both. Investment advisors who manage more than $25 million will be registered with the SEC, while those who handle less will be on file with their state.

Effectively, you are looking for information from the Investment Advisor Registration Depository (IARD), which you can get from the Investment Advisor Public Disclosure program. Late in 2009, the SEC unveiled a new consumer site—www.investor.gov—which has the easiest links yet to the search functions.

To get the contacts for your state securities administrator, go to the North American Securities Administrators Association website, www.nasaa.org.

There are also a few services that promise to do the legwork of a background check for you. Combing Better Business Bureau records and the databases of FINRA and the SEC, they come out with a recommendation that an advisor has been "approved" by the service.

Truthfully, these services—like AdvisorCheck or AdvisorRating—make me nervous, because they typically use you, the consumer, as a shill to drum up business (which is why I am not including Web addresses for them). When you request information on an advisor, they contact the planner and suggest that person pay a fee to sign up for the service; if the advisor pays the fee, he or she then gets checked out or rated. If that advisor is already on the service, you're in luck, but if that person never subscribes, the service is worthless to you. Moreover, there's no telling what these services will discount in a planner's history; they're being paid by the advisor so they have an incentive to be, shall we say, "forgiving." You might want to know about everything a planner has done wrong, but these services might be willing to overlook consumer complaints arising from, say, the advisor's sales practices during the market meltdowns of 1988 and 2000.

It's free to do the search yourself; unless you can't process the information in the reports—and it can be dense, but give it a try—do it yourself.

If you intend to use a planner for your insurance needs, make sure he or she is licensed with the state; you can find your state insurance commissioner's office by looking at the "states and jurisdictions map" on www.naic.org, the website of the National Association of Insurance Commissioners.

If you can't find an advisor in any of the public databases, be prepared to call the agencies and authorities; if they can't help you find accurate records, something is amiss. Even the newest advisors have records; there may be no details listed yet, but they are on file somewhere.

Registered Rep, Registered Investment Advisor, Investment Advisory Representative?

A "registered representative" is licensed to sell securities, having passed two key examinations required for brokers. While many "account executives" at brokerage firms call themselves by a title akin to "financial planner," if it turns out that they are a registered rep, then they function legally as a broker. This is important in terms of the standard their advice must live up to, as well as how you will check out their background and disciplinary history.

By comparison, a "registered investment advisor" is on file with the SEC. These advisors aren't recommended by the agency, simply regulated by it. As an advisor, they must uphold the higher "fiduciary standard" for the moves they encourage, but there is no certification necessary to be an RIA.

Many financial planners function technically as "investment advisory representatives," meaning they are registered with the state to provide investment advice, but they are not in charge at the highest levels of the investment advisory firm they work for. IARs can only provide advice on topics on which they have passed appropriate examinations, which can mean a wide variance in their expertise; they run from newbies just starting out and working up the expertise scale to learned, experienced hands who are more comfortable working for a big firm than putting out their own shingle.

Interview Questions for Financial Planners

Because "financial planning" covers a lot of ground, it can be hard to find the right match of skill and service to meet all of your needs. But if you enter the relationship with the right expectations, and then ask the right questions, you are likely to come away with an advisor you can trust for a lifetime.

Your First Meeting

Here are the questions you will want to answer as you go about selecting and working with a financial planner.

Do you have experience in providing advice in . . .

Make a list of everything that is important to you, every concern or issue that has you ready to hire a financial advisor. Stack them up and click them off.

Does the advisor have experience in retirement planning? Investment planning and portfolio management? Tax planning? Estate planning? Insurance planning? Cash-flow and household debt management? College planning? Integrated planning?

Whatever you think you will need, start the interview by asking if the advisor does it and how many years he or she has been doing it for. If he tells you, for example, that he is new to insurance planning, then you will need to decide if you want him involved in that facet of your overall plan, compared to an insurance agent who is a real specialist.

If the advisor doesn't have experience doing the things you feel you need the most, you're interviewing the wrong person.

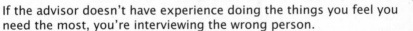

Smart Investor Tip
If the advisor doesn't have experience doing the things you feel you need the most, you're interviewing the wrong person.

What is your role? What is your approach to financial planning?

Now you have a mental picture of what the advisor is capable of doing, but every advisor has his or her own vision for how he or she likes to work with clients. You may want just a "fiscal physical," a snapshot of where you stand now and what actions you must take to reach your long-term goals, or you may want to hire someone to move your money into specific investments that will lead to a lifetime of financial security. There are advisors to fit each of those roles; sometimes one person is willing to work either way, sometimes she only does things her way.

One of the very best planners I know is a woman named Sharon, who works only on an hourly basis, developing plans; she leaves implementation of the plan to the client. That doesn't frustrate her clients because she tells them up front that they are responsible for putting the plan into action. If they are not confident, in advance, that they can properly execute the transactions, implement the plan and get their money's worth from her advice, she suggests they hire someone else.

Plenty of people using the title of "financial planner" are more like "money managers," interested mostly in your portfolio and managing your stocks, bonds, and mutual funds. If you are looking for an active day-to-day manager of your financial affairs, you want to make sure you're not getting someone who is mostly interested in executing trades. Since the generic titles of "financial planner," "investment advisor," or "wealth manager" cover such a vast territory, make sure you know what the advisor is talking about when applying his or her services to your situation.

Selecting investments should be a small part of a planner's role; if the only reason you want to hire an advisor is to get the names of good mutual funds, chances are you are paying too much money for a service that will let you down the first time any fund pick fails to pan out. Worse yet, an advisor whose role is defined as picking investments can be made obsolete at little or no charge by any number of websites, magazines, or computer software programs. Or you can go to a broker or money manager and get services that are more tailored to your specific needs.

Whether you are seeking periodic check-ups—plenty of planning clients see their advisors once every two years after an initial consultation sets them on the course toward their goals—or an active day-to-day manager of your affairs, the planner needs to either work the way you want, or must convince you of how his or her preferred role will work out properly for you.

This is one of the key reasons why you interview multiple candidates.

Years ago, Walter R., one of my friends and colleagues at the *Boston Globe,* asked me to recommend a financial planner; I would not give one name and pick an advisor for him—because the selection process is so personal—but instead gave them the names of several candidates to interview. Walter interviewed three candidates before making his selection; afterwards, he came to me and said, "I talked to three different people about working with me and, from the sounds of it, each of them looked at me as a completely different type of job."

You know the job you want done, and the advisor knows the job he or she prefers to do; make sure those jobs are actually one and the same.

What is your responsibility to me?

This is all about where your interests lie in comparison to the advisor's personal interests in you as a client.

Legally, if you are dealing with a registered investment advisor, he or she must uphold a fiduciary standard, meaning that he or she must act in your best interests at all time. By comparison, a broker functions under a suitability standard, meaning he or she must only give advice that is appropriate. When someone who has the legal standing of a broker functions in almost every way like a financial planner—but does not have the fiduciary requirement —there is tremendous potential for conflict of interest. The advisor can suggest moves that are "appropriate" for you, but particularly good for him or her, such as putting you into the financial product that provides the biggest commission.

As the planning industry has moved toward a fiduciary standard (see Chapter 4 for a discussion of this concept), the number of planners who must put your interests ahead of their own has grown. With titles being practically meaningless, however, you always must ask whether the advisor plans to act like a fiduciary. Any advisor who claims to be a fiduciary should be willing to sign a pledge to that effect, confirming that your interests come first.

"Fiduciary" Is an Imperfect Safeguard

Plenty of people in the industry and in Congress want to see a fiduciary standard applied universally to all stripes of advisors, thinking it will resolve conflict of interest issues.

No legal standard will stop an advisor from becoming a crook. I've interviewed plenty of advisors who were working under a fiduciary standard, and who broke it—and the law—by stealing client funds or selling fraudulent investments.

If someone is sufficiently desperate to turn to crime, he or she won't be dissuaded by the "responsibility" to put your interests first. Even if this person doesn't go all the way to theft and fraud, there are plenty of cases where an advisor could act in a way that looks like your best interests at heart, but which is designed, first and foremost, to maximize the advisor's payday. Customers must always be vigilant, even if they are working with a fiduciary.

The Price You'll Pay, and How You'll Pay It

Now that you know the questions you need to ask when selecting your advisors, here's what you'll need to ask to figure out how much you should pay.

How Do You Charge for Your Services?

The entire financial planning community has been moving away from traditional methods of payment (read: commission) for over a decade now. While there are still many advisors who work on a commission basis—if only because that allows them to serve people with less money to work with and still make a supportive wage—a percentage of assets under management is increasingly common. Some advisors charge on an hourly basis, and still others use a fee-offset approach. (For a full discussion of compensation methods and the pros and cons to each method, read Chapter 2.)

Despite the fee-only trend, or perhaps because of it, it is more important than ever not to assume how a counselor exacts his fee. Be sure to find out if costs are associated with products or with overall services, and be careful when those lines are blurry.

For example, some advisors claim to be fee-only, but the moniker applies only to their investment products. The minute they sell you insurance, they are back on commission.

Likewise, advisors may get a piece of the action for helping to keep you in certain mutual funds. A "12b-1 fee," for example, is a marketing charge that some funds apply to accounts every year. Essentially, the fund takes as much as 1 percent of your account balance to pay for "marketing and distribution costs," and then pays a portion of the fee to your broker. This charge is added to the fund's management costs to come up with your total expenses for ownership. (If you fire your advisor, the fee keeps going to her so long as you own the fund, unless you direct it to a new helper; if the advisor changes firms or quits, the fee—often known as a "trail commission" typically continues to flow to the firm.)

If you are changing advisors, make sure any applicable trail commissions get credited to the new planner. This encourages your new helper to retain those holdings that are appropriate, which may have tax benefits.

Your planner may offer you an investment management account with something called a "wrap fee," which combines management and brokerage fees. These fees can run as high as 3 percent of the assets under management, which is steep. Something closer to 1.5 percent or 2 percent is about average for a stock wrap account; 1.0 to 1.5 percent is the norm with mutual fund wraps. A wrap fee lets you know in advance what you will pay a money manager, but it will be worthwhile only if the manager trades actively and if you have a significant amount of cash—at least $25,000 and preferably $100,000 or above—to commit to the program; if you and the manager employ a buy-and-hold strategy, run the numbers to make sure you aren't better off with straight commission.

Last, there are some occasions where a planner works on a salary-and-bonus basis for a financial-services firm, so that he or she will tell you that you are not paying anything for his or her services. There is no such thing as a free lunch in financial services; you will pay planners' salaries through the costs associated with the investments they sell, and they will earn those bonuses by selling you products. Make sure you understand their incentives, because human nature says they will take the actions that earn them the most money, and you're paying the costs even if it doesn't look like it.

What Can I Expect to Pay?

Now that you know *how* planners charge, you want an idea of *what* they charge.

Whether it's a flat-fee, an hourly rate, or a percentage of assets under management, they can give you an idea of their standard charges and how they are likely to apply to you. If they can't provide this estimate early in the process, they shouldn't get your business.

Remember, too, that there are thousands of financial planners out there; if you can't afford the services of one, there will be others whom you can hire without breaking your bank.

Don't Forget the Nuts and Bolts

And of course, you must ask the following administrative questions that let you know more about the advisor's background.

What's your status? Are you a registered investment advisor, an investment advisory representative, or a registered representative? What states are you licensed in?

By now, your need to have the very basic information should be obvious. Use this for background checks and for confirming the advisor's legal responsibility to you.

What is your educational and professional background?

Look at a planner's background to see if he has a stable employment history. You want an advisor who will be there for you in the years ahead, as well as one who has not bounced from job to job because his work did not satisfy previous employers.

If an advisor has had more than two jobs in the last three years or has a regular pattern of job-switching, find out what's going on. While a planner may switch firms to get better career opportunities or to specialize in a personal field of interest, she also might move after having disciplinary or other troubles. If necessary, call the previous employer for a reference check.

A planner's educational and pre-financial planning background also is interesting to know. Many planners come to the field as a second career. Their first interest may have been teaching or money management or art. You can often learn a lot about an advisor—and get a feel for the human skills he or she brings to the job—by learning what he or she did before becoming a planner.

What credentials do you have? Are there areas in which you specialize?

Consumers (and advisors too) sometimes place too much emphasis on credentials and not enough on chemistry, but there's no denying that you want someone who has the expertise to handle your situation. Just as telling for the future of your relationship may be the credentials the planner doesn't have. A financial planner who lacks insurance credentials probably will pass you on to an insurance agent or consultant and will focus her efforts on your more liquid assets. That's a smart move, and it's the right thing to do, but it may disappoint you if your hope is to hire one advisor who can handle all of your current needs.

There are also some amazing specialties that may be worth asking about, depending on your personal situation. There are advisors who are particularly adept at helping parents with disabled children, or parents who plan to adopt, who focus on single women or widows, who work with people facing terminal illness, and more. If you have what you think is a unique situation, you at least want to know if the advisor is prepared to handle it or willing to learn about it.

Remember, too, that some specialties are only important for a time. I know of advisors who specialize in helping parents amass college savings and pay for tuition bills without going into hock. That's terrific, but you've got several decades of life left once the kids are through college; if you hire an advisor for their specialty, consider whether that will someday mean changing advisors to handle future needs that are your lesser concerns right now.

What continuing education classes have you taken? What certifications, if any, do you have?

Finding out what an advisor has been learning recently is a good way to know what is on her mind. It also shows where her practice is headed. If you hear that she has used her educational credits on some esoteric subject that will never come up in your finances, you should wonder about the scope of the practice and whether you're a great fit.

Can I have your Central Registration Depository (CRD) number or Investment Advisor Registration Depository (IARD) number?

When you do your background checks, you want to make sure you get the right person. By having the appropriate registration depository identification number, you are certain to get the right guy in the right place. Advisors may not know their CRD/IARD number—and it can be just one even if a financial planner is in both databases—off the top of their heads, but they can find it easily enough. If the financial planner sold securities in the past, separate from being a registered investment advisor, get his CRD number so you can make sure disciplinary problems did not lead to the career change.

When you ask this question, the advisor should be pretty sure you are going to check her out; if she doesn't get you the numbers, she's trying to hide something.

Can I have a copy of your complete Form ADV?

Form ADV is an investment advisor's registration form. They're required by law to give you a copy, which you would think would make this question unnecessary, but it's not. Specifically, you are asking for a complete ADV, when the law only requires them to provide Part II.

Some advisors—mostly those who are brokers providing some measure of financial planning service—will not have an ADV, but instead will have a U-4 registration form for you to review.

Yes, you can get this form on your own; you shouldn't have to. In fact, ask the advisor if there is anything he thinks you should discuss about the information in the form, anything he thinks will raise a red flag with you. If he tells you there are no red flags and your subsequent review of the document shows you otherwise, you know he tried to sweep trouble under the rug.

Dealbreaker

By rule, advisors must give Form ADV to all new clients. The same rule, however, only requires the advisor to give you only Part II of the form.

The problem is that Part I is where all disciplinary actions and potential conflicts of interest are listed.

Advisors know you can get this information (in fact, you will get to it through the websites for checking an investment advisor listed earlier in this chapter), but most only give Part II unless you specifically ask for both sections of the form. (In fact, the Certified Financial Planner Board of Standards, in its list of interview questions for advisors, suggests that you request only Part II or its state equivalent.)

Do not let anyone dissuade you from getting Part I.

Request a "complete" Form ADV (make this request even if you already have the information). If a financial planner only gives you Part II, clarify your request and say you'd like to see Part I. If the advisor declines—and cites the rules in doing so—the interview is over. Just walk away. Planners who won't give you information you want *before* you are a client will be tough to work with *after* they have your money in house. Moreover, a planner who knows you intend to do a background check but refuses to honor a simple request for information you can get on your own is acting as if he has something to hide. Don't risk it.

Do you provide a written client engagement agreement?

For many planners, this is the document where they pledge to be a fiduciary and to always act in your best interests. It also puts the terms and conditions on paper, which may help you if anything goes wrong down the road.

Expect to have an engagement agreement; new account forms are standard when you first give money to an advisor, and they actually help form the basis for your relationship, as well as prove what you agreed to in the event of trouble. Make sure you get a copy for your files.

If there isn't a new account agreement, find out why, because it's a big red flag that there could be trouble. (A crooked advisor might give you a document to look legit, but any reputable advisor will want the protection that the document gives him or her every bit as much as he or she will want you to feel comfortable.)

Learn about Clientele and Scope of Practice

Below are some questions you should ask to learn about the advisor's clientele and scope of her practice so that you can make an informed decision of whether you fit within her niche.

Who is your typical client?

If the average client looks like you, financially speaking, and has concerns like yours, chances are the advisor has already dealt with whatever situation your personal finances can dish up. In addition, planners generally put the bulk of their educational time toward figuring out how to better serve their core client base, which means learning about things that will benefit their average client.

Make sure the planner's answer doesn't focus solely on age, income, and size of portfolio. If you are a union worker with a particular type of pension plan, for example, you want someone who understands the workings of those plans, as opposed to a consultant whose clients are largely self-employed and setting up their own retirement plans.

If you resemble an advisor's average client, there is a good chance he will want you as a customer because you fall comfortably within his circle of confidence.

How many active clients do you work with?

There are only so many hours in the workweek. If a planner promises regular attention, but then tells you he has 200 clients, something doesn't add up. Either he palms off a lot of work on subordinates, or he doesn't live up to his promises.

Many of the top financial planners in the country work with no more than 60 clients at any one time. When their calendars are full, they simply stop taking new customers.

An advisor is not necessarily doing you a favor by squeezing you into his datebook, particularly if you won't be satisfied with the attention you get.

Will anyone else be working with me?

Financial planning firms come in all shapes and sizes. I know of one prominent planner who functions largely as a rainmaker, bringing clients into the firm and then passing them on to subordinates; the big guy does the initial meeting and dispenses the advice, but he is little more than a puppet for the back-room personnel that do the grassroots work of strategizing.

If others besides the planner will work on your account, find out why. Then learn who they are and how they are qualified; if they will be critical to your success and happiness with the planner, you want a meeting, and enough details so you can review their backgrounds, too.

Do you take possession of, or have access to, my assets? Do you have discretion to change my investments without my approval?

Generally, the answer to these questions is "No."

Beware of signing any form that gives the planner the right to manage your money in accordance with your wishes, but without your direct approval. If you pick a planner who turns out to be a crook—or who is simply dumber than advertised—agreeing to a discretionary account is like giving him the keys to your investment vehicle before seeing how he can drive.

Some financial advisors ask for "limited discretionary powers," especially if they are managing money in accounts at mutual fund supermarkets, such as those offered by Fidelity or Charles Schwab. Typically, this allows them to execute trades on your behalf, rather than forcing you to pull the trigger yourself, but make sure you understand why there's a need for the advisor to have this power, how full or limited control really is, and why it's necessary.

The rule in these situations is to walk away from any financial advisor who pressures you for too much control over your assets.

There are extremely rare circumstances under which an advisor might hold assets—or be able to access them at will—but you should be wary of a planner who wants this access, as it is a cornerstone of many financial fraud cases. Expect the advisor to tell you that there is a custodian for your assets and a clearing firm for the trades, and that your checks and deposits will be made out to that firm. You want to know this before dealing with an advisor, because the one thing your background checks and due diligence can't stop is the advisor who goes rogue after you are a client. By knowing up front where your checks will go and who will handle them, you will be alarmed if the advisor ever asks you to change directions and make deposit checks out to his firm.

There are many fraud cases where advisors had personal issues and dipped into customer funds to bail themselves out, hoping they could recoup the money and replenish the accounts later. As a general rule, their easiest way to access the money was to have the checks made out to the wrong party.

What will my plan look like? Can I see a sample?

You want to know what you get for your money, and you are paying for a financial plan. Many advisors have samples—with the real names scratched out and replaced by Prince Charming and Cinderella, or Mr. and Mrs. John Doe—and they'll let you see what you get for your money and whether you like the form and format.

Make sure you understand the information that is presented—and that your spouse or anyone else involved in your decisions can make sense of it—because if you think it would keep you bamboozled, rather than informed, you're interviewing the wrong advisor.

Can I get the names of a few clients to act as references?

Just because you've now seen work samples doesn't mean you don't want to check with real people. See Chapter 14 for a list of questions you will want to ask references in order to make sure that that clients believe the advisor delivers services in the manner being described to you in the interview.

> ## What a Planner Should Want to Know about You
>
> The short answer is everything financial, from your debt and investment picture to your tolerance for risk, your insurance, and more.
>
> Most advisors have a questionnaire that they may ask you to fill out in advance of the first interview. Do your homework, and be forthcoming. They can only determine if you are a good fit for their practice—and you want them to be as excited about adding you as a client as you are to have found a good advisor—if they have a complete picture. Don't start them out with bits and pieces of your information and then give them the rest once they are hired; you can provide details of your investments without giving up so much information that you fear identity theft.
>
> The scope of information that the advisor asks about should give you a clue about the focus of his or her practice. With that in mind, pay attention to the questions that are *not* asked. If the advisor doesn't ask about insurance coverage, for example, he may have you rely on another specialist to do a needs assessment. If he doesn't want to know your debt picture, he may not provide credit counseling to help you eliminate the debt while adding to your investments.

Inquire about Relationship and Investment Style

With this information in hand, below are questions you should ask to learn about the advisor's relationship and investment style.

How often will I hear from you and what will prompt your calls?

This question covers both phone calls and statements. You should find out how often you will get a statement of your account, as well as when you might expect a phone call from the planner.

Some financial planners do a lot of hand-holding, stroking clients to preserve the emotional discipline necessary for long-term investing. Others call only when there is a need or an investment recommendation to make. Good planners talk about many things besides immediate sales.

Why do you want to hire me as a client? What kinds of people do you NOT want as clients?

You want a planner to "hire" you as a client every bit as much as you are anxious to work with her as an advisor. In that way, the relationship becomes a partnership, where she is excited to work with you and your assets, while you are anxious to have a pro guiding you. The hope, of course, is that you make money together, that she profits as you profit.

Presumably, the answer to this question gets back to the fact that you are within the advisor's target client range, with a situation she finds appealing. But listen carefully when an advisor tells you what kinds of people she turns away or dislikes working with; if she is describing you—but doesn't know it because this is a first interview—you will be better off going elsewhere for your financial help.

Signs of Trouble

- **Paperwork you don't understand.** If you are asked to sign any agreement that does not make sense to you or does not seem in keeping with what you and the planner have arranged for, get nervous. Some planners pass discretionary agreements in front of customers as a matter of course; the authorizations make it much easier for mismanagement to go unnoticed, so don't sign unless you agree to the terms.

- **Statements that don't arrive on time or no statements from anyone but the planner.** You should receive regular statements from the investment or insurance companies with whom your planner works. If all you get is a statement from the planner, something is amiss. Don't forget that a scammer can mail fake statements, making everything seem fine while he is robbing you blind. Be prepared to follow up directly with the company if something is wrong with your statement; if an advisor is mismanaging your money, you almost certainly will have to go around him or her and get to the investment company for copies of your statement showing how much of your investments, if any, actually made it to an investment account.

- **"It's just a computer error."** Glitches are extremely rare; when they happen, they should be corrected in a snap. Do not tolerate this excuse if something shows up on your statement that does not belong there. Do not brush off an anomaly or abnormality on your statement; many frauds and Ponzi schemes have gotten so big and hard to manage that the cheat behind them makes errors on statements and simply explains them away as input or data or computer errors. If it is not corrected immediately, you have a problem; even if it is fixed, make sure it doesn't surface again.

- **The only products being offered are run by the house.** This is a bad sign for two different reasons. First, planners sometimes get more compensation for selling products developed by their firms or selling fund families they have a relationship with. Just as important, however, is that you want a free thinker, someone who does not give you formulaic, one-size-fits-all planning.

- **Significant declines in investment value for which you were not prepared.** As bad as 2008 was on the stock market—and it was ugly, with the market off more than 30 percent—your financial planner should have taken every step of the journey with you, so that you were prepared to endure your share of the carnage. Surprises in your investment portfolio are a bad sign; the wrong time to find out that your investments are hard to sell or that they are overly volatile is when it's too late to sidestep trouble. If you are consistently being surprised, it's a sign of poor communication. There may be nothing illegal going on, but no advisor worth his salt would let a client get bushwhacked by bad news.

- **You are consistently passed along to people you barely know and never checked out.** If an advisor promises to work with you but regularly hands you off to a subordinate, you may be in a situation where your real financial planner is the underling. It may be the size of your account, the nature of your transactions, or you personally, but if it's not what you signed up for, you'll want to know why you are getting the brush-off.

- **The planner does not return your calls or e-mails promptly.** To be an active partner in your financial life, a planner has to be interested in you and your case. You're not dating or married, and you shouldn't abuse the privilege you have by calling incessantly over nothing at all. But if you keep your requests reasonable and your planner doesn't get back in touch promptly or answer your questions at his first convenience, he has lost interest in you. Once you sense that lack of interest, start the search for someone who can serve you better.

What is your investment philosophy? What criteria do you use before deciding what to buy? Under what conditions do you sell?

You may be hiring an expert, but the logic behind all investment choices must be something you agree with. If the planner tells you that astrology plays a key role in decisions, for example—and there actually are some planners and brokers who use star charts for guidance—you may decide to hit the road if that's not your cup of tea.

While that example is extreme, many advisors have a certain bent, where they prefer to be a value investor (buying securities that are cheap and waiting for the market to recognize their worth and bid the prices up) or a growth investor (looking primarily for securities driven by current revenue and profit growth). Some advisors are dedicated to buy-and-hold strategies, while others like to trade so that they can ride the hot sectors and try to surf the market's wave.

Find out how a planner selects investments, because those criteria will be the basis for all recommendations made to you. If it doesn't sound good now, imagine how nervous it will make you when there is money on the line.

Do you personally research the products you recommend?

If an advisor relies entirely on someone else's research, she may just be pushing product. Good advisors know how to analyze financial products and which investment analysts they trust; they make decisions based on their own experience and intuition, rather than on something they got in the firm's sales manual or a recommendation from a service they subscribe to. If an advisor does not do her own research, ask whether she puts her own money into the products she recommends.

Ask These Questions before Buying an Investment

With the slew of questions you will have asked in simply selecting the financial advisor, you'd like to think there's not much to do after you hire someone but sit back and enjoy the ride. Alas, it's not that easy, especially when the relationship is new.

As your relationship starts—and perhaps for the life of the relationship, depending on how certain questions are answered—you will want the advisor to answer a raft of follow-up questions before putting your money to work:

How much will you and/or your firm earn on this investment?

You should always know what a transaction will cost you; remember, even fee-only advisors sometimes charge commissions on certain transactions (and may accept 12b-1 fees and other investment-related charges in addition to their prescribed fee). Some financial planners will work on a fee-only basis when it comes to financial planning and money management, but are on commission when selling insurance products.

This is particularly important when your financial planner is turning funds over to a money manager, in which case you want to know how that manager is compensated, too. For example, the standard hedge fund arrangement is what's known as "2-and-20," meaning 2 percent of the assets under management, plus 20 percent of any profits. That's enormous, but you won't complain if the return numbers are big enough.

Let's remember, however, that your advisor is being compensated for putting you into the hedge fund, too. It may be that this just falls under "assets under management," so that it's a part of your regular fee, or it might be that there is some type of arrangement with the hedge fund. Bernie Madoff made a lot of deals with advisors, who plowed funds into his Ponzi scheme.

If the cost structure makes you nervous, speak up.

Smart Investor Tip
If the cost structure makes you nervous, speak up.

After all fees are paid, how much must this investment gain in value before I break even?

Again, this looks at the cost of making an investment, showing you in dramatic fashion whether a trade puts you at a financial disadvantage. If nothing else, layers of compensation—for the planner, for the fund manager or insurer, or for anyone else—should make you think twice about the effect costs have on returns. If you pay a fee of 1 percent of assets under management and the advisor puts you into a fund with a 1 percent expense ratio, then you're paying 2 percent off the top for advice and management. If you are expecting your portfolio to be up by 10 percent on average annually—roughly the long-term historical return for the stock market before expenses and transaction costs—then your expected gain would actually be 8 percent once you factor in the costs, meaning that one-fifth of your expected potential gain will go to the people who sold you the investment and managed it.

Some "separate accounts" and "private-equity" deals sound great, until the costs are completely factored in. Factor costs in before giving your approval.

What is your rationale for picking this specific investment/product? Do you have a business affiliation with the company behind this product or service? How does it suit my needs and risk tolerances? What standard will we set for performance and how will we monitor progress?

A planner should be able to justify decisions and mesh advice into your personal circumstances. If a planner can't put investment selections into the context of your individual circumstances, then you are getting off-the-rack counsel, or you are being put into the same "box" as the bulk of the clientele, even though you thought you were paying for a custom tailor.

Will this sale help you win any prizes or sales contests?

Federal regulations have gone a long way toward eliminating the contests and other incentives that used to motivate brokers and planners to sell something awful, but there are still times when the advisor has extra motivation to close your deal in a certain time frame. I have friends in the planning business who have won trips all over the world, literally, for being top producers; no one product or investment pushed them to the top, but the honest ones acknowledge that they urged clients to follow through on a part of a plan because closing the deal would help the planners earn the bonus.

If the financial product meets your needs, there's nothing wrong with selling it, though the incentive should be disclosed. That said, contests and product-specific bonuses lead advisors to produce cookie-cutter plans, putting all clients into one basket to earn the prize, even as they pass off their service as being individualized.

How long do you expect me to hold this investment? Why?

Most financial planners pursue a buy-and-hold strategy, although there may be a portion of the portfolio that is actively managed (or they may hire a money manager to do regular moves and tactical allocations).

When you buy a new investment, your file on it should start with a sheet of paper that includes notes from your advisor, specifically his or her rationale and reasons for making the purchase and how long he or she expects to hang on. This is a particularly good tool for allowing you to revisit your thinking periodically to make sure the investment remains a good fit. It also helps you hold the advisor's feet to the fire, especially one who works on commissions.

Smart Investor Tip
If an advisor who gets paid by the transaction comes back and suggests selling in a few months—unless there is a significant change in the investment's status that warrants a move—your notes are a wake-up call that he is straying from the original plan.

If an advisor consistently sells more quickly than anticipated, it could be a sign he is mostly interested in the commissions your account can make him or in proving to you that your portfolio requires active management and that his fee is justified.

Can I get out of this investment quickly?

You may be expecting to hang on for a lifetime, but you need to know if what you are buying will be hard or costly to unload. There may not be many buyers for an individual municipal bond, for example, and private-equity deals can become illiquid, making it hard to cash out if you see the company starting to falter.

Other investments, such as annuities or mutual funds, may be easy to get out of, but could carry steep penalties, surrender charges, exit fees, or back-end sales charges.

You've said what it costs to buy this investment. How much would I get if I were to sell it today?

This is about "spread," which you may face if you use a planner (or a broker who functions as a planner) to buy stocks and bonds. Think of it like a new car, for which you pay the sticker price but could not sell it back to the dealer at the same price the second after you drive it off the lot. The bigger the spread, the more certain you must be that you will hold this investment until it pays off.

What is the worst-case outcome for this investment?

Financial planners sell you the good stuff but, before buying any investment or implementing any financial strategy, find out what the worst possible outcome for your investment could be.

What NOT to Do in Working with a Financial Planner

- If you are buying an investment, never make the check out to the representative. The money goes to the firm that is processing the transaction—usually the brokerage firm that clears the advisor's trades or the company offering a particular investment product, such as a variable annuity—to be invested in your account. The firm will pay the commission and use the rest in accordance with your instructions. If you make a check payable to the planner—or even the planner's firm—you leave an opening for trouble. Brad Bleidt, the Boston advisor whose $20 million Ponzi scheme I have talked about a few times in this book, only stole money from clients who made their checks payable to his firm, Allocation Plus Asset Management. Those checks, effectively, went into a personal checking account; by comparison, investors whose checks were payable to the clearing broker didn't lose a penny.

- Never send money to any address other than that of the firm or of an operation designated in the prospectus (such as a transfer agent). Again, this avoids a rogue planner diverting money into his own pocket.

- Never allow transaction confirmations and account statements to be sent to your advisor instead of you. These are your record of what is happening in the account; without them, you don't have the paper trail necessary to build a strong case when things go wrong. If an advisor wants confirmations and statements, he can help you arrange for duplicates. In the Brad Bleidt case, victims allowed him to say they had investments without showing paper from the brokerage firm confirming it; they got a monthly statement from Bleidt's firm that was a complete work of fiction, and they would have uncovered the fraud if they had simply confirmed with the brokerage the status of their account (which they would have found to be nonexistent).

Prepare for Trouble, Just in Case

Charles Wilson, one-time chairman of General Motors Corp. and a former U.S. Secretary of Defense, once said that "No one can prevent a stupid person from doing the wrong thing in the wrong place at the wrong time—but a good plan should keep a concentration from forming."

Your plan to keep a concentration from forming involves knowing what you will do if and when there's trouble. An advisor who knows you are vigilant and knows that you are prepared to take action if it's ever needed knows that you're the wrong person to mess with. That's never bad.

Conclude your interview with an advisor by asking about problems.

How will we resolve complaints if I am dissatisfied?

Chances are you will sign an agreement to try arbitration before turning to the courts; some arbitration agreements—the good ones—do not take away your right to pursue action in court, they merely attempt to settle things using lower-cost, faster-working arbitration. That said, the arbitrator typically is someone with industry ties, so the process is harrowing and difficult.

Legislation in Congress as this book went to press would give the Securities and Exchange Commission the authority to invalidate mandatory arbitration clauses in broker-dealer and investment advisory agreements, a change that would potentially open up the courts system and provide better chances for recovery.

Still, expect that arbitration will be the first step and find out how you can fix problems long before you get to that extreme. Find out how the planner would handle a problem in your account, whether it is a technical glitch, a transaction you don't recall approving or making, investment outcomes outside the realm of what you are prepared for, or anything else.

Many planners try to reassure you that this stuff never happens, but consumers who lived through the market meltdown of 2008 seeing their portfolios gouged and unprepared for the massive hits they took know better. The number of cases filed against advisors has been on a steady rise over the years, but it shot up after the market slowdown in 2008.

That's why you want a planner to guide you through the complaint process, just in case. If the planner works for a large firm, get introductions to the office manager and, if possible, the firm's compliance officer, the first people you are likely to deal with if there is a problem. Get business cards from these people and keep their numbers handy.

All of these actions tell the planner that you won't stand for any shenanigans; a diligent customer is the best deterrent to fraud.

Smart Investor Tip

A diligent customer is the best deterrent to fraud.

How can I terminate this relationship if I am not satisfied?

An advisory agreement should favor you, not the planner. That means it should come equipped with some sort of ejector seat. Most advisory contracts can be terminated with a month's notice—with fees prorated—at any time.

Still, be sure you know how to open the escape hatch before you climb into the cockpit.

Have you ever had complaints filed against you by customers? How have those complaints been resolved?

The planner knows you are going to check his record with the state; this is when he gets a chance to come clean and explain what, if anything, you will find in his records or Form ADV. You want the advisor's side of the story, whether the complaint was the result of miscommunication or unrealistic expectations or whatever.

If the planner tells you he has never had these kinds of problems and the state tells you something different, the game is over, and you should turn elsewhere for financial help. If a planner tries trickery when he knows you are looking, what will he do when you have an established relationship and your guard is down?

That said, most complaints are run-of-the-mill differences of opinion. Even the best advisors sometimes run into bad relationships, people who believe they were entitled to investments that only rise in value in all market conditions, or who sign off on investments without really understanding them and who get angry when the risks they agreed to take don't results in the rewards they envisioned getting.

How do we make sure that I will not have similar problems?

Once you know what the advisor's past problem cases were, you should see what the advisor has learned from his troubled clients. Find out what he intends to do to make sure you do not become his next problem client.

Describe your nightmare client, the worst one you ever have had.

This is an old hiring technique, in which you ask the job applicant to describe her worst day on the job. More than once, when I was a boss, an applicant describing her worst day was actually talking about an average afternoon in my shop.

It not only makes for good stories that lighten up the whole interview process, it helps you see if you are the planner's next "nightmare" before actually becoming that horrible client. If the planner's description of her worst client ever sounds just like you and the things you want and expect—or if you think the worst client's feelings and actions were justified—you may want to go elsewhere.

Where to Complain if There's a Problem

If the advisor can't resolve your complaints, your advisory contract most likely will put disputes into arbitration or mediation before allowing you to go to court (be sure not to waive your right to seek restitution through the legal system).

If the problem is operational—such as failure to deliver securities or checks due to you—and the planner is not solving the situation, put your complaint in writing and seek a higher-up. If the planner is a sole practitioner, go immediately to the state securities commissioner's office (you can find contact information at www.nasaa.org).

At the same time you are making your case in arbitration or court—and it generally takes 8 to 12 months between filing an arbitration case and getting a hearing—pursue the matter with state and federal securities regulators. They generally do not have the power to get your money back, but they can lean on an advisor—who knows what a black mark on his record might do to future business—and may help speed a settlement. Look through enough ADV forms and you will undoubtedly find some in which advisors settled cases—even those where they felt they had done nothing wrong—rather than face the expense and reputation damage that could come from a fight with authorities.

Don't let a complaint sit around unfiled; the statute of limitations on these issues varies, but the general rule is to file the paperwork as soon as you recognize there is a problem that is not being solved amicably.

Building the Relationship

Whether an advisor is a regular partner in your financial decisions or just someone you turn to for a checkup and fine-tuning of your own strategy, you will be best served by building a relationship over time.

That means calling with questions and concerns, arranging the occasional meeting or lunch when there is no pressing business to transact, and more. Many advisors produce a client newsletter, or get one from the financial services firm that clears their transactions; read them, and correspond with the advisor when something strikes a chord.

That's particularly true when you know that the newsletter is the advisor's "baby," her personal platform. For years, my brother Rob worked with an advisor named Jack, who produced a regular client newsletter that covered everything from his thoughts and feelings on the market to his favorite vacation spots and recipes. When Jack retired, he kept the newsletter going, as a means of expressing his views and sharing his thoughts and feelings with his friends and former clients. One time, my brother asked me about something he read in Jack's newsletter—which Jack graciously sent me, though I was never a client—about a certain rule and how it might affect him; I told him to follow up with Jack. Suffice it to say the change was a very big deal that truly will help my brother live out his days more comfortably, but Jack was particularly anxious to be helpful and look into how the change affected Rob because he knew the call was spurred by the newsletter.

Advisors don't necessarily have time for chit-chat, so plan your calls and meetings. Gather your concerns and questions, the articles that spark your questions, and more. If your planner encourages e-mails from clients—and you should ask—don't be afraid to forward items that you believe could affect you.

Over time, you and the advisor both will get a better sense for each other. That will be important in the long run, as circumstances change and you need to adjust your financial plans to suit your new reality.

Future Considerations

Planners sometimes change firms, and that leaves you trying to decide whether you want to go with them. Truth be told, it depends on the circumstances and on what you expect to happen if you stay or go.

Start by asking your advisor about the reasons for the change. If she is moving from one firm to the next, do a background check on the new employer. While you are doing that check, you might want to recheck your advisor. I know that sounds strange, given that your advisor has done nothing to make you scared, but one reason why a planner might jump to a new firm is that the old one has shown her the door when she played fast and loose with the rules. The planner is not likely to tell you that happened, so make the check while you are investigating the new advisory firm just to be safe.

If you decide to follow the planner, find out if he or she gets a bonus for bringing over new customers. Also find out who pays any transfer fees involved or whether you might incur taxes because you'd be forced to sell some investments to follow along (which could happen if you have to sell out of the "house funds" run by the advisor's old firm).

If you choose not to follow your advisor, your current firm will give you someone as a replacement. While you can make the assumption that the firm will not give you a bumpkin, you need to start the interview and background-check process over again. You may find that the new advisor is technically proficient, but not a good personality match for you and your family. If there is any uncertainty, be prepared to interview other candidates and commit yourself to going through the complete hiring process all over again.

Don't Ignore Your Gut

As much as this book is about weeding out the bad guys and the poor fits, you should go into your search confident that the vast majority of advisors are fair, competent, honest, and anxious to do the right thing.

That's why choosing a planner is like mixing art and science. The science is the investment and money-management work, the art is that "good fit" between you and an advisor.

As you come to know an advisor, you should also recognize changes in the relationship and in his or her persona. You never want to be fooled for being too trusting.

A number of Brad Bleidt's victims—he was the Boston advisor who ran a $20 million Ponzi scheme—told me they saw changes in Brad's behavior as his crisis was coming to a head. It was his demeanor, a sense of pressure they had never felt before, and more, but they wondered if he was all right; in hindsight, they should have been wondering whether their investments were all right.

Gregg Rennie, a financial planner who was a primary sponsor for my "Your Money" radio show in 2007–2008, clearly went through some issues that changed his demeanor. He had passed every test—complete background checks, an interview, and more—and I had seen his presentations to groups, which were impressive. I could see why someone would want to work with the guy.

When he started to have business and personal finance problems, he backed away from the show, so I never gave it a second thought. His clients, however, might have wanted to put things together, because somewhere during his dark period he allegedly turned to fraud to make ends meet. He may have been meaning to put the money back on account—many Ponzi schemes start just that way—but his actions had turned criminal; his clients were in the dark until charges were filed and were mostly lucky that his first bad turn with an investor generated the complaint that brought him down. It might have been worse—with many other clients taken in—had the deception gone on longer.

It proved, again, that while due diligence and background checks and everything prescribed in this book will root out the guys with a past that runs from bad service to theft, it can't stop you from being victimized by the person who "goes bad" once he has you as a client.

Keep that in mind. Over time, your advisor should become a confidant and trusted friend. If something seems amiss, ask questions. Put your feelings aside for a moment and take stock in where you stand, and to know that the information you have been given is real and backed by your actual dollars and not just by a paper statement.

Smart Investor Tip

Over time, your advisor should become a confidant and trusted friend. If you don't have that feeling, something's wrong.

It's like those times where you leave the house and wonder if you have your wallet and find yourself suddenly patting yourself down to make sure it's in a pocket somewhere.

When all of the questions and credentials and forms are out of the way, your gut and intuition will still play a big role in finding the right advisor and protecting yourself against the potential betrayal that is a client's worst nightmare.

Interviewing a Broker

With an evening coat and white tie, anybody—even a stockbroker—can gain a reputation for being civilized.

—Oscar Wilde

Oscar Wilde's assessment of stockbrokers stems from the many decades when the brokerage business was less than civilized, a mysterious, dangerous place that most individuals didn't understand. It was the Wild West, where the good guys and bad guys were hard to tell apart, but impossible to avoid because they were the only ones with access to both information and data and the markets themselves.

In addition, those brokers were, until recent years, always paid on a commission basis, meaning that many encouraged selling and trading in order to generate their own income at the customer's expense.

It made people wonder whether they were called "broker" because that's what you were once you had dealt with them.

The brokerage industry has, in many ways, reinvented itself over the last 10 to 15 years, though there are still plenty of pockets where the Wild West mentality lives on. The metamorphosis of brokers—guys who traditionally sold stocks, bonds, and mutual funds—into financial advisors, who go beyond making transactions and recommending investments to oversee the entire financial picture, has largely been created by public demand.

It has also generated a tremendous amount of public confusion. Between the different regulatory standards and documents for brokers versus financial planners, the range of names that loosely fall under the terms "broker" or "financial planner" or "money manager," there are many times when consumers believe they are getting one type of help, and instead are talking to someone who plays a different role.

It is entirely possible for you to think you are hiring a broker, but to wind up with someone who acts more like a financial planner or money manager, or vice versa. As this book goes to press, the federal government is wrestling with these inconsistencies and trying to decide if it will require broker-dealers who "provide advice" to work under the same standards as investment advisors. If it does, then a brokerage account executive who gives investment advice would have the same fiduciary, put-the-client's interests-first standard that an investment advisor must currently live up to.

That doesn't put an end to the "suitability standard" that brokers have been living with, it just leaves that in place for the guys who sell products and investments, rather than advice.

Of course, plenty of people who have worked with a stockbroker feel like they have been getting advice, even if that's not what they have actually been paying for. It's unlikely that part of the confusion will end.

The reasons for this evolution have to do with changes in the rest of the financial services industry, but they boil down to brokers' efforts to survive amid the financial planners who offer complete service and the do-it-yourself crowd that buys stocks and funds without help from anyone.

While the changes in the brokerage business were supposed to make things easier for consumers, they made vetting a broker more complex. In fact, if you are meeting with a broker, but looking for someone to provide investment advice and function as a financial planner, you may need to ask the interview questions that apply to both specialties in order to feel comfortable with your decision.

As with all financial advisors, the key to finding a good broker is having a good idea of what you want, and knowing how to look for it.

Can I Do This Myself?

No one actually "needs" a broker. The average individual investor can take care of a lifetime's worth of investment needs by purchasing no-load mutual funds and stocks—and the number of stocks that are being made available to the public on a commission-free, no-broker basis has grown to the point that you can assemble a nice portfolio that way, too. Treasury bonds also are available on a no-commission basis, direct from the government.

Likewise, anyone working with a financial planner, investment advisor, money manager, or the trust department of a bank could find a broker's services redundant and unnecessary.

But if you intend to invest in municipal or corporate bonds or want stocks beyond the universe of the few hundred that currently sell shares directly to the public—or you simply want a specialist to suggest moves and implement strategy—you will need a broker in there somewhere, either the full-service variety, a discount broker, or an online service (there are details on picking an online broker later in this chapter).

Some people work with several brokers, each specializing in meeting a specific need or handling a particular type of transaction, such as a fixed-income specialist selling bonds and an equity specialist recommending stocks.

What to Expect from a Broker

The traditional broker is a "full-service broker." As the name implies, this is someone who can handle all manner of transactions and provide information to guide your investment choices. Technically, if he is a broker, he is selling you products and services, rather than selling you advice.

That said, many full-service brokers go by other titles, notably "investment consultants" or "asset managers." Thus, no matter what an advisor gives as a title, you want to qualify her services, not only in terms of what she provides you but what her responsibilities are. Unless she is registered as an investment advisor, she does not currently have to live up to a "fiduciary standard" to put your interests first.

Unfortunately, millions of customers pay the full-service rate without getting full service.

A relationship with a full-service broker should be part-guidance, part-research, and part-execution. In an ideal relationship, the broker gathers information, passes it to you, outlining each prospect and supporting it with analyst recommendations, research reports, and other data. Once you have made your decision, the broker makes the trade.

Where to Start the Search

Brokerage services tend to be a word-of-mouth business, but the truth is that many established, experienced brokers started working their way up taking the people who walked in to the office, and making cold calls—dialing for dollars—hoping they might find an interested customer. Don't assume, therefore, that you'll be poorly served if you get a phone solicitation or simply walk into the most reputable firm in town; just do your due diligence to make sure you're not walking into trouble.

Many brokers hold local seminars, designed to educate consumers, then, draw them in as clients. Don't be bashful about attending these seminars, which usually are free, and which may include a lunch and promise a no-obligation financial analysis. Just remember that the fact that someone can fill an auditorium or a fancy restaurant does not make him the right broker for you.

If there is a local stockbrokers club, put a call in to see if you can attend a meeting. Most of these clubs have regional executives in to talk about their company; you can watch a broker ask questions and do some personal research.

Defining "Suitability"

The broker functions like a salesman but, unlike someone pushing vacuum cleaners or refrigerators, simply persuading you to write a check does not legally constitute doing his job.

Brokers have a legal responsibility to make sure that each and every recommendation they make is suitable for you, your financial circumstances, goals and objectives, and level of understanding. Anything less than that, whether done out of greed for a commission or mere stupidity, leaves the broker liable for resulting losses.

"Unsuitable investments" are inappropriately risky, such as junk bonds for a conservative retiree. It may also be something that is inappropriate, such as a costly insurance product like a variable annuity with a "life insurance kicker" sold to someone with no real need for the insurance feature; if the insurance tie-in significantly increases costs or erodes the client's investment— and those things can happen—then the investment was unsuitable.

It's also worth noting that "unsuitable" does not necessarily mean investments that lose money when they were purchased expecting a profit; a broker is not liable for losses that are a normal part of investment ups and downs, so long as they clearly explained in advance the possibilities and circumstances that could lead to losses.

Smart Investor Tip

"Suitable investments" can lose money. While that's obviously not the intent, the market makes fools of many money managers and brokers; a broker is not liable for losses that are a normal part of investment ups and downs, so long as they clearly explained in advance the possibilities and circumstances that could lead to losses.

What is suitable, therefore, is defined by you and not necessarily the broker.

An interesting anecdote about that involves my father, who once had a broker who suggested what amounted to a high-cost, high-risk regional bank mutual fund. My father asked for my thoughts, and I told him the investment was inappropriate given his conservative nature, his outlook, and his needs. When my father told the broker that he would not be investing, the broker went off, asking whether my dad thought that he knew more about investments than the broker did. My father explained that the broker knew more about investments, but not enough about my father. (He subsequently stopped doing business with the broker.)

While you want a broker to present you with opportunities and reasons why you should—or should not—buy or sell a stock, bond, or mutual fund, the broker's first job is to get to know you well enough to only present you with opportunities that meet your needs. If the broker doesn't know you—if he has just called on the phone, for example—and he does not ask a number of detailed questions, you should wonder whether he has enough knowledge to adequately do his job.

If a broker continually suggests investments that you consider inappropriate, that he thinks are "perfect" for you—like the idiot trying to sell my father the regional bank sector fund—he has failed at Job One, getting to know you.

Do It at a Discount?

Discount brokers are exactly what they sound like. They execute trades at reduced commission rates, but typically with fewer services like research and counsel. Thus, if you are seeking an advisor with whom you can have a lifetime relationship, cheaper may not be better.

Typically, a discount broker does not offer the same breadth or research that you might expect from a full-service broker, but may make additional research available for a fee. And unless you plan to trade regularly, you may not work with anyone at a discount brokerage firm on a regular basis. Instead, you will get the broker who is available to process your trade, a far cry from the comfort and assurance you can get from a long-term relationship with a full-service broker.

With the evolution of online brokers and the incredible suite of tools many offer, the traditional "deep discount" broker has pretty well been moved to cyberspace. It's ideal for the do-it-yourselfer, but the person who needs more assistance will need to pay for it.

Do Name Brands Matter?

It is more important to have a broker who is expert at what he or she does than to have someone who is affiliated with a national wirehouse like Merrill Lynch, Morgan Stanley, or the other big names.

Yes, the big names have access to their own big stable of researchers and may sell exclusive products, but there are few other operational differences. Moreover, both the brand-name houses and the boutique brokerage firms have their own cases of "selling pressures," where brokers feel management's push to reach certain sales quotas.

Additional research is important, but you want a broker who does his or her own research, rather than relying solely on the firm's reports. In fact, you want a broker who is unafraid to do things that are out of step with the firm, advising you to stay away from industries or companies that she is nervous about, even if the brokerage house analysts are on television or in the papers talking those stocks up.

Smart Investor Tip

You want a broker who does his or her own research, rather than relying solely on the firm's reports.

Finally, the bigger firms typically have programs that try out a crush of newbies, trying to see who can hack it in the business and who is better off finding a different profession. The advisor who calls on you from a big firm may be the latest recruit trying to build a clientele; the experience of the broker in the office matters more than the name of the brokerage firm above the office door.

Picking an Online Broker

If you don't need the counsel and guidance of a broker to buy stocks and funds—or if you have hired a financial planner for advice but it's left for you to execute the trades—you probably want to forget about picking the right person and look instead at picking the right online brokerage firm.

Unlike the interviews you do with real people, the selection process for an online broker is an "interview" that typically involves reading the frequently asked questions from the firm's website and maybe having a discussion with a customer-service representative.

But because this is a do-it-yourself kind of business, you need to know your plans in order to find the right fit. Frequent traders have different needs than buy-and-hold investors; savvy investors need less hand-holding than newbies. Match your needs to what the firm offers. Here are your key considerations:

- **Commission costs.** Commissions vary by the frequency of trades, number of shares, and even price of the shares. Plenty of firms offer a certain number of free trades, although they may require that you open a bank or money-market account with a minimum balance to get those no-cost transactions. There can be a huge jump in costs if a broker is required to execute the trade. The lowest cost provider may not be the one with the ads screaming about cheap trades, it will be the one where its system best meshes with your expected account activity.

- **Trading/investing pattern.** Try to put your trading/investing pattern into the cost grid from the online broker; the one advertising the cheapest trades may not actually be cheapest for you.

- **Hidden costs.** Commissions are just one part of the equation. If there are fees for delivery of stock certificates, for transfers, for wired payments, for annual "account maintenance," and even for terminating your account, you may wind up an unhappy camper. The firm with the lowest trade commissions may not be cheapest if it nickels and dimes you all the time.

- **Trading capabilities.** Most online firms can serve most online customers. Make sure you fall into that category. You're outside the norm if you are frequently trading penny stocks, options, futures contracts, foreign currencies, bonds, foreign securities, and more. If you can't handle all of your business with the firm, you may want to look elsewhere.

- **Real-time abilities.** This was a big-time selling point in the past, but it's par for the course now. If a firm is bragging about its real-time abilities now, it's kind of like a shopping center bragging that it has indoor plumbing. It's nice, but not much of a selling point. However, if rapid trading is important to you, you will want the most live action you can get; make sure the firm can deliver.

- **Support.** Ask online traders for their biggest beef about brokerage firms and the most common answer will have to do with how the firm responds to questions and complaints. Yet the amount of support you receive should be pretty well spelled out by the firm in advance. If you go for the ultra-low-cost trades, you can expect virtually no hand-holding whatsoever. Find out the support levels that come with basic service and know who to contact if there is a problem or dispute.

- **Account minimums.** Some firms have no minimum investment to open and maintain an account, while others have clearly defined levels and charge fees when you fall below the specified target. Depending on your means, a big investment requirement can be off-putting.

- **Sweeps and money-market features.** Most online brokerage firms have money-market accounts, which is where new deposits—plus any dividends or money received from the sale of your stocks—sits while awaiting your next instructions. Find out if the firm automatically sweeps idle money—such as dividend payments—into your money-market account at the end of the day. (If it waits longer, you are losing interest on that money.) Find out what the firm's money-market account pays in interest, and whether you must use the house fund or if you can pick one on your own. Inquire about check-writing privileges and fees, too.

- **Research and other goodies.** Consumer research firm J.D. Power & Associates says customers rank decent research ahead of things like trade execution and customer service in determining their overall satisfaction. Each brokerage firm has its own resources and access to other providers, too. At some, everything is free; at others, certain services come with a cost. Check out an online broker's tools—like portfolio planners, stock screeners, and the like—and compare between sites to find the tools you find most helpful and easy to use.

- **Crash protection.** We're not talking stock market crash here, as there is nothing any brokerage firm can do to help you then. System crashes are another matter altogether. Find out what a broker will do someday when an emergency strikes. Will you be working by telephone or have a personal contact? These problems are few and far between, but you'd like to know what happens if you get blitzed by one.

- **Easy navigation and your gut feeling.** As with a traditional broker, once you sort through the details, it's still going to come down to where you feel most comfortable and which service you like the best. Remember, too, that with online brokerage firms there is seldom a drawback to having accounts at two different firms; if it doesn't promote confusion and make your accounting difficult—and if you have an affinity for the offerings and niceties at two different firms—you may opt to get the best of both worlds.

Checking out Candidates

Stockbrokers typically file a Form U-4 to register with the Financial Industry Regulatory Agency (FINRA), which covers the details on the advisor's past. As this book was going to press, FINRA had proposed stepped-up disclosure requirements that would make it easier to discern when a broker had committed violations of securities law or had disciplinary hearings or customer complaints.

Further, the new form would more easily enable "statutory disqualification," which happens when an advisor is barred from the investment industry; under current rules and existing paperwork, a registered investment advisor could be tossed from the business for violating securities laws, but resurface as a registered representative, working as a broker. When approved, the new U-4 form will make that kind of disingenuous act hard to pass off.

Because brokers, account executives, and whatever else you want to call a "registered representative" are regulated by FINRA, start your background check by using the agency's BrokerCheck service. It will provide information on an advisor's previous employers, disciplinary actions, and customer disputes filed against him or her, states he or she is licensed to do business in, industry exams he or she has passed, outside business affiliations (which may show conflicts of interest), and more.

The service is free and takes just minutes. If you can get the broker's Central Registration Depository (CRD) number, you can go directly to his or her record, which is helpful if the broker has a common name. To use BrokerCheck, go to www.finra.org.

Your second background check stop should be your state securities commissioner's office, for which contact details are available at www.nasaa.org.

If your broker candidate also functions as an investment advisor, she will be a registered investment advisor, meaning she files a Form ADV with either the state regulator or the Securities and Exchange Commission. To check out the Investment Advisor Registration Depository (IARD), which you can access through the SEC's Investment Advisor Public Disclosure program, go to www.investor.gov to find an easy link.

Some brokers also sell insurance products. If your candidate does, be sure to check the insurance license—and to look for disciplinary problems—with your state insurance commissioner. Find your state insurance commissioner's office by looking at the "states and jurisdictions map" on www.naic.org, the website of the National Association of Insurance Commissioners.

The Price You'll Pay, and How You'll Pay It

Unless he or she charges an asset-management fee—meaning he or she takes a slice of the assets managed each year—or a flat fee for account management (as in the "cash-management accounts" common to many brokerage firms), you should expect any broker you meet to be paid on commission.

It's not always easy to figure out just how much commission, or how the broker gets paid at all for some services, which is why you will need to ask. Moreover, the broker's pay scale may change depending on the size of your investments; the more money you are putting into play, the more you may feel like you get the volume discount.

With stocks, for example, smaller trades and low trading volume generally result in higher commissions per share. If you want to buy the grandchildren five shares of Microsoft, your commission could be as expensive as one or two of those shares; by comparison, if you buy a round lot (100 shares), you might be laying out roughly the same dollars to get the trade completed.

On mutual funds, investors pay a "load" that can either be taken off the top as a front-end charge (typically 3.0 to 5.5 percent) or paid in the form of higher expenses over several years of owning the fund, plus a back-end charge if the fund is sold during the first few years of ownership. Some funds drop the sales charge—meaning no money comes off the top to pay the broker—but charge higher expenses for the life of the investment, with the broker capturing the "trail commission" the whole way.

On bonds, there usually is no explicit commission amount. The broker buys the bond at one price and sells to you at another; the "spread"—the difference between the two prices—represents the commission. As in stocks, the more bonds bought, the smaller the spread.

Then there are other products, ranging from limited partnerships to annuities, life insurance, new stock and bond issues, and more. Commissions can get as high as 10 percent in these cases.

The general rule on these types of financial products is that the more complicated and harder to sell, the bigger commission the broker will get for convincing you to buy it.

Brokers may also be compensated on an ongoing basis. The "12b-1 fees" charged for sales and marketing on some mutual funds apply to accounts every year. Essentially, the fund takes as much as 1 percent of your account balance each year and pays a portion to the broker; the charge is in addition to the ongoing management fees charged by the fund, but it is calculated into the fund's "total expense ratio." Annuity companies and partnerships often charge similar ongoing fees.

Because these ongoing fees are removed painlessly—without a bill or confirmation statement that lays out the exact cost—they are easy to forget about. Don't. If you should decide to change brokers, make sure that any and all ongoing fees are transferred to the new broker; if you do not specify the change, the broker (or firm, if your broker changed firms or left the business) will continue to receive these ongoing payments in perpetuity, without providing you with one shred of the ongoing service you are actually paying for.

Last, if your broker is functioning as a money manager—essentially developing and executing an investment strategy on your behalf—she may charge something called a "wrap fee," which combines management and brokerage fees. These fees can run as high as 3 percent of the assets under management, which is pretty steep. Something closer to 1.5 percent or 2 percent is about average for a stock wrap account; 1.0 to 1.5 percent is the norm with mutual fund wraps. A wrap fee lets you know in advance what you will pay a broker/money manager, but make sure you are actually getting your money's worth; if you and the broker/manager employ a buy-and-hold strategy, run the numbers to make sure that you aren't better off with straight commission.

Credentials Worth Looking For

Brokers sometimes pursue the same credentials of a financial planner. Like a planner, however, no credentials are necessary. A broker, however, must pass exams in order to practice, the basic tests being known as "Series 6" and "Series 7" exams.

Those will not necessarily be much help when it comes to lifetime financial advice, since the typical licensing review course takes only two or three days. Moreover, the exams are more concerned with a broker's technical proficiency—understanding of investment issues, legal and regulatory requirements—than with developing a real-world understanding of risk, diversification, and more.

The National Endowment for Financial Education has done several studies that have consistently shown that rookie brokers are trained without a significant emphasis on "understanding a client's overall financial picture and assimilating the role of individual investments within that picture." (That's not a problem, so long as you only want them to facilitate your trades; the minute you want something bordering on planning, it's a problem.)

Until a decade ago, brokers did not have to even undergo continuing education to retain their license, although it is now required at certain anniversaries of licensing.

Smart Investor Tip
Don't be fooled by an advisor telling you he is a "registered representative," a "registered investment advisor," or both.

As such, advanced credentials are a good thing; while there is no substitute for the School of Hard Knocks, you don't want to go through *that* course while riding on your account. With that in mind, you may want to look for advanced credentials. Don't be fooled by an advisor telling you he is a "registered representative," a "registered investment advisor" (RIA), or both. The former is a fancy way of saying that someone has passed the exams needed to sell the products they represent; RIA, meanwhile, is not a credential, it's just proof that the advisor has registered. That said, an RIA qualifies as an advisor—and not just a broker—so he or she must live up to the fiduciary standard of care; that's a plus, but it doesn't make anyone a more skilled counselor. These credentials will:

- *Certified Financial Planner, Certified Fund Specialist, Chartered Mutual Fund Consultant,* or other designations that are described in Chapter 5, among many others, typically are more common to financial planners, but have found a home with some brokers looking to raise their education and prove their expertise.
- The *Chartered Financial Analyst* (CFA) designation, one of the most prestigious of all credentials, awarded by the CFA Institute, requires several years of experience, a study course, and exams in securities analysis, portfolio management, financial accounting, economics, and ethics. The designation is common among institutional money managers and Wall Street analysts; it is held in high regard in those circles, so if you find a local stock-picker with a CFA, he or she may merit strong consideration in your selection process. At the very least, he or she will have some chops for doing his or her own stock-picking, rather than relying mostly on company research.

Interview Questions for Brokers

With brokers, you have an initial interview and then subsequent mini-interviews whenever you discuss making additional investments or changing your portfolio. The first interview should define the relationship and establish your comfort level with the broker; the other is part of ongoing maintenance and is designed to keep you informed, the broker honest, and the relationship moving forward.

Your First Meeting

During your first meeting with a broker, start with these questions:

What is your educational and professional background?

A broker's background will provide you with clues to his competence. If he has been jumping around from one firm to the next, there could be trouble ahead. Many firms don't fire brokers, but simply encourage them to leave before they get the axe; when that happens, a poor performer packs up and moves to the next firm. (Good brokers sometimes jump ship, too, especially if they have been lured by bonuses and improved commission schedules.)

Smart Investor Tip
If a knowledgeable and experienced broker has moved several times in recent years, be prepared to call the broker's previous employers for a reference.

If you find someone who appears knowledgeable and experienced but who has moved several times in recent years, be prepared to call the broker's previous employers for a reference. Ask the manager of the old office whether she would hire the broker again and whether there were any discipline problems; some office managers will feel constrained by confidentiality rules not to tell you, but most will warn you away if there were real problems. (After all, if someone warns you away from the advisor, he or she may also be able to capture your business.)

What continuing education classes have you taken? What certifications, if any, do you have?

Classes aren't a necessity, but they do show commitment to staying on top of available products and laws. This is particularly important if you plan to have a broker advise you on more than just plain-vanilla, pick-a-stock/fund/bond issues.

What is your CRD number?

This is one of the few deal-breaker questions in all of financial services, so don't waste your time and save it for the end of an interview. CRD stands for Central Registration Depository, and it is the centralized clearinghouse used by regulators for filing complaints against brokers. When a broker passes the exams and gets a license to sell securities, he or she gets a CRD number.

When there are complaints filed against a broker—even if he is cleared of wrongdoing—they go into a file listed by that number.

You can do a background check without the broker's CRD number, but why risk confusion? Having the specific number guarantees that you get directly to their record. This is particularly important if the broker has a common name, as asking the state regulators or FINRA to find "John Smith in Pennsylvania" could lead to reviewing the wrong file.

Brokers may not know their own CRD number. Chances are they have never been asked and may not have it handy. That's an honest excuse, but they can look it up quickly; suggest they find themselves in the FINRA BrokerCheck service, since their record will have the number on it.

If the broker also works as a financial advisor, he or she may have an Investment Advisory Registration Depository (IARD) number. That's a suitable alternative.

If a broker will not give you his or her CRD number, end the interview immediately. No kidding, just walk away. Think of it like a walking into a room and finding your children with something in their hands; when they see you, they put their hands behind their back. Presumably, they're hiding something. When a broker knows you intend to check backgrounds and refuses to help you check his own, he must have some idea of what you are going to find. Don't take chances.

What a Broker Should Be Asking You

The short answer is everything about your investment habits, notions, and ability to tolerate risk. The more services the broker provides—if he acts as a financial planner or also sells insurance products—the more he will delve into your entire background.

Even if he will only handle a portion of your money, let him see the whole financial picture. Only with that knowledge can he fully understand your strategy and then implement his piece of it properly.

Remember, too, that the questions the broker asks typically support your new account agreement, so if you have left him with the wrong impression or an incomplete picture of you, he acts on that information, and it ultimately leads to trouble, your failure to make complete disclosure will be used against you in arbitration. If the broker's recommendations were "suitable" based on the information you gave, he'll win the case even if a big-picture, complete review shows that a prudent man would have made different choices if he had known the full situation.

The Price You'll Pay, and How You'll Pay It

Now that you know the questions you need to ask when selecting your advisors, here's what you'll need to ask to figure out how much you should pay.

How do you get paid?

Always ask about the money, especially because it can lead to discussions of your payment options. If the broker can act as a financial consultant and get paid a percentage of the assets you give her to manage, you may be better off than paying straight commission.

And some brokers put you on a flat fee basis that covers the basic costs of your account; the annual fee gives you a limited amount of "free" trading, so that there won't be traditional commissions until you make sufficient trades to use up the freebies.

Can I get a copy of the firm's commission schedule? Is it negotiable?

Discount brokers will give you their fee schedule in a flash, because it is a major selling point that they have lower prices than a full-service shop. Full-service brokers may not be so willing, hemming and hawing about how the schedule is not really fixed and how the commission can vary on each trade.

If at all possible, get the commission schedule, even if it means going to the office manager. With the schedule in hand, don't be afraid to negotiate for a discount; you probably won't get it, but if the advisor wants your business badly enough, there may be a deal that can be cut.

What service will I get for the commissions I pay?

If all you get from a broker is processing trades—with no measure of portfolio management, investment research, and suitability analysis—you might as well go with a deep-discount broker.

Keep in mind that "full-service" means different things to different people. To some people, it's an occasional phone call; to others it means a weekly e-mail.

For years, my in-laws had a "cash management account" with a very big brokerage firm. It was, as my father-in-law put it, their "chance to feel like a big shot." However, when my father-in-law died in 2008, I found that it was mostly a cash-mismanagement account. In fact, the account was almost completely in cash stuffed in a pathetically low-yield money fund run by the house. When account-management fees were factored in, they swallowed the annual returns on the cash and then hit the balance for more. (I eventually replaced their "cash management" for my mother-in-law with an online savings account; it generated better returns without the expenses.) I will forever believe that my in-laws were never properly served for the amount they paid in fees.

Will I pay account management fees?

It would be a simple world if brokerage houses earned all of their money on commissions.

They don't.

Some will nickel-and-dime you at every turn, for everything from failing to maintain a certain balance to not generating a prescribed amount in commissions every year. Others offer accounts like the one my in-laws had, charging high fees for the convenience of check-writing and credit card privileges. While my in-laws stopped making trades—and thus generating commissions—for several years prior to my stepping in and closing the account, the broker in charge of the account collected fees like clockwork. My in-laws were, effectively, a small-scale annuity making regular payments to the guy (for doing absolutely nothing; he didn't even call my in-laws to see if they needed anything).

You may even pay a fee for opening and closing your account.

Fees like this add up—especially at the discount firms—so make sure you know about all potential ancillary charges before you sign up.

Are there any contests right now for signing up new clients? Do you get anything special if I decide to do business with you?

You may have gotten a cold call because you were the next name in the phone book or because a friend gave out your name; your broker might also be working to sign up new clients in order to get some sort of prize from the firm.

It's not that signing up during a contest period is necessarily bad, but make sure that you believe that the broker's interest in you extends beyond a potential prize for bringing you into the fold.

Learn about Clientele and Scope of Practice

Below are some questions you should ask to learn about the advisor's clientele and scope of his practice so that you can make an informed decision of whether you fit within his niche.

Who is your typical client?

As with all forms of financial advisor, you want a broker whose average client looks like you and has concerns akin to yours. Typically, brokers look for good investments and then try to match those selections with good candidates from within their clientele.

If the bulk of a broker's clientele is singles and young couples, that is likely to push her to spend her time looking for more aggressive stocks, college-tuition plans, and other investments that fit that demographic group. If, by comparison, you are nearing retirement age, you need to worry if the broker is mostly looking for investments that are better suited to someone else.

In getting the answer to this question, don't focus solely on age, income, and size of portfolio issues. Look instead at what the typical client wants to buy. This will give you an idea of whether the broker has a particular specialty. Remember that just because a broker is adept at picking stocks does not make him ideal for picking corporate bonds; make sure he will be able to meet your needs or be prepared to split your business between a few different specialists.

How many active clients do you work with at one time?

Because their job involves finding investments that fit any number of their clients, brokers can work with a fairly large number of people on an ongoing basis. Once they find the right investment, they may spend the whole day just calling customers.

But if you want guidance, you want someone who will give you more than a sales pitch.

Do the math. You know how often to expect the broker to call because you've asked. If the broker has a huge clientele and calls the average client once a week for five minutes, you will know quickly that he spends more than half of his time selling rather than researching.

The broker is not just supposed to be a conduit for trading, so make sure the size of her client base allows her to have the time to adequately research and come to conclusions about investments and how they fit in with your needs. The broker who was upset when my father didn't take his suggestion, for example, was pushing a product rather than making sure that he had a good fit for his clients.

Will anyone else work with me?

Some brokers have so many clients that they have sales assistants. These people call you on the broker's behalf. Very often, the assistants get the clients who are less likely to make a trade. (In my father's case, when he decided to think for himself and not take the broker's tip, the broker threatened him with having to work with an assistant in the future. Ironically, my father moved his account to a firm where, for years, he was very satisfied working with the big broker's assistant; he got the broker's counsel when he needed it, but found that the assistant was more than qualified to work with his less-demanding needs.)

Sales assistants generally have a sales license, but not always the full expertise or knowledge concerning your situation. That could make it tougher for them to answer your questions.

If you will field calls from someone in the firm besides your broker, find out why. Then find out who; arrange to meet that person and, at the very least, get his or her CRD number.

If a broker promises to work with you but consistently lets you deal with the sales assistant, chances are that he has focused on the accounts with the most bucks in them—and yours doesn't qualify—or that you have a transaction-oriented salesman who is more interested in generating commissions than in developing a good long-term relationship.

Learn Relationship and Investment Style

With this information in hand, below are questions you should ask to learn about the advisor's relationship and investment style.

How often will I hear from you and what will prompt your calls?

This helps set expectations for the relationship and allows you to direct the broker on the right way to work with you. If you don't want a call every week pressuring you to invest, this would be the time to speak up.

At the same time, if the broker promises to call weekly and those calls become more sporadic, you will know immediately that you have a "loss-of-interest" problem.

You want to know why the broker will call because you may not want continual sales pitches. Good brokers call to talk about a lot of things besides immediate sales. They act as emotional disciplinarians to help clients stay the course when the markets turn volatile, to suggest when it might be time to add more of a stock that the market has knocked around, or when to consider taking a tax loss and making a sale. They notify clients of changes in tax laws, talk about how their opinions concerning certain market segments are changing, and more. If a broker only plans to call when she believes she has something appropriate for you, you will eventually have the problem my father encountered, namely a broker who values your contact only for the commission it can generate.

How do you react when a client doesn't take your advice?

You'll get a better answer from the references than the advisor, but a good broker should know that not every suggestion will spin your fan. Hopefully, she will talk about using a "no" to better figure out what will create a "yes" in the future.

What criteria do you use before deciding what to buy? What makes something a sell?

It's time to figure out how the broker puts expertise to work. You want to know how he picks the stocks and mutual funds that he recommends and how he matches different types of funds to the individual needs of an investor.

If a broker can't tell you in plain English what gets her excited about an investment, then all you are getting is a practiced sales pitch rather than the benefit of real knowledge.

You also want to know up front why a broker buys or sells securities to make sure those conditions hold up later in the relationship. If you have been working with a broker and he or she suddenly changes stripes and starts recommending buys and sells that are out of character, you will recognize immediately that something is wrong and that the broker appears to be pushing trades—which generate commissions—even if they are inconsistent with the broker's approach to the market.

What's your preferred market strategy or investment style? How do you invest your own money?

You may have a preferred strategy or no clue at all, but you want to make sure that the way the broker invests makes sense to you, that it's something you can believe in and stick with.

Many people claim to be buy-and-hold investors, and they are so long as the market makes their picks look good. As 2008 proved, however, the market sometimes works against investors. Ask how this broker's clients did in 2008 and 2009, and whether his or her strategy allowed investors to sidestep the carnage—but possibly miss out on the subsequent rally—or whether it provided a smoother ride.

Don't Forget the Nuts and Bolts

And of course, you must ask the following administrative questions that let you know more about the advisor's background.

Can I get the names of a few clients to act as references?

References will help you determine the character of the broker-client relationship and decide if the broker works with people in a way that you expect to be comfortable with. No advisor is going to tell you that she reacts badly when you decide not to take one of her suggestions; it will just happen if that situation comes up. By asking clients about those situations, you can learn a lot more about the tenor of the relationship. (See Chapter 14 for questions to ask references.)

Can I review the papers you want me to sign when I open an account? Can I review and get a copy of my "new account form?"

Some brokers have clients routinely sign up for margin accounts or options agreements. Some also push discretionary agreements, giving them control over the trading activity in the account.

Don't do it.

In addition, brokers fill out new account forms whenever they get a new client. These forms include information on your net worth, income, and investment objectives; they get filed away and may never again be seen—let alone signed—by customers. Unless, of course, there's a problem, when the new account form will be brought out to show all of the things you first said you might be interested in, thereby justifying the suitability of almost anything.

Rogue brokers have been known to fictionalize these forms, putting incorrect information in so that it looks like you want commission-generating activity. Some brokers may tell you they have a great investment that they can't sell to you unless the forms say your net worth exceeds $250,000; if you fudge the paperwork to get in on the deal, you might be killing yourself in arbitration if/when things go wrong. This is precisely what happened with a number of the victims of the Bernie Madoff and Robert Allen Stanford Ponzi schemes; in that case, it was the money manager and not the advisor who was crooked, but breaking the rules to get in on the investment yielded disastrous results.

Help the broker fill out the new account form, coming up with a definition for your investment objectives; get a copy—preferably signed by the advisor—for your own records. It could come in handy if there is ever a problem with how the broker managed your account.

Smart Investor Tip

Lawyers at arbitration cases put tremendous value on "predispute correspondence," written instructions about goals and objectives. If the broker will not let you participate in the new account form or give you a copy but you still want to work with him, put your investment circumstances in writing in a letter to both the broker and office manager. If a dispute ever arises, this letter from the start of your relationship will go a long way to building your case.

Who will hold the securities? Why?

Most brokerage firms prefer to hold securities "in street name," which means that they keep the shares registered in their name, but in an account registered to you. This makes it easy to buy and sell and to complete trades (rules provide that transactions must be closed—the money or shares turned over—within three days of the trading date). They also like this because safekeeping the shares means you will likely use them when the time comes to sell instead of redeeming shares through a discounter.

Most investment customers keep shares in street name, but make sure your broker explains how to get stock certificates if you want them. As a general rule, brokerage houses charge a fee—the highest I have heard being $100—for issuing certificates. If you want to hold the paper, know the costs and the rules.

How frequently will I get statements? Will you go over a sample statement with me?

It's not the broker's fault if the firm has statements that are hard to read; it is the broker's fault if she doesn't prepare you on how to read them. Get a look at the firm's statements, confirm that you will get them at regular intervals rather than only when there has been trading activity, and make sure you understand how to read them.

Who will control the decision making in my account?

If you sign a "discretionary agreement," you are giving up control of your investments. For your own financial safety, this is a bad idea. Make sure that trades will not be made in your account without your approval. As obvious as it seems, make sure the broker acknowledges that this is your wish and that he or she promises to contact you and get your authorization before moving your money. Churning cases—where a broker makes a lot of transactions to generate commissions—have been on the wane for a decade now, but they haven't disappeared completely.

Ask These Questions before Buying an Investment

Because each trade is a chance to reconnect with the broker and build the relationship, every purchase or sale becomes its own mini-interview. Beyond wanting to get enough information to be comfortable with the security itself, you'll want to get these questions answered:

Is this in keeping with my investment strategy?

This question applies only in those cases when the broker is providing investment counsel or portfolio management services. A full-service advisor should always be able to explain how an investment choice fits into the overall scheme of your portfolio. If he or she can't answer this question, chances are that you have not done enough work together for him or her to know your best interests or what's suitable and appropriate.

You want to be aware when a broker's selections represent a drastic shift in your portfolio, such as the regional bank fund that was an oddball choice for my father. If the investment raises a red flag, investigate the broker's choices further.

How much commission will you and your firm earn on this trade?

Yes, you asked about commissions and asked for the schedule during the initial interview, but you still need to check it out again with each and every trade. At most firms, a broker can get extra commissions for selling stock that the firm wants to get out of inventory. The firm may also offer extra money whenever it is a "market maker" in a stock, meaning that it buys and sells a certain issue from its own inventory.

Similarly, brokers may get a commission boost when they sell the house mutual funds.

Your confirmation slip should tell you whenever the firm is a market maker, and it will give you the total outlay on the trade, but by then it is too late; you already have paid the commission. I once got a surprise when my broker's commission schedule changed, and I only recognized the new deal when it hit me in the wallet.

By asking, you get a chance to maybe get some of that commission back, in the form of a discount. Some brokers have the authority to cut commissions by anywhere from 20 to 60 percent, although your chances of getting that discount probably depend on just how good a customer you are and the firm you are dealing with. Increasingly, firms are loath to cut any deals, fearing that if you get special treatment, your neighbor might sue to get the same pricing.

If you find out that the broker has a special incentive attached to the deal, ask if the recommendation would be the same if she wasn't getting paid more. If you question her sincerity, make her justify the decision by comparing the investment to similar choices on which the commission would be lower.

After all fees are paid, how much must this investment gain in value before I break even?

This is another way of getting at the costs involved in the trade, but it helps you see in dramatic fashion just how big a hurdle trading costs are. If trading costs are a big nut to crack, it will make it harder for an investment to deliver real, after-expenses returns that meet your expectations.

What NOT to Do in Working with a Broker

- Never send money based entirely on a telephone sales pitch. Even if you like the cold call—and I hate them, but they must work because brokerage firms keep doing them—you need more information about the firm and the security than you can get in a quick sales call. If you want an advisor for life—rather than a hot stock tip for today—you need to be able to go to a broker's office, meet him or her and check things out; lacking that, hang up the phone and go find a broker who can shake your hand and look you in the eye.

- Never make a check out to the representative. The money goes to the firm to be invested in your account. The firm pays commissions and uses the rest in accordance with your instructions; if your check is payable to the broker, it just might be cashed rather than invested.

- Never send money to any address but that of the firm or of an operation designated in the prospectus (such as a transfer agent). Again, this avoids schemes where money is diverted into a rogue broker's pocket.

- Never allow transaction confirmations and account statements to be sent to your broker instead of you. These are your record of what's happening in the account; without them, you don't have the paper trail necessary to build a strong case if things go wrong.

If a broker asks you to do any of these four things, contact the firm's office manager or compliance officer immediately. Chances are you will want to end a relationship in these circumstances, because any broker who asks for these things—even if he or she has not taken any of your money yet—is playing fast and loose with the rules.

Will this sale help you win any prizes or sales contests?

Yes, you asked something similar during the initial interview, but that was a bit different. Contests to sign up new clients aren't bad, because there is no inherent conflict; if you need brokerage services, and the brokerage house needs new clients, your interests are aligned.

But if the broker gets a bonus for selling you an investment—whether it's a health club membership, a fancy dinner, or some bigger incentive—that's a problem. If the broker is selling all of his clients the same product to win a prize, his interests are misaligned.

FINRA has cracked down on contests and wiped out the worst abuses, but even minor paybacks can sway some advisors. If the broker's advice doesn't feel to you like it's a great fit and you then find out there is a contest involved, you probably can develop enough of a gut feeling to decide whether to do the trade; without the knowledge of the contest, you might shrug off your uneasiness and assume the broker knows better than you do.

How long do you expect me to hold this investment? Why?

Most investors are better off pursuing a buy-and-hold strategy, but commission-based sales make a broker want to trade. Unless a security shoots up in value, short-term profits may be swallowed by the costs of the trade. Make a written record of the reasons why you are buying the stock and your expectations for it, including the likely holding period; that way, if the broker suggests dumping your shares without a significant change in the company's status, you can find out why things went off the plan.

Smart Investor Tip
Make a written record of the reasons why you are buying the stock and your expectations for it, including the likely holding period.

Can I get out of this investment quickly?

This may seem a strange request given the previous question, but there is a difference. Brokers should tell you, before you invest, whether a product is hard or costly to unload. There may not be many buyers for an individual municipal bond, for example.

Other investments, such as annuities or mutual funds with a back-end load, are easy to get out of but only if you pay steep penalties. Make sure you know about these charges in advance, too.

Are there other available share classes or any cheaper ways to pay for this?

Sometimes the broker has payment options, such as Class A, B, or C shares for mutual funds, each of which charges a different load/fee structure. Make sure the broker does the math and shows you how the costs vary over the life of the investment. One share type will be less expensive in the short run, another over 10 years, so mesh the answer to this question with the answer on how long the broker expects to hold the security. (There's a discussion of how share classes work in Chapter 2.)

You've told me what it costs to buy this stock (or bond or mutual fund). How much would I get if I were to sell it today?

This is not just a commission issue, but one of "spread" and market value. In some cases—as with mutual funds—it serves to remind you of the sales charges or surrender charges. You're worried that your new investment will be a bit like a new car, where someone pays sticker price to buy it, but the vehicle will sell for a lot less the moment it's driven off the lot. If the spread is too big, find out why, and decide if the investment is really worth it.

What is the worst-case outcome for this investment?

Not every investment makes money or hits its target. Before buying a security, understand what it could cost you under dire circumstances. If a broker "guarantees" something, make sure she is offering your money back—and that you know how to get it and have it in writing—and that she is not just using an expression that shows she is confident a security will make money.

Danger Signs

It's not important whether a stockbroker wins or loses; it's where she places the blame. That's not just a clever play on words for a famous maxim, it's a true statement. When things go wrong, listen carefully to the explanation, as it will speak volumes as to whether the relationship is in trouble.

Here are signs of trouble in the relationship:

- "Happiness letters." They sound innocuous, which is the problem. In reality, these are "activity letters," where the brokerage firm has spotted a lot of trading in your account. You get a letter from the office manager, sounding like an introduction, recognizing your trading activity, wanting to make sure you are "happy" with the firm, and offering you the chance to sit down and discuss more opportunities there. If the trading continues, you may get another one of these. This is a hint that perhaps your trading pattern is not normal. The firm is trying to alert you without making you unduly alarmed. (At the same time, this letter is designed to give the brokerage firm proof that it warned you of the abnormal activity in your account.) If you get a happiness letter, review your account statements immediately.
- Paperwork you don't understand. Just because the broker says you will have control of investment choices doesn't mean that he won't pass a

discretionary agreement or a form to allow him to trade in options in front of you. Some ask all clients to sign these agreements as a matter of course, but the authorizations make it much easier for the broker to mismanage your money.

- "It's just a computer error." If there is an unauthorized trade in your account and the broker tells you not to worry because it's a computer glitch, get very nervous. Technology is so good that there are virtually no computer errors in brokerage statements. It is the proverbial needle in a haystack. If you're facing a "computer error," see the office manager and get the problem straightened out immediately.

- Inside information, allegedly confidential stuff, an upcoming research report, merger rumors, or "dynamic new products." Hot trades like this tend to have bigger commissions. They may also be excessively risky, and you may not have a good shot at capturing the kinds of profits that attract you in the first place. Hot new-issue stocks are distributed to big favored brokers and customers, and your broker most likely will not be among the lucky few. That's why a deal that sounds too good to be true probably is.

- Being "quota bait." Generally, this means the broker is trying to increase a monthly paycheck or reach sales goals, all about five days ahead of the end of a billing cycle. That would be around the 19th of the month. If that's the only time you hear from your broker—and all he or she does is talk sales and not strategy—you should question whether he or she is interested in you as a client or merely as a commission.

- "The deal is done," "It's too late," or "You have no choice" on a trade you did not authorize or understand completely. Just because the broker says something is a done deal does not make it so. Sometimes, there are errors and trade disputes, and the broker knows that anything you do to set things straight is going to cost the broker some money. If there is a problem and your broker throws this line at you, see the office manager.

- The only products being offered are run by the house or are stocks in which the firm is a market maker. The broker may make more money on these trades, but you also want a broker who is a free thinker, who makes his own evaluations and does not rely entirely on the firm's research. Brokers know which analysts in the firm are the most on-target, whose judgment they trust the most, and they should be able to sort out the firm's recommendations for what to sell all customers from what is right to sell you. Remember, you are paying for expertise, not just for the brokerage firm's latest tip.

- Significant declines in investment value for which you were not prepared. This is the biggest bugaboo of all, and many consumers lived the worst-case scenario of it in 2008 and early 2009. It's a broker's job to explain the possible downside of your investments. It's not that losses are the broker's fault, but you should never be shocked by what happens in your account. A good broker will never let you be caught unaware.

Prepare for Trouble, Just in Case

As mentioned in Chapter 7, your plan to keep a concentration from forming involves knowing what you will do if and when there's trouble. Therefore, conclude your interview with an advisor by asking about problems.

How will we resolve complaints if I am dissatisfied?

The firm will have you sign an agreement that says you agree to try arbitration before turning to the courts; you would prefer not to lose your right to pursue action in court, keeping arbitration as a lower-cost, faster-working means to an end. The same legislation that may apply the fiduciary standard to brokers who sell advice would also give the Securities and Exchange Commission the authority to invalidate mandatory arbitration clauses in broker-dealer and investment advisory agreements. After years in which mandatory arbitration clauses have been the norm, limiting investor access to courts, the new legislation may open up more venues for recovery.

Before your case gets that far, however, you want to know what would happen if there is a problem in your account, how the broker would handle it, whether it is a technical glitch or a trade that you don't recall authorizing.

The broker may laugh off the likelihood of this happening. Make her humor you and walk you through the complaint resolution process anyway. In addition, ask for an introduction to the office manager or compliance officer, the first people you are likely to be dealing with if there is a problem. Get business cards from these people and keep their numbers handy.

All of these actions serve notice to the broker that you won't tolerate trouble.

How can I terminate this relationship if I am not satisfied?

Never enter any financial arrangement without knowing how to get out of it.

> **Smart Investor Tip**
>
> Never enter any financial arrangement without knowing how to get out of it.

Have you ever had complaints filed against you by customers? How have those complaints been resolved?

The broker knows you are going to check his or her record using FINRA's BrokerCheck, so this is fess-up time. Complaints that require outside help in order to be settled—even if they clear the broker of wrongdoing—will be in the CRD file.

Essentially, you want the broker's side of the story for anything you'll find in the CRD (although don't describe it this way, because you'd also like to hear about complaints that may have been resolved before hitting the file, and many brokers don't know exactly what their CRD includes).

If the broker tells you he or she has never had these kinds of problems and BrokerCheck shows something different, run away. If a broker tries to slip one past you when he knows you are looking, what will he do when you have an established relationship and your guard is down?

Over time, even the best brokers run into customers who didn't understand what they agreed to, who sue over normal market losses, and more. What you want to hear is why these problems happened.

How do we make sure that I will not have similar problems?

This is a direct follow-up to the last question; the broker does not want you to be her next problem child. If she's learned from what went wrong the first time, she knows what she would do differently to avoid the problem again. You'll want the remedy—which may boil down to something as simple as improved communication—to be a part of your relationship.

Is your firm a member of the Securities Investor Protection Corp. (SIPC)?

SIPC provides limited protection to customers if a brokerage firm becomes insolvent or tries to shut down in the face of its financial responsibilities. SIPC does not insure against losses created by a decline in the market value of your securities.

In addition to SIPC protection, ask whether the firm has other insurance that carries over beyond the SIPC limits. SIPC coverage is standard, but many firms provide this extra insurance, too; chances are that you will never need it, but it's a comfort if you're the type of investor who worries that your brokerage firm will disappear overnight.

For more information on SIPC, check out www.sipc.org.

Where to Complain if There's Trouble

If the problem is operational—such as failure to deliver checks promptly or to correct an error—start with the broker. If it's not fixed quickly, contact the branch manager, and follow up in writing. A written record of your complaint is important, so write letters detailing your dispute and how it is not being resolved.

If the manager is not responsive, contact the state securities administrator's office.

The same path applies to misconduct on the part of the broker. Keep all records—give copies only to the office manager—and be prepared to pursue an arbitration or court case if necessary. Most brokerage agreements state that disputes will be settled in arbitration whenever possible.

Don't let a complaint fester; the statute of limitations on these issues varies, so file the paperwork as soon as you recognize there is a problem that the broker, office manager, and firm are not able to resolve to your satisfaction.

Building the Relationship

There's an old saying that the best way to get good market information is to "take a broker to lunch." It's not far from the truth.

The best way to develop a relationship with a broker is to be able to talk about money and investing when there is no commission on the line and no sale to be made. The more you learn about your broker and his or her attitudes toward money and the markets, the better your working relationship is going to be.

These meetings don't have to be regular, just often enough to get a feel for how the broker operates and to give the broker a better understanding of who you are and how you tick. It takes more than an initial interview and subsequent phone calls to do that.

At the same time, a busy broker doesn't have all day to schmooze. When you have questions, spend a few minutes planning your call to the broker so that if he has other business to do you can be efficient and get the information you want without tying him up. Not only will he appreciate that approach, but he will be happy to take and return your calls.

What if My Broker Changes Firms?

There are many reasons why brokers switch firms. It's a normal part of the business, but you will want to know why.

I once met a couple whose broker was changing firms for the second time in three years, moving from a national firm to a regional one. They worried about the small firm but wanted to keep the broker.

Whenever a broker changes companies, do a fresh background check on the new firm and the broker. A broker's record can be sullied quickly, so get current details. Just because the broker was clean when you started working with her doesn't mean things have stayed that way.

In this case, the couple had never done a background check on their broker. He explained that he had left the big firm for a pay raise and less sales pressure. A background check uncovered problems, however, notably several complaints concerning the suitability of his choices for older couples. That was enough to convince the couple not to follow the broker.

If you end up following your broker, find out if he or she gets a bonus for bringing over new customers. Also find out who pays any transfer fees for the securities or whether you might incur taxes because you'd be forced to sell some investments to change firms. If you choose not to follow the broker, you will have to start the interview and background-check process over again with a new advisor who works for the old firm.

Intuition Is Important; Greed Is Not

Ideally, you'd like to be able to introduce your broker to your children one day as "the person who helped us reach our goals." For all of the questions, background checks, and concerns, there will be no substitute for your sense that the advisor can deliver on that potential.

Do what you can to get a great sense of the advisors you meet; you want this to be a hard choice, a decision where you feel like there's no wrong answer. In the end, however, listen less to promises of future wealth and more to what your gut tells you to do.

Smart Investor Tip

Anyone can say they'll make you lots of money. Follow your gut instinct more than your greed instinct.

Remember, there's no limit to the promises stockbrokers can make, only to the promises they can keep.

Chapter 9

Interviewing a Money Manager

If there is any easy money lying around, nobody is going to stuff it into your pockets.

—Jesse Livermore (legendary trader)

Financial planners can act as money managers. Brokers can, too. The guys who run your mutual funds are money managers. Hedge fund managers, guys who trade "separate accounts," and virtually anyone who promises to oversee your investment capital are money managers. In fact, so long as you follow a few regulatory rules, you could hang out your shingle as a money manager, even if you don't have a lick of financial sense.

As such, that makes "money manager" an odd job among the financial experts you will work with in your lifetime. It can be completely personal and one-on-one, or it can be as impersonal as the nameless, faceless guy who makes sure your index fund actually replicates its benchmark.

To show just how much confusion there is over the role of a "money manager" and how confusing the titles can be, consider that MoneyManager.com is a service that is designed to introduce consumers to financial advisors. That said, in telling you to "find your advisor," it lists specialties such as portfolio management, retirement planning, estate planning, education planning, 401(k) rollovers, and debt-relief services.

With the exception of portfolio management, I would suggest that those are not the roles of a money manager at all. The idea in hiring a money manager is finding a specialist who is focused on running the money, not doing the rest of it.

Yet here was a site on money managers where the "featured" advisors were all typical, neighborhood financial-planning types (not surprisingly, I did not find the online service particularly worthwhile).

That confusion is commonplace. In Chapter 7 on interviewing a financial planner, I noted a message board posting that was in search of a money manager, but which was really all about finding a planner instead.

For the purposes of this book, however, a money manager is someone who looks after your investments only, implementing a financial strategy that is less targeted to your goals than it is to making money in all market conditions. Where the broker has a suitability standard and the financial planner a fiduciary standard, there's a question as to how well a money manager may actually know you; in many instances, you will be referred to a money manager by a broker or planner who knows your big picture and believes a specialist is exactly what you need.

Think of it this way: The money manager's job is to give you the kind of performance that Bernie Madoff's clients *thought* they were getting from him. He was their money manager; as we have heard from victims since his massive fraud came to light, what is clear is that some of Madoff's victims knew him and dealt directly with him, others were funneled his way by other financial advisors and intermediaries.

All were attracted by his performance claims and purported results, right up to the moment it all came crashing down.

But the Madoff case shows precisely why choosing a money manager is difficult, and why it's important not to take a money manager's credentials, history, record, or reputation at face value.

The scope of money managers runs a wide gamut, beginning with local financial planners and brokers who like managing money and working portfolios, and who may leave the other parts of the planning to colleagues to guys working in the towers on Wall Street. In some cases, you get to talk face-to-face with the money manager, in others, you are really asking your broker or planner questions before agreeing to take his or her recommended step of turning money over.

That can make it hard to get comfortable with a money manager. The good news is that, if you can't get comfortable, you don't have to hire one. You can stick with ordinary investments—stocks, bonds, and traditional mutual funds—and not go the private account route.

But if you have the money and the thought of a professional money manager is appealing, there is a lot you will want to know before you should be comfortable writing the check.

Finding Candidates for the Job

You're not going to want to go dialing for dollars or using a referral service here; instead, you may be introduced to a money manager by a current advisor, or you will find one by looking at a database that looks at performance, such as Morningstar Inc., the Chicago research firm known for its ratings of mutual funds, but which also tracks private-account management.

Recognize, however, that if you get the referral from a financial planner or investment advisor, that he or she may get a cut right along with the money manager. Think of it the way you do a sales charge for a mutual fund, where the fund manager charges you a management fee, but your sales load or trail commission goes to compensate the advisor who sold you the fund.

Under most circumstances, professional money managers don't come cheap. The typical structure of a hedge fund is "2-and-20," meaning that the manager gets 2 percent of the top, plus 20 percent of the profits. That's every year. If you are paying your broker or advisor for putting your money in place, that can make things worse.

Madoff's structure was unique in that he charged nothing for his purported money-management services (that should have been a red flag right there . . . there are no financial-services charities). He claimed to be happy just earning the commissions on the trades made in his money-management business. He also didn't dip into the management fees that advisors charged customers to put money with him; that created an incentive for advisors to throw money his way, because they could collect a fat fee for the privilege.

Perhaps the most heinous case actually involved a Connecticut "money manager" (it's in quotation marks because his actions made it clear he wasn't really managing money himself) whose idea of handling a client's portfolio involved giving all of the money to Bernie Madoff. The customers were aware that the money manager invested with others, but had no idea that they effectively were paying their advisor a 1.5 percent fee for handing the money over to Madoff and doing nothing else. On a $1 million account, the intermediary scooped up $15,000 for not actually running the money. That would have been bad enough with a legit manager who simply had a bad year; when Madoff's fraud was exposed, it had the consumers thinking their trust was violated twice.

Madoff's Gift to Investors

For all of the pain Madoff caused, he left others with a lasting legacy, namely the importance of doing your due diligence and looking for the red flags in the relationship. His case personified many of the things that any investors considering a money manager should have worried about all along; now, they're aware of the cost of ignoring the problem.

One thing that has not been discussed much in the wake of Madoff's fraud is why investors were so trusting. The guy didn't send regular investment statements, seldom talked to investors—preferring to deal with the advisors who brought in the bucks—did very little to discuss how he made his magic, stood stubbornly up against observers who thought his way was strange or different.

Smart Investor Tip

When investors are lured by big returns coming from an investment they can't easily research, they will have Madoff as a cautionary tale to get them to do their homework.

In 2009, I read a biography of Warren Buffett, arguably the greatest investor of all time, that discussed the things the "Oracle of Omaha" did while building up his reputation. They included being secretive and not telling everyone precisely how his system worked, sticking by his guns in the face of criticism, not paying dividends (it's why Buffett's Berkshire Hathaway is the highest priced stock on the market), and more. If you had removed Buffett's name from the description, and inserted Madoff's (prior to the scandal), you might have thought they were the same guy.

And that's why investors chase some money managers, hoping to find the next Warren Buffett. Madoff's Ponzi scheme was able to continue for so long because he never promised outrageous returns, but rather tried to be the picture of consistency. With big promised payouts, a Ponzi scheme quickly collapses under its own weight; with more reasonable numbers, the scam can work until market conditions become unfavorable and redemptions can't be met.

Now, at least, when investors are lured by big returns coming from an investment they can't easily research, they will have Madoff as a cautionary tale to get them to do their homework.

After Madoff, All Backgrounds Get Checked

It's unfair to say that a simple background check would have saved investors from Bernie Madoff. His firm had gotten into trouble over some small compliance issues and was fined a small amount; those items would have shown up in a background check, but they might not have scared many people off.

> Coupled with other concerns, however, they might have helped to tip the scales against an investment. That's why you will do some basic checks on any money manager you work with:
>
> Run the name of the advisor and the investment firm past both the Financial Industry Regulatory Authority (FINRA), through its BrokerCheck database at www.finra.org, and the Securities and Exchange Commission's Investment Advisor Registration Depository, which you can access through www.investor.gov.
>
> Money managers who oversee less than $25 million in assets will be regulated by their state securities administrator. Even if you are working with a big-time firm, there's no harm in taking the extra precaution of checking with your state. Sometimes, a consumer reports an issue to the "cop on the beat," which will be the state office, so you will unearth something at that level even if nothing shows up at the national level. You can get the contacts for your state securities administrator from the North American Securities Administrators Association website, www.nasaa.org.

One other key lesson of the Madoff case is that the easiest way to become a victim of affinity fraud is to let your affiliations color your judgments. Madoff's victims included a whole lot of people and institutions who should have known better: well-known Wall Street economists Henry Kaufman and Irwin Kellner (a colleague of mine at MarketWatch), countless celebrities, big banks that have staffs to vet investment advisors, and a host of golf and country club buddies who thought Madoff's handicap was his crooked swing, rather than his crooked mind.

He even sucked in Stephen Greenspan, a psychology professor who is the author—and I'm not making this up—of *Annals of Gullibility: Why We Get Duped and How to Avoid It.*

What Is a "Separate Account"?

Most times, if you are hiring a money manager, it is to run something called a "separate account." It is "separate" from other pooled monies, such as mutual funds and hedge funds, and is instead managed to the owner's general specifications.

Separate accounts differ from traditional funds because you, the investor, will own the securities yourself, rather than having a share in a big investment pool. Say the XYZ Fund has big stakes in Coca-Cola and PepsiCo, and you believe after a taste-test that Coke is finally going to wipe out Pepsi. The fund

Separately Managed Accounts Offer:
• Direct ownership of individual securities such as stocks and bonds.
• The ability to eliminate certain types of securities—think tobacco stocks or companies that pollute—based on the investor's preferences.
• Tax-management strategies, including tax-loss harvesting and offsetting of gains. Unlike mutual funds, separate accounts offer individual tax lots, meaning you're not going to suffer the tariff on someone else's gains when you buy in.
• Monitoring of the individual investor's other securities, which may be able to be transferred into the separate account.

would not allow you to reduce your exposure to Pepsi, since the manager can't make decisions based on the preferences of one investor. In a managed account, however, the money manager could dump the Pepsi and double down on Coke, if the strategy is in keeping with your goals.

In reality, money managers probably don't want that kind of input from customers, but the point is that the portfolio is customized to you, rather than to a mass of somewhat like-minded shareholders.

As a general rule, separate accounts require a minimum initial investment of $100,000 or more, but there are now some brokers and planners looking to get into the business by accept small accounts, so that you may be offered the service by someone trying to build a practice and willing to oversee your $25,000 or $50,000 account.

Interview Questions for Money Managers

In light of the Madoff case, I am often asked what types of questions a person should ask his or her money manger to ensure that person is working for the client. So, here they are:

Your First Meeting

Here are the questions you will want to answer as you go about selecting and working with a money manager.

Who is your custodian?

Prior to Madoff, this might have been the last question asked, now it comes first.

Registered investment advisors must place client assets with a qualified custodian, usually a bank or brokerage firm. Advisors can use an independent custodian—providing an extra layer of security—or an affiliated custodian.

Madoff's firm acted as both investment advisor and broker-dealer, and that affiliation removed one key check and balance from the system.

Before you hand over your money, know where it goes. Whoever manages your portfolio should use an independent financial institution, known as a custodian, to hold your assets. Get the name of the firm and its contact information.

Instead of relying on your advisor's word, check out the custodian yourself.

One of the custodian's jobs is to generate a quarterly statement, which either gets sent directly to you (preferable) or which goes to the advisor to pass on to the client. That step—where the advisor gets the paperwork and can fake it up—is where the potential for fraud lies. Madoff allegedly faked statements to look like his clients owned securities when, instead, their money was being used to pay off other investors.

When checking with the custodian, you might ask what current statements look like; if the sample statement you get from the money manager looks different—and you will ask for a sample statement—you will want to know why there's a difference.

Smart Investor Tip

Ask to see a sample statement from the custodian; if it looks different from the sample you get from the money manager—because you'll want one of those too—find out why there's a difference.

If the custodian for your money is affiliated with the money manager, find out what safeguards are in place to make sure the advisor can't just swipe your money. In this case, because of the close ties of the advisor and the broker-dealer, you really want to make sure that statements come directly to you. Further, if your money manager wants discretion to make trades in your account—which is common—you should make sure that you don't actually give the permission to withdraw funds. He can move money around within the account, but you don't want him to have an ability to take it out.

Who is your auditor?

Auditors have traditionally gotten a free pass. Not anymore.

When the client receives statements from the advisor, rather than the custodian, the advisor must in turn submit to an annual surprise audit by an outside firm. Madoff's auditor was a three-person firm operating from a tiny office in suburban New York, hardly the presence necessary for an advisory firm that was purportedly trading a good chunk of the volume of the New York Stock Exchange every day. A legitimate firm the size of Madoff Investment Securities should have employed at least one brand-name auditor.

Independent auditors are critical to keeping things in line; they verify the existence of the assets in your account (and others run by the advisor). If your advisor has an auditing firm whose name escapes you, fish around to make sure it's reputable and licensed to work in your state. Your state securities regulator, typically, can help you with that information.

Learn about Clientele and Scope of Practice

Below are some questions to ask about the advisor's clientele and scope of his or her practice so that you can make an informed decision of whether or not you fit within the advisor's niche.

Who is your typical client?

You are paying for personalized money management, or something close to it. The truth is, however, that the less personal it has to be—because you are right in the sweet spot of the practice—the better off you are likely to be.

If you are the epitome of the average client, the money manager presumably has your issues down cold and manages just right for your age and circumstances. If, however, the description of the average client sounds very different from you, that's a concern.

How many active clients do you work with?

Again, you are paying for a separate account, not "the same thing as the next guy, just with a personalized wrapper." The more clients a money manager has, the less attention any one account can get, the more the advice and execution becomes cookie-cutter. That's not necessarily bad—an advisor using her proven strategy in every account will produce roughly similar results—but you still want to have an idea of how much attention you are getting for your dollar.

Will anyone else be managing my money?

Some money managers turn big chunks of their portfolio over to other managers. As previously noted, that's how Madoff got a number of clients.

Whether it's a subordinate in the office, or a subadvisor to run some or all of the money, you want to know who has responsibility for your cash. One of my favorite stories of the Madoff scandal involved the consumer who said his initial reaction upon hearing the news was, "Wow, that's bad . . . I feel badly for those people," only to find out that his own money manager's idea of running the portfolio was to give everything to Madoff.

Can I see a sample statement? Is it prepared by your firm or the custodian?

Given your questions about the custodian and auditor, you want to see what the advisor's statement looks like, and find out who prepares it. That way, if the document you end up getting looks different, you can find out if anything is amiss.

What is your educational and professional background? How long have you been doing this?

Some money managers come to the job from the mutual fund world or the traditional Wall Street mold, while others percolate up from being a broker or financial planner, finding that what really interests them—and what they have skill at—is managing the portfolios, rather than the ancillary jobs of those other advisory roles. Either way, background and experience count for something.

Have you ever had complaints filed against you by clients? How have those complaints been resolved?

The money manager knows you will check the record and background, so this is the time to fess up to what you are likely to find, and to give his side of the story. He knows that you are going to check his record with the state; this is when he gets a chance to come clean and explain what, if anything, has gone wrong, but was eventually set right.

Most complaints against money managers amount to a difference of opinion over what was provided versus what was expected. Still, if there's any history of those problems, you'd like to know in advance that you can avoid the same kind of fate.

Inquire about Relationship and Investment Style

With this information in hand, below are questions you should ask to learn about the advisor's relationship and investment style.

What role do you see yourself playing in my finances? What is your responsibility to me?

We started this chapter pointing out that even money managers—or at least the ones at moneymanagers.com—are sometimes confused about what this job involves. Fundamentally, however, it is portfolio management, and nothing more.

If the advisor tells you she wants to provide more, you need to decide if you really are interested in buying the services she is selling. You should also decide if you are better off with a generalist—typically, the financial planner—than with the specialist money manager.

In some cases, you may be able to get the best of both worlds. There's a Boston firm, for example, where the wife is the financial planner and the husband is the money manager. Each has a distinct role, but you can't get one without the other.

How do you charge for your services?

Compensation is always an issue with investments. The bigger the fee, the more the investments must return to justify it. Costs are guaranteed, results are not.

Always know what you are paying and how you are paying it.

What is your account minimum?

You don't want to have to stretch or ruin your asset allocation plan to throw money at an advisor. Ask the people who did that and went all-in with Madoff about the dangers of that strategy. Know how much you must invest to work with the advisor, and then you can figure out how much you should invest.

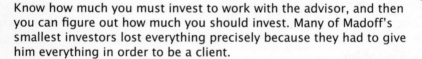

Smart Investor Tip
Know how much you must invest to work with the advisor, and then you can figure out how much you should invest. Many of Madoff's smallest investors lost everything precisely because they had to give him everything in order to be a client.

How do your interests align with mine?

Most money managers—but not all—fall under the broad classification of investment advisor, meaning they have a fiduciary standard and must put your best interests first. That said, how able they are to actually do that may depend on how much contact you have.

As previously noted, some money managers are right there, local and in the office for you to see, while others are down on Wall Street somewhere. For the former, they will have a good sense of your needs, hopes, and fears. For the latter, they pretty much uphold the fiduciary standard by trying to make money and profiting more when their moves pay off and less when their moves are wrong.

How much input do I really get?

If one of the benefits of a separate account is that you can get personalized counsel and can drop a stock when you are nervous about it, or push to pick up something additional that you like. That said, the money manager probably doesn't want to be on the phone with you all day, hashing out your ideas and customizing your portfolio.

Be sure you understand how much input you will have. Money managers have discretion to make trades on your behalf; that's a lot different from a broker or planner who must run their moves by you for approval.

Investment Philosophy Is Critical

Before Bernie Madoff, all of your first (and most important) questions would have been about the manager's style and philosophy. Ultimately, these are the important questions that help you determine if the manager has the mindset to deliver the heightened returns you are hoping for.

What is your investment philosophy? What strategies and securities do you use? What criteria do you use before deciding what to buy? Under what conditions do you sell?

You're hiring an expert, but the actions he or she takes need to make sense to you. That may be the most critical mistake of the Madoff victims; his spoken strategy left people scratching their heads, wondering not only exactly how it worked, but whether it was possible to trade the kind of volume purportedly needed to carry it off.

While many experts have said that Madoff's trading strategy should have been a red flag, I believe that's wrong. Madoff's "split-strike conversion" options strategy looked to me—from the marketing materials—like a more straightforward options approach, but I don't know anyone who could reverse engineer the whole thing to see if it ever truly had a chance. With most strategies, the pros try to see if the execution and idea lead to results that can be replicated over time, so that if the fund tops the market by 1 percent this month, it can be expected to do the same thing next month and the month after that.

The mind-numbing complexity of Madoff's concept—because the experts failed to duplicate it—was much less the red flag than the fact that no one could explain how it worked or why it worked, let alone tell their loved ones what this great new investment they were making was actually doing with their money. Buying something you don't understand is always a big, honking danger sign.

You may be hiring an expert, but since you live with the consequences of his or her actions, the strategy needs to make sense.

Keep in mind that you do not need a special money manager to get the job done. You can stick with ordinary stocks and bonds and mutual funds.

But if you believe that there are investors—the ones generally recognized as "the smart money"—who know the secret to beating the market and you want to invest with them, you'll need to hear more than just "it's a secret formula" to get comfortable. Many people believe that trying to outguess and out maneuver the market is futile. Personally, I believe managers can add value, but not so much that I am willing to pay exorbitant costs for it.

Smart Investor Tip

Managers can add value, but not so much that I am willing to pay exorbitant costs for it.

If this money manager has a distinct approach, you want to know what it is, and how it might affect you when your account grows and shrinks, and also on taxes, income, and more. If his or her approach doesn't mesh with your own—you favor buy-and-hold, he is a market timer—consider whether you will have the fortitude to stick with the strategy long enough to truly see if it can work.

You're Paying for Results, Not Complexity

A few years back, I was asked to put together a panel discussion for a meeting of the Investment Management Consultants Association in Chicago. The panel included one traditional fund manager, one private money manager, and a guy running a hedge fund.

Mark Sellers of Sellers Capital was the hedge fund manager, and he talked about his strategy, which is very disciplined about its buying approach, and which then functionally uses some options as a form of "insurance" on his stock bets. He explained that his fund gets paid the traditional 2-and-20 fee structure. And then, one audience member—wrestling with the complexity of the investment structure—said, "How many holdings do you have?"

Clearly, for the big dollars involved, everyone expected a huge portfolio. Instead, you heard audible gasps when Sellers said, "We've got five stocks right now."

So I asked the audience—all qualified investment managers themselves—how many would put their client money into a hedge fund with just five securities, and not a single hand went up. My next question was whether they would buy a hedge fund that had shown a consistent ability to crush the market and to minimize downside pain. Virtually every hand up.

The results, of course, were from Sellers fund. The moral of the story: You need to be convinced that the style will deliver the results, but don't make any assumptions of what a money manager does until you hear it from him or her.

What kind of returns should I expect? How much should I expect returns to vary?

This is where the rubber meets the road. If the money manager can't generate sufficient returns consistently enough to make you believe this strategy is better than what you can get by going with a few mutual fund manager, you probably don't want to go to the trouble or expense of bringing him or her on board.

Make sure any projected return is in sync with your needs and your risk-reward profile. If the money manager believes she can consistently deliver a return that beats the market by 5 percent, but you believe that you will only reach your financial goals if you can outperform by 7 percent, then something needs to be worked on with your overall financial advisor. You may need to save more or you may need to adjust your expectations.

What percentage of my assets do you think should be managed this way?

Every great money manager thinks he should handle all of your money. So does every crook. That's the problem.

Many Madoff victims had nearly their entire net worth tied up with his firm, thereby violating the first rule of investing: Don't put all your eggs in one basket.

Ask for the advisor's input, because it will give you a good idea of whether he is looking at the strategy for you to be a big-picture, one-portfolio-serves-all-goals thing, or if he, too, sees himself as bringing one style of investing to your portfolio and running that piece of your money and leaving the rest to other managers or investments so that you can be broadly diversified.

Can I see past results? Has your performance been measured and monitored independently anywhere?

It's easy to check the record of a guy running a mutual fund; it's a lot harder figuring out the skill level of a local, regional, or national money manager who runs separate accounts. After all, he could deliver like gangbusters for one client, and be a dog for the next customer.

You are paying for personalized money management, but there is only so much variation between one client and another. You have asked about the manager's average client, now you need to see how the manager has done on behalf of that average guy.

This will go a long way to convincing you that the manager can live up to his promise.

Firms like Morningstar are now looking at separate account performance and rating private money managers, but these databases are not always readily available to the general public. Typically, the ratings would be something your financial planner would see, to help her decide which money manager she would recommend you use.

Still, if the data is out there, you want to see it. In fact, if the money manager is a referral from your broker or planner, you need to ask up front if she has independent research on the manager.

Prepare for Trouble, Just in Case

Conclude your interview with an advisor by asking about problems.

How will we resolve complaints if I am dissatisfied?

Chances are you will sign an agreement to try arbitration before turning to the courts; the best arbitration agreements do not take away your right to pursue action in court, they merely attempt to settle things before that step. Legislation in Congress as this book went to press would give the Securities and Exchange Commission the authority to invalidate mandatory arbitration clauses in broker-dealer and investment advisory agreements, a change that would potentially open up the courts system and provide better chances for recovery.

Still, expect arbitration to be the first step and find out how you can fix problems long before you get to that extreme.

Find out how the planner would handle a problem in your account, whether it is a technical glitch, an error in your account statement, investment outcomes outside the realm of what you prepared for, and more.

Remember, the market downturn in 2008 pushed a lot of money managers out of the business; someone who never expected it to happen—who gave clients a rosy outlook—made up those statistics.

How can I terminate this relationship if I am not satisfied?

Depending on the agreement and the type of account the money manager runs, you may not just be able to walk away, or if you do leave early, you could face stiff penalties. An advisory agreement should favor you, not the planner. That means it should come equipped with some sort of ejector seat. Find out what happens if you pull the lever and bail out.

In the Event of Trouble, Contact Authorities

After suffering the black eye of Madoff, Robert Stanford, and many lesser scam artists and frauds, regulators are tired of being punching bags and are acting aggressively if they see potential cases.

That's why you shouldn't be afraid to go to your state securities regulator, the Securities and Exchange Commission (start with the closest regional office), and even the Federal Bureau of Investigations and local law enforcement with your concerns. The more documentation you have the better, so take copious notes and get copies of every agreement you sign, as well as retaining your statements from the advisor.

Smart Investor Tip

Take copious notes and get copies of every agreement you sign, as well as retaining your statements from the advisor.

When in Doubt . . .

Consider whether hiring a private money manager really is the best idea for you. Yes, there can be performance and tax advantages, but maintaining control, working with financial planners and brokers, staying involved in the process and using mutual funds—which are much more tightly controlled—may still give you the highest sleep factor, and no amount of extra theoretical return is worth it if you spend every waking moment terrified of what happens next.

Remember, too, that for every scoundrel and rogue advisor, the vast majority are up front, honest, and will not be trying to get over on you. If you can couple that with the basic competency to live up to financial promises, you will have found someone you can work with for a long time.

Interviewing an Insurance Agent

Insurance—an ingenious modern game of chance in which the player is permitted to enjoy the comfortable conviction that he is beating the man who keeps the table.

—Ambrose Bierce

For most people, insurance is their leaky roof. When it's sunny, everything's fine. When it rains, it's too late to fix it.

An insurance agent, therefore, is like a roofer, building shelter for clients by providing coverage that protects against storms that could not be weathered alone. But in insurance, as in homes, there are many ways to build or fix that roof. Plain shingles, or fancy wooden ones; old coverage ripped off, or simply covered over and improved. Warranted for a few years or guaranteed for a lifetime.

The quality of the craftsman will go a long way to determining how happy you are when the repairs are done. Enter the insurance agent, your financial roofer.

The basic premise behind insurance is simple: Protect those things you cannot afford to replace yourself and cover yourself for outcomes you could not otherwise afford to pay for.

That means, for example, that you might want insurance to replace a new luxury car, but might not carry collision coverage on an old clunker. If the former gets smashed up, you don't have the $30,000 to $50,000 to buy a new one, while if your old beater is in an accident, you can probably replace it for the same money you were paying in annual premiums.

In financial circles, the saying is that insurance is always sold and never bought, meaning that no one purchases protection unless required to or compelled by a convincing pitch. No one wakes up and says, "I need to go to the grocery store today, drop off the dry cleaning, and then go buy a universal whole life policy." That kind of thinking applies to most forms of insurance; you may know you need it, but you're not getting it without some pushing and prodding.

Face it, no one wants to face up to his or her own mortality, the potential to spend a long stretch of time in nursing home or hospice, the potential to be involved in accidents, the loss of home or property, the loss of income from disability or death, and more. Moreover, no one wants to spend today's hard-earned money to protect against something that may never happen; after all, the best insurance policies are the ones that allow you to feel safe at night, but that are never cashed because you never have the crisis.

The other reason why insurance products are sold versus bought is that they can involve complex jargon and illustrations. The combination of stomach-churning topics with mind-numbing specifics is a real turn-off.

And so, people put it off, enjoying the sunshine and promising to fix their financial roof before it rains. Sadly, they can then fall victim to the very sales process that makes them uncomfortable, delaying purchases until the day they meet an agent at a party or receive a cold call after they did a Google search and visited an insurance website. They take the chance encounter as a sign that it's time to get protection, and the agent with the fortunate timing becomes the lucky advisor with a client ready to fall for the whole sales pitch.

The best way to avoid that problem is to tackle insurance head-on, hiring an agent early and working with him or her to develop, upgrade, and maintain a program of financial protection that will always keep the roof protecting the family, without leaks.

Can I Do This Myself?

If you have no insurance, you *are* doing this yourself. You are "self-insured," meaning that if something happens to you tomorrow, you're liable for all costs associated with the problem. The bigger the issue, the bigger your problem; if you suffer a major disability for which you have no coverage, you'll find out quickly how inadequate your resources are.

If you want insurance, but not an agent, you are looking at the low-load insurance market, where insurers sell directly to the public or work through a quote service like Insure.com or Insweb.com. The sites will do some quick comparison shopping and give you an idea of what's available and at what cost; while pricing is good, the best deals may require you to meet with an underwriter who does a basic check of your physical condition.

If you can understand the terms and conditions in the policies you are being offered, you don't need to hire an advisor. If, however, you're going for cheap and easy and you are kidding yourself about your real knowledge of what is in the policy, then you are building your roof from straw and hoping the winds won't just blow it off.

Agent or Broker? Independent or Captive?

You can hire an insurance agent, who represents the insurers as they sell you products, or you can hire an insurance broker or consultant, someone typically on your side, to represent your interests. You can compare the agent's services with those of so-called "low-load insurers," which sell policies direct to the public. Because both agents and low-load services are not allowed in all 50 states, there are circumstances where an agent will be the only choice, although the trend nationally has been moving toward choice, not restriction.

When it comes to agents, there are independent agents and "captive" or exclusive agents. The difference is pretty much what you'd expect from the titles.

Independent agents represent any number of insurers and may change the firms whose lines they carry depending on whether they are satisfied with price and service. In theory, independent agents offer you more choices because they work with more companies that are competing for your practice dollar; in practice, however, they may only sell the options that bring them the most money.

Captive agents, as the name suggests, can work with only one insurer. The good news is that they will know the provisions of the policies better than an independent agent, because over time they will come to learn the company's offerings inside and out, rather than simply well enough to sell them. The independent agent may have too many insurers to become that well acquainted with the minutiae of each product.

Exclusive agents tend to learn lower commissions than their independent counterparts. Still, the lack of competition means that the independent agent may have lower-cost competition to bring to the table.

Meanwhile, insurance quote services may sound like a direct-purchase choice, but that's not quite true. The telephone and online quote services—which promise the best available rates on simple policies such as term life—effectively are independent insurance agencies representing many companies. By doing a bulk business, they cut costs and offer basic policies at a discount.

Still, the effect is buying a policy through an agent, without the benefit of the service you might expect from hiring someone local. In addition, the great prices don't always turn out any better than what you can get from an agent in town, because the quote services offer bare-bones "teaser" policies to get you interested. You may not qualify for the policy—your health isn't way above average, for example, or you fall above age restrictions—or the agent does a needs analysis that shows you need coverage beyond the basics, and suddenly you are looking at a higher-priced policy that is no better than what you could have gotten from your local seller.

Ultimately, however, your choice may come down to completely personal feelings about whom you want to represent you. My own insurance situation is a perfect example of this.

Years ago, when I was the rare consumer who went looking for insurance products, my wife Susan—the most patient and understanding woman in America—told me to do the legwork on my own, using my resources, and to get her involved only when I was ready to hire an agent or sign a policy.

So I did my background checks and other work to pick an advisor. I also worked with an online quote service. Ultimately, I settled on George as the independent agent I most wanted to work with. He picked a policy from a Michigan insurance company; the quote service offered me identical coverage from the same company for $72 per year less. (It's not that George's actual commission was $72, it's that the policy through him cost that much more when all costs were factored in.)

So I had George over to the house to show me the details of the policy and his service. Now my wife was involved, getting a sense of the man and his products. So when George left that morning, I offered her the choice: In the event of a disaster, she could have George or she could have a toll-free phone line and have to tell a stranger that she's policy number X and that there's been a disaster.

"So it's $72 a year for George," she asked. "I'll take George."

Finding Candidates for the Job

Nothing beats word of mouth, especially when it comes from someone who has had claims experience with an agent. The best minds in the insurance industry say the place to start your search is with friends, relatives, and co-workers to determine whom they use as an insurer.

Beyond that, the national accreditation and membership organizations have lists of advisors in your area. The National Association of Insurance and Financial Advisors, for example, has a "Find An Advisor" function at its website, www.naifa.org. You can find an independent agent or broker by going to www.iiaba.net, the website for the Independent Insurance Agents and Brokers of America, and clicking on "Find an Agent." You can do credential-specific searches too; the CPCU Society, for example, has a search function that will help you locate Chartered Property Casualty Underwriters in your region; go to www.cpcusociety.org.

If you currently work with an agent but need to find a new one to handle a special need, be sure to get a referral from your current advisor. For example, the agent for your home and auto coverage may not do life insurance or long-term care coverage, but probably knows a few agents who do.

Credentials to Consider

Credentials aren't a necessity, but they are a way that good agents typically distinguish themselves. Because insurers tend to set prices uniformly, you can't really play one advisor against the next. If they both quote policies from XYZ National Life, your costs should be nearly identical; it will only be by searching for more and different providers that an agent may be able to create an edge. Since you will pay roughly the same regardless of the agent working with you, choosing someone with a high degree of professional achievement—whose expertise might help you find ways to make your coverage more efficient—helps to ensure you'll get the most for your money.

The other key reason to pursue agents with credentials is the codes of conduct and ethics that generally go with membership in these groups.

Insurance agents are dual agents, working on your behalf while representing the insurer; they are supposed to serve the best interests of both masters. Professional standards certainly give them perspective that makes it easier to walk that tightrope.

For life insurance agents, the Chartered Life Underwriter (CLU) and Chartered Financial Consultant (ChFC) designations are generally considered the top credentials. Both are administered by The American College, with the ChFC being the financial-services add-on to the insurance-oriented CLU mark. Agents who have one or both of these credentials agree to abide by the college's code of ethics and conduct.

A Chartered Property Casualty Underwriter (CPCU) has completed property and liability coverage education requirements from the American Institute for Chartered Property Casualty Underwriters, a group that has a strict code of professional ethics.

Insurance is one area where advisors often have sub-specialties, and there seems to be an association for each of those groups. There's the Association of Health Insurance Advisors or the Association for Advanced Life Underwriting. That said, the overarching group for many of these niche specializations is the National Association of Insurance and Financial Advisors. Membership does not require the same kind of training as some of the other programs, but there is a code of conduct to follow.

Beyond the credentials, insurance agents frequently pursue financial planning designations, such as the Certified Financial Planner mark. This is helpful, but you need to make sure that the agent understands the role you expect him to play, especially if you already have a financial planner to oversee your personal finance needs.

Perhaps the most confusing, confounding credential in all of financial services is the MDRT mark used by insurance agents who have achieved status in the Million Dollar Round Table. When the group was formed in the 1920s, the Million Dollar Round Table was all about the biggest "producers," insurance agents who sold more policies for more dollar volume in premiums than anyone else. The idea was that the industry's best sales pros would share their ideas.

Over the years, the Million Dollar Round Table has evolved and taken on a more industry-minded, general training role, and has developed a code of ethics. Still, it is a status symbol for top sales people, and someone who can sell tons of insurance is good at his or her job, but might not be the best one in terms of developing close one-on-one relationships with customers. If an advisor says she has this status, ask how it actually helps you.

If a prospective agent offers credentials beyond these basics, find out what it took to earn them, and what they mean for you. The industry seems to be churning out new designations at a rate of one or two per year, trying to see which specialties resonate with practitioners and have staying power.

Protection versus Financial Growth

One of the key decisions you will make in buying life insurance—and in choosing the right agent to sell you coverage—is determining what you really want insurance to achieve.

Your basic need is replacing lost income and protecting your loved ones from a future without you. That means a basic term insurance policy—where you buy coverage for a set period of time—can work very well. When you are a young married parent, the coverage protects against catastrophe, but it lapses when you are a senior, when your life's savings and any pensions protect your family.

Many consumers, however, want to have their insurance premium dollar generate a long-term investment return. Cash-value policies are more expensive, and tend to generate bigger commissions for the agents, so it's cheaper to "buy term and invest the difference," provided you have the discipline to actually capture and invest the savings.

Policies that build investment value can be a type of forced savings, by comparison. My father-in-law used insurance this way, saying he might not always feel like scrimping and saving to make investments, but that he always paid his bills on time. "Insurance is like a bill for savings."

There are plenty of arguments in the industry over which is the best policy and for whom. There's also no one right answer. That's why you will want an agent to run you through all of the potential options, so that you can figure out the coverage, cash-flow, and investment option works best for you. Remember, too, that many policies can be converted, so that the term coverage you buy at age 30 to protect you while the kids are young may be convertible into a whole or variable life policy before the term ends at age 55. That's a big reason why you want an insurance agent who will work with you over a lifetime.

Sins of Commission

Most agents are paid on commission, which is not surprising given the fact that most policies are sold, not bought. Commissions can be hefty; depending on the type of insurance, fees can be up to 50 percent of first-year premiums, falling to 3 to 5 percent over time thereafter.

Commissions also depend on the quality of the insurer. A high-quality company does not pay as much in commission as one that is in tougher financial straits, because the good company's high ratings make its products easier to sell. (Commission structure is why the low-load and fee-only advisor options were able to gain a foothold in the industry.)

The differences between one company and the next are so minimal that good agents will simply bring you the best available policies; they aren't likely to gouge on commissions if it puts their reputation at risk.

What's good about the commission structure in insurance is that you can easily make side-by-side comparisons to see if one deal works best. Say an agent shows you two life policies charging, say, $200 per month in premiums; both policies offer virtually identical coverage and are sufficient for your needs. If the price is identical, the commission becomes irrelevant, at which point your sole deciding factor will be the quality or service reputations of the insurers.

Checking Them Out

There is no substitute for checking in with your state insurance commissioner to see if there have been complaints, disciplinary problems, or licensing actions taken against an agent. You can find your state insurance commissioner's office by looking at the "states and jurisdictions map" on www.naic.org, the website of the National Association of Insurance Commissioners.

If the agent's credentials impress you, make sure they are real. Contact the agency that awards the credential to make sure the advisor is in good standing and without any disciplinary actions.

Smart Investor Tip
If the agent's credentials impress you, make sure they are real. Contact the agency that awards the credential to make sure the advisor is in good standing and without any disciplinary actions.

And since many insurance agents come to the business from financial planning—or they practice in several specialties—be sure to check out their background in those areas too. There have been plenty of cases where someone wears out his welcome as a broker or planner and turns to insurance because it uses the same skill set but allows him to dodge his troubled past.

If the agent ever functioned as a broker, check his record by using the Financial Industry Regulatory Authority's BrokerCheck service (www.finra.org). If he acted as a financial planner, you can get his history from the Investment Advisor Registration Depository via www.investor.gov.

Finally, while insurance agents typically fall under the eye of the state insurance commissioner, it's not a bad idea to contact your state securities administrator, especially if the agent has a history of selling investments and

> ### What an Agent Should Ask You During an Interview
>
> Every advisor should have a bunch of questions for you during an initial sit-down but, unlike those other specialists, the life insurance agent isn't doing his or her job if you don't hear certain queries.
>
> An agent should be asking you about your income, assets/net worth, the makeup of your investment portfolio, marital status and children to support, employment status, salary, insurance benefits offered by your company, and how much money your family needs to maintain its standard of living if you die. Without this basic information, an agent can't determine your needs.
>
> If an agent starts to talk about a policy's price or earnings potential before asking you for these basics, you've got a salesman, not someone who wants to be a true advisor.

not just insurance. (Technically, insurance is not considered an "investment," but certain products have piqued the interest of securities regulators and attracted some attention from regulators over sales practices.) You can get contact details for your state securities administrator from the North American Securities Administrators Association website, www.nasaa.org.

Interview Questions for Insurance Agents
Your First Meeting

Here are the questions you will want to answer as you go about selecting and working with an insurance agent.

Do you specialize in any particular areas?

Some agencies are full-service, others are limited to specific lines and types of coverage. For example, I have one insurance agent for my home and auto coverage and another agent who handles my life-insurance needs.

Who you can work with may be determined by your needs. Some agencies specialize in high-risk drivers, for example, or work mostly on long-term care insurance. While you can pick individual agents for each specialty, that gets complicated and cumbersome. Generally, you will want to pick one agent for your mandatory insurance needs—home and car coverage—and then find a specialist, if necessary, to round out your protection.

That said, you may not want to be an agent's first foray into a new area. If, for example, your life insurance agent doesn't focus on long-term care protection but is "willing to look into it for you," you need to question whether you really need a specialist to make the best possible decisions.

How long have you been in insurance? How long with this particular agency?

Experience counts, but it isn't everything. If an agent has bounced around from one firm to the next, there may be a problem; at the very least, it should make you question whether the agent will be there to service your long-term needs.

Remember my story about my wife and George, the insurance agent she wanted on our side in case of emergency? Well, for her to get her wish and have George in place during an emergency, George needs to still be in the business and working with us. If he were changing firms all the time, chances are that we'd be stuck in the event of a disaster, with Susan frustrated about having to deal with a stranger (and if she wanted to deal with a stranger, we'd have saved the $72 in annual premiums and done the deal on our own, without the agent).

Like many financial services disputes, problem agents can sometimes get off without a scratch on their records by settling cases and resolving complaints before problems reach the state regulator. The firm that employs the agent may not be so lenient; that's why having too many past employers in a short stretch of time needs to be checked out.

How many insurance companies do you represent? How long have you worked with each company?

The more insurers an agent represents, the more options she can present you with. At the same time, an agent may have a few favorites she prefers to work with. Captive agents, of course, work with only the one firm, but those companies are likely to provide cradle-to-grave coverage options on virtually every type of protection.

Ideally, an agent with a long history in the business has longstanding relationships with the insurer(s) she works with. If not, that raises a concern that she has not been the kind of agent an insurer wants to keep. That said, there are also legitimate reasons why an insurer might drop an agent, not the least of which is state regulations that make a company decide to no longer participate in the market.

If there have been a lot of changes to the product line, find out why.

What companies get most of your business and why?

"Independence" is great, but it doesn't mean an agent won't play favorites. That's okay, so long as the agent's favorite consistently provides proper coverage, rather than the best commission structure.

The reason for asking this question in advance of doing business, however, has to do with how you will size up the agent's advice. If, after a needs analysis, the agent is recommending companies that are not the primary carriers he works with, you will want to know why. If he picks his fave, you'll want to know what makes this a better policy than other available options.

How are the companies you deal with rated?

You'd like to know about an insurer's financial strength before you buy one of its policies. The major independent research firms—Standard & Poor's, Moody's Investor's Service, A.M. Best, and the like—measure a company based on the depth of its reserves, the spread of its risks, profitability and investment income, the quality of management, and more. From there, the service assigns a grade.

Your agent should be willing to give you at least two ratings reports on any insurer you are considering. If he can't deliver, question what is being hidden here. While insurance company failures are rare, they are not unheard of, especially since the financial crisis that swept the country in 2008.

Unless you have a special need and a highly limited number of providers, you will only want to deal with companies that have ratings of excellent or superior. Have the agent not only show you the ratings, but explain how they work, since each system is just a little bit different.

Smart Investor Tip

Have the agent show you the ratings and explain how they work; each ratings system is unique.

What continuing education classes have you taken? What credentials, if any, do you have?

Insurance, like the other financial services specialties, is evolving; you want someone who is current on the law and on the best procedures to follow to maximize your insurance dollar. With pricing being less of an issue in insurance than other specialties, expertise is at a premium (so to speak), so make sure you are getting an expert and not just a salesman.

Can I have your insurance license number?

Ask this one early in the process and you could save some time. It's a deal-breaker.

Insurance agents are licensed by the state. Getting the license number speeds up your background check with the state insurance commissioner; it sends a clear message to the agent that you intend to do a background check.

You can laugh it off as being precautionary and being a waste of a phone call if that gets the agent to show you a license, but you should make it clear that you won't hire an agent who can't prove that he or she is currently licensed. Some states give agents a card to show, others a certificate for the wall. It doesn't matter; ask for proof, look at the document, check the names and dates.

An agent without the license on the wall may not remember the number and may not have it handy—you should be able to search for the records based on his or her name—but that person can look it up. Refusing to give you the number is as good as an admission of trouble. Without a problem past, there is nothing to hide.

The Price You'll Pay, and How You'll Pay It

Now that you know the questions you need to ask when selecting your advisors, here's what you'll need to ask to figure out how much you should pay.

How do you charge for your services?

All advisors must spell out their cost structure. Insurance may be more product or commodity than service, but you still want to avoid surprises, particularly if you intend to develop a relationship and get on the phone periodically seeking advice

Insurance agents get paid more for selling new policies than for maintaining older ones, and some recoup this decline by adding hourly costs for offering ancillary financial planning services. If an advisor will put you on the clock when you call for advice, you should know it up front, especially if the charges are in addition to ongoing commissions from your insurance policies.

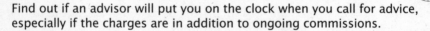

Smart Investor Tip

Find out if an advisor will put you on the clock when you call for advice, especially if the charges are in addition to ongoing commissions.

How much of my initial premium payment goes to commissions and fees, and how much of that commission do you get?

This is a big issue with life insurance products, for which the agent is going to get a big cut of what you spend up front to buy coverage. A big chunk of your first premium payment is going to the advisor, no matter what, so be sure the agent has shown you several options and given you the information necessary to pick the best one for you. That won't necessarily be the policy that provides the agent with the biggest payday.

How can I reduce my costs?

In all types of insurance, there are ways to cut costs, jettisoning unnecessary coverage, consolidating policies under one insurer, qualifying for discounts, and more. Ask for a list of all potential discounts. Insurers offer discounts for everything from people who stop smoking to those who enter a weight-loss program or get good grades.

In addition, discuss any situation that is "abnormal."

Say your child—covered by your auto insurance policy—goes to college for several months at a time and has no access to a car. During that time, you may be able to remove the child from your policy and save on premiums. Likewise, if you stop driving to work for a long stretch of time—such as a maternity or sick leave, or if you leave a car in the garage while you travel extensively—you may be able to stop coverage temporarily, saving on the cost of unnecessary protection.

A good agent can unbundle standard policies to at least see if you are better off financially with a menu of services customized to your needs than with the more generic, one-size-fits-all standard.

Don't Forget the Nuts and Bolts

And of course, you must ask the following administrative questions that let you know more about the advisor's background.

How does your firm operate? When is it open? What about after-hours contacts? How will claims reporting be handled?

There are plenty of reasons to get these questions answered before you have to put the agent to the test.

Say you decide to buy a car on Saturday afternoon, but don't know whether your current policy offers sufficient protection for the new car. If you drive off the lot and get in an accident, you could be in for a heap of financial troubles; if your agent isn't available until Monday and has no off-hours number to check in on, you may not have any way of knowing whether you are sufficiently covered on the new car.

Likewise, you have a car accident on the weekend and need to know if you can rent a car and bill it to the insurer, or there's a fire in your home and you want to know how quickly you can get people working to weatherproof the parts of your home that survived.

And because insurance affects your spouse and family, you want to make sure they know how to deal with the agent if something unexpected happens to you.

That's why you want to know how an agent pursues claims—some walk customers through the process, others leave everything to adjusters—and make sure you are comfortable not only with the sales pitch, but with the service you'll get after the sale.

What is your philosophy on working with insurance companies and consumers in settling disputed claims?

This is one of those areas in which an independent agent may have an edge. If your agent believes the insurance was wrong in denying a claim, she should step in and lobby on your behalf. When an agent represents one company, she may not want to put up too big a fight or could wind up out of business. An independent agent, meanwhile, has the threat of moving business to another company.

Under any circumstances, beyond knowing how an agent will help in processing claims, you want to know if they will go to bat for you when a claim goes against you.

Who will have the primary responsibility for handling my account?

If an agency is big enough, the salesman may only close the deal, leaving subordinates or clerical staff to do the actual paperwork and much of the research. If that's the case, find out who will have responsibility for your account.

Could I get the names of a few recent clients who you have worked with?

Ideally, you'd get the names of customers whose cases are similar to yours and who use the advisor for the same types of situations.

Extra Questions for References

Aside from the standard questions to ask references in Chapter 14, be sure to ask about the claims experience the customer has had and whether the agent was involved in producing a satisfactory outcome. Be sure to ask about how the insurer was to deal with, too, as you will also have to deal with the company if there are issues in the future.

Have you ever been the subject of any complaints to the insurance commissioner or any lawsuits? If so, for what and how do we make sure that situation does not happen again?

The advisor knows you are checking. Lying will only get him or her tossed from your list of candidates. Still, if anything comes up, make sure the explanation jibes with what you learn of his disciplinary history, and that it sits well with you and does not give you the shakes. If you believe the action that landed him or her in trouble is unforgivable, move on.

Inquire about Relationship and Investment Style

With this information in hand, below are questions you should ask to learn about the advisor's relationship and investment style.

After the initial sale, when will I hear from you, and why?

If the agent is transaction-oriented, you'll get calls only when there are other products to pitch, most likely at policy renewal time when he might convince you to upgrade.

If the advisor wants to pursue a relationship, he should call periodically, notably when he notices a major life change in the offing (kids getting ready to leave for college, mortgage debt almost retired, etc.)

Good agents can be good salesmen, but they earn that distinction by taking care of their clients first and filling their sales ledgers second. If you plan to have a long-term relationship with an advisor, make sure he is willing to work with your other financial advisors and will meet with you at times when there is no pressing need for service, just to do an insurance checkup and make sure you have not outgrown your financial safety net.

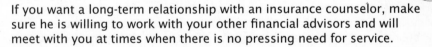

Smart Investor Tip
If you want a long-term relationship with an insurance counselor, make sure he is willing to work with your other financial advisors and will meet with you at times when there is no pressing need for service.

Do you value my business enough to look after me?

This question sounds odd, but it comes from a disturbing personal experience. After the death of my father-in-law, I took over most of the finances for my mother-in law, who was in poor health herself. In sorting through the family's various insurance policies, I came across a surprising find, seven small term policies—none valued at more than about $2,500—that had been purchased over a few years about a decade earlier.

They had been allowed to lapse.

Truth be told, I still am not quite sure why they were started, but my assumption is that my father-in-law got them to help cover funeral costs, to protect the family without doing a prepaid funeral (which was not his style).

Whatever the reasoning, what made me angry was that the agent—who had worked with the family for more than a decade, taking over from his partner, who had been the family agent for a quarter century—never called my in-laws to say the policies were lapsing. As my mother-in-law's health declined, she apparently thought she had paid the premiums when, in fact, she had made payments on their primary insurance contracts (and thank goodness, in her mounting confusion, she never missed any payments there).

Truth be told, the advisor should have recognized that something was amiss the moment a family that had never missed a payment suddenly goes into arrears on the account. It's no big deal to him if the policy lapses—he had made his money on the sale—but the moment he saw a notice that the account had not been paid, he should have been checking in with the octogenarian customers. I believe he owed it to long-time customers to look after them.

He never did, the policies lapsed while no one noticed, and I will forever be frustrated, not by the lost money but by the fact that decades of doing business didn't inspire the advisor to step in. Make sure your insurance agent looks after clients the way you want to be looked after.

Smart Investor Tip

Find out how involved the agent is in your community. A top independent agent once told me that "the more ingrained in the community an agency is, the more it has a selfish reason to serve customers to its utmost ability."

Unlike someone who is transient and just passing through, an advisor who is tied in to the community can't just pull up stakes. The business will not necessarily survive a move, so the agent is stuck where he is. That's good news for you, because it means that preservation of reputation is crucial.

Remember, an agent has the inherent conflict of working for both you and the company, a firm that may have no ties to your community. His ties to the community strengthen your safety net, because no agent in your community wants the bad word-of-mouth that occurs when he or she can't orchestrate a fair, if not happy, ending.

Prepare for Trouble, Just in Case

Conclude your interview with an advisor by asking about problems.

How will we resolve complaints if I am dissatisfied?

Most times, real problems will wind up in mediation, but find out how the process works and which chain of command your complaint will follow. That way, if problems do arise in the relationship, you can pursue redress immediately.

How can I terminate this relationship? How do I get out from under these insurance contracts?

You may be able to walk away from the agent, but not the insurer. Your contract may specify a period of time during which your policy is in force, with financial penalties for early cancellation.

If you are satisfied with the coverage but not the agent's service, you might call the company and ask for names of other agents in your area; the insurer will be happy to oblige because it is less likely to lose your business.

As with any financial arrangement, however, it is important you know ahead of time how you can get out if you are not satisfied with products, service, or performance.

Knowing Your Rights Illuminates Relationship Warning Signs

Years ago, the leading insurance industry groups got together and drafted the "Insurance Consumer's Bill of Rights." Essentially, as a customer, you have right to protection, to be informed, to choose, to be heard, to redress, and to services. The danger signs of a bad relationship with the advisor show up when these "rights" are violated.

Let's examine each situation separately:

- **The right to protection.** Obviously, you are paying to receive adequate protection. If your policies do not meet your need, or you find out through dealing with other financial advisors that your needs were not properly met, you have not received the guidance you were paying for.

- **The right to be informed.** Insurance is a mysterious business, cloaked in jargon and with so many subjective, hard-to-assess judgments. If you are not kept abreast of changes in your policy, in laws that affect you, of the basic assumptions made in calculating your needs, and in adjustments made to those assumptions over the years, you're in the dark. The less informed you are, the more you are one of those customers who is sold a product, rather than given personalized advice and solutions.

- **The right to choose.** Your choice may come down to finding another agent, but you always have options. If an agent says that you have no choice and no options—remember, giving up a policy and paying surrender charges is an option, no matter how unattractive—something is wrong.

- **The right to be heard.** You are the leading voice in decisions that affect you, and you should be treated with the respect accorded the key decision maker. That means prompt response from your agent and insurance company. If your agent is not listening to your concerns or keeps pushing something at you that is not in accordance with your wishes—or if your agent is not quick to resolve problems—the agent has stopped listening to you.

- **The right to redress.** Legitimate claims should be settled quickly. If not, and the agent isn't taking up your cause, be prepared to pursue a case with your state insurance commissioner's office.

- **The right to service.** You are entitled to prompt, fair attention. An insurance agent should want to be a part of your financial team and should never be afraid to justify your policies to the other members of your advisory squad; if she can't show your other experts how she has served you well and acted in your best interests, something is amiss.

Beyond those basic rights, the other big sign that may there's a problem you're your insurance agent is surprise. The whole idea of insurance is protection. The catastrophe that forces you to make an insurance claim—whether it is an auto accident, a house fire, or a death in the family—is traumatic enough. If the coverage or service in those times of need does not live up to expectations, or if the protection you thought was sufficient turns out to be faulty, the relationship probably was based more on making a sale than on your needs.

Pursuing Complaints

If the agent is a sole practitioner—and your beef is with the agent and not the insurance company—your first place to turn may be the insurer to see if it is willing to intervene on your behalf or step in and correct the perceived wrong. With an agent at a large firm, your complaints will start with a supervisor.

In both cases, you may have signed an agreement to mediate any disputes between you and the advisor. Do not wait to pursue other remedies (lawsuits) before any statutes of limitation expire. If your problem is severe enough to require a mediator, it also warrants a call to the state insurance commissioner's office, which has the power to frighten most agents into a least reviewing tough cases.

Don't stop there. The insurance agent's responsibility is to sell you products in your best interest and suitable for your need; if he has failed to do this, your remedy is likely to come in court.

Building the Relationship

There are still a lot of insurance agents whose idea of a relationship is that they send you a calendar at the holidays and figure that when you see their name and contact number at the bottom every day of the year, you will call when there is an issue. That may be fine; after all, once you fix your leaky financial roof, you wouldn't expect to need additional repairs for years or decades.

Still, as with a will or an estate plan, insurance coverage must be reviewed periodically, particularly when there are major life changes. Take the time to do this in person, to have an insurance checkup that brings the advisor up to date on your needs, desires, and how your financial picture has changed over the last few years.

Make sure the advisor knows you welcome his or her input to your financial team; most will want to work with you in that fashion—and to interact with your other advisors—because it provides a refreshing change from the routine, and it creates the best chance to represent you well.

Chapter

Interviewing an Accountant/Tax Preparer

I have no use for bodyguards. But I have a very special use for two highly trained certified public accountants.

—Elvis Presley

Most Americans need more brains to figure out their tax return than to earn the money necessary to pay it.

That's certainly true for anyone earning a decent amount of money.

For those without a big income or who have simple, uncomplicated lives (single, no children, no deductions), filing a tax return can be pretty EZ (to quote the code of the Internal Revenue Service form for a straightforward tax return). Once you leave the realm of simple tax returns, however, you must decide if you are the best-qualified person to deal with the tax code, get the most from its credits and give-backs, and to properly make your case to the IRS. You must also decide if you are hiring someone to complete your tax return now, or if you want someone who will take the job for years to come.

If you are picking a preparer to use for the foreseeable future, you should start your search by acknowledging that the person who prepares your tax statements knows your deepest secrets, things not even your family may know about you, such as household income, investment returns, and more. It must be someone who can draw out that information, be trusted to keep it confidential and use it to your advantage, while staying securely within the boundaries of the law.

The challenge for an individual looking to hire a tax preparer for the long haul is finding the right match of competence, expertise, price, and attitude toward dealing with the IRS.

Can I Do This on My Own?

Of all financial jobs, the only one that comes with an instruction booklet to get you through the task on a do-it-yourself basis is tax preparation. The IRS sends you that instruction book with your tax return forms.

Since you are entitled to prepare your own return, you don't need a preparer or accountant to do the work. The problem is that taxation without representation may be a really stupid idea.

In every tax situation, there are three solutions: the "right" way, the wrong way, and your way.

The right way gets every allowable deduction without stretching the truth or making you vulnerable to penalties or a problem if you get audited. It generally involves not only doing the paperwork necessary to complete a tax return, but occasional phone calls throughout the course of the year to allow for tax planning. The right way is not necessarily letter-of-the-IRS tax advice, because officials in that agency acknowledge that there are many ways to do a tax return. It depends on how aggressive you want to be in taking deductions and pursuing opportunities; go for too much, and you get into trouble, pursue too few opportunities and the IRS gladly will accept all the extra money you are willing to pay.

The wrong way is slap-dash and sloppy, thrown together to beat the deadline or simply to get out from under the pressure of filing. It may involve stretching the truth or trying to take deductions that you fear the IRS will disallow. It will cost you interest charges and penalty payments, or will simply result in your paying more tax than you need to pay.

Then there is your way, which is probably somewhere between the other two. You will likely find that aiming for the perfect tax return involves shooting at a moving target. The idea is as come as close as possible to the ideal return for someone in your particular situation.

If you don't feel comfortable doing that on your own, hire someone who can. A good advisor will earn back his or her fees—and save you time, stress, and aggravation—by properly minimizing your taxes due.

That's harder than it sounds because anyone—literally, anyone—can be a tax preparer. By law, you might be unable or unwilling to do your own taxes, but you could hang out a shingle, promise to help people and sell your miserable tax-preparation services to others.

While tax preparation seems like one of the easiest roles to fill on your financial team, it is also one of the most subjective spots, because the right relationship depends so much on the two of you having the same approach to dealing with Uncle Sam. If you want to minimize taxes and are willing to risk raising the proverbial "red flags" that can increase your chance of audit to do it, you'll want a preparer who is comfortable taking those same risks when handling your documents.

Finding Candidates for the Job

Aside from asking friends or relations who does their taxes or walking into a storefront tax-preparation shop, the groups behind the main credentials and designations for tax preparers all have online programs to help you find a pro in your area. Some also have telephone services. Not only can you use these services to find an advisor, but you can use the same contacts to verify the credentials of any advisor you meet with, so that if a friend recommends an enrolled agent, you can make sure the person's qualification remains in good standing.

Start your search for a tax advisor by contacting:

- Accreditation Council for Accountancy and Taxation, www .acatcredentials.org (for advisors with the ATP or ATA credentials)
- American Institute of Certified Public Accountants, www.aicpa.org (look for the "Consumer Information" tab, then search for "Find a CPA")
- National Association of Enrolled Agents, www.naea.org (look for "Find an Enrolled Agent")
- National Association of Tax Professionals, www.natptax.com
- National Society of Accountants, www.nsacct.org (click on "Find a Professional") or call 800-966-6679

Your state society of CPAs is another good resource, and you can get the contact details through the AICPA website. The more localized database may not be any better for your search, but it typically is better when checking an advisor's background, as most problems with a CPA tend to be reported first at the state level and may be settled before ever going any further.

Referrals from all of these groups should not be considered endorsements, just a list of practitioners in your area. Some agencies require advisors to pay a fee in order to get any referrals from the group's website; that doesn't mean the referral is bad, but it does suggest that the referral database will be incomplete, in that advisors who don't pay the fee may not show up on the list. If there is a discrepancy, talk to a real person at the organization to get the scoop.

Interview Questions for Tax Preparers

Few people actually sit down for an interview with a tax preparer, outside of "Here's my last return. Do you think you could handle it?" Even if you want someone to simply put you out of your misery and do your return before your head explodes, you will want to go a little bit deeper. Remember, too, that the reason most tax preparers don't face interview questions is that the customer comes in around tax time with an immediate problem. The best time to be shopping for a tax preparer is right after the close of tax season, around the time you are thinking, "I never want to go through the pain of filing on my own ever again."

That way, you can contact potential advisors early and take the time to get complete information. Here are the questions you should ask:

Your First Meeting

Here are the questions you will want to answer as you go about selecting and working with a financial planner.

How long have you been preparing tax returns?

Tax law is always changing, but experience counts for something. Think back to the first time you faced any tax form on your own, and you'll understand why you don't want to be any preparer's test drive into a new area of the tax code.

Looking at my return from last year, how do I compare to your average client? Am I more or less complex, or about the same?

Bring previous tax returns to an initial interview so that the advisor gets an idea of what is involved and can accurately forecast a cost.

By asking how you compare to a typical client, you should find out what concerns the advisor might have in preparing your returns. ("Most of my clients don't have self-employment income [or fill-in-the-blank unique need]" is a big red flag.)

Get the advisor to describe his or her average client, using specifics of age, family situation, average income, and so on. His idea of "average" may come from the paperwork—"a 1040 with Schedules A, B, D, and other standard forms"—rather than personal data, but if you want him to provide counsel beyond merely filing returns, you will need to resemble the average client in more than just the forms you fill out. If you will have questions about removing money from annuities while the typical client is worried about getting money out of a college savings plan, you may be asking questions the preparer is unprepared to answer. If he isn't used to doing a return like yours and answering questions for clients in the same situation, find someone who is.

Another way of getting at this information is to ask for the range of forms the preparer filed the previous year. She may have done a lot of Schedule A and B forms, but not a single Schedule SE, which affects people who are self-employed. If the range of forms is narrow, make sure your previous returns do not eclipse the advisor's comfort zone.

Are there any areas on which your practice is focused or in which you specialize?

Tax advisors can be generalists or specialists. They may focus on a particular clientele—doctors or small-business owners, for example—or type of situation, such as cases of divorce. Just because an advisor has a specialty doesn't mean she won't branch off into other arenas depending on a client's needs, but make sure your needs fall in the trunk area of the practice, and not out in the tree limbs.

What continuing education classes have you taken? What credentials, if any, do you have?

Tax-preparation credentials require ongoing classes or certification exams. Find out what makes the preparer qualified to be your personal expert; you will find that many people with similar professional designations have different backgrounds, with some opting to do the minimum and others going back to school for master's degrees in taxation or extra schooling to handle specialized situations.

Regardless of credentials, your preparer must be current on the law, which changes almost daily. The IRS does not care if you—or your preparer—are unaware; ignorance is no defense for overzealous deductions or underpayment of taxes due, so be wary of advisors who haven't been to continuing education programs in more than a year. Remember, you'll be the on the hook for the bill if your advisor makes a mistake.

Smart Investor Tip

Regardless of credentials, your preparer must be current on the law, which changes almost daily.

The Price You'll Pay, and How You'll Pay It

Now that you know the questions you need to ask when selecting your advisors, here's what you'll need to ask to figure out how much you should pay.

What can I expect to pay? How do you charge for your services?

Tax-preparation service fees can vary wildly, which is good reason to shop around before settling on the advisor you intend to work with.

Typically, tax preparers charge either by the form or by the hour. Expect less-personalized service if you are charged by the form, because the preparer has an incentive to crank out the paperwork and move onto the next return. Advisors who charge a flat fee per completed return also have their compensation tied to how quickly they can get the job done, rather than how correctly or whether it has the best tax outcome.

Beware the urge to save a few bucks now, while leaving yourself exposed to big-time costs later; make sure any advisor who charges a flat rate per return tells you how he handles complex cases—in case yours falls into that gray area—and how much time he spends on the average return. Compare the hours he expects to spend per return to the estimated hours given by other advisors, and you may find out whether the flat-rate preparer spends too little time on the case (or the hourly advisor too much).

No matter how the advisor charges, you will pay less if you deliver your papers in good order, rather than dumping a cigar box worth of receipts on the preparer's desk. In fact, many tax preparers will turn you away if there is too much work involved in your return; they don't make money sifting through your receipts and trying to decipher your notes.

How Tax Advisors Set Their Prices

Your costs for hiring a tax pro will be based on one or more of the following:

- A set fee for each tax form or schedule. (A National Society of Accountants survey found the average cost of preparing a non-itemized Form 1040 to be $115 in 2007, the most recent data available. The average charge for an itemized Form 1040 with Schedule A and a state return was $205. Average prep costs for other types of tax returns ranged from $165 to more than $1,700, depending on the forms' complexity.)

- Last year's fee plus an additional charge for any changes in your tax situation that require additional research or paperwork.

- A minimum charge, plus additional fees based on the complexity of the client's situation (so that you pay a set fee for a basic return, but then pay more if you add a Schedule C for your sole proprietorship, etc.).

- A value-based fee based on the subjective value of the tax preparation service (this is where you will pay fees for handing the preparer a shoebox full of receipts, expecting her to do the work and the math rather than compiling the data yourself).

- An hourly rate for time spent preparing the tax return (the NSA study showed that the average hourly fee for accountants providing tax services was $122.12, with variations from roughly $90 to $140 depending on geographic region).

- A set fee for each item of data entry.

Ask what goes into your bill and ask for an estimate. Per-item, per-form, or per-hourly rates sometimes make it hard for a preparer to provide an accurate price quote, especially if your tax situation is in flux, but most can provide a price range if you can show them your returns from the last few years.

Smart Investor Tip

Ask what factors determine your bill, and use your last tax return to get an estimate of what you're likely to pay.

While pay scale is tied to expertise, going a step up the hierarchy doesn't always translate to bigger costs. There are enrolled agents who are more costly than accountants. The national preparation services aren't always such a bargain either; my enrolled agent—who fills voids in her calendar by working at a tax-prep service—charges less in her individual practice than if you met her at the storefront practice because she has less overhead.

In addition to shopping around on basic return preparation, find out how a tax advisor will bill you for time spent during the year that does not translate directly to what appears on your tax return. If, for example, you want tax advice before selling an investment, or want to make sure that another advisor's take on tax law is correct, you could pick up the phone to call your advisor in, say, June.

Some advisors just add that time to your next return, others will bill you for a consultation, and others answer straightforward questions for free.

As you schedule interviews with a preparer, ask whether an initial get-to-know-you meeting is free. If you wait until tax time to find a preparer, you should expect to pay a fee because it's the advisor's busy season; if you are lucky, the preparer will put the money toward your first bill if you become a client.

What do I get for my money?

Once you know how fees are structured, find out what you get for your dough. If your hope is that the preparer will go through your shoebox trying to make out every chicken-scratch note you've left on the back of a receipt, you need to be sure he's willing to do those chores for you (most aren't); he may sift the paperwork with you or tell you what to look for, but you won't be satisfied if you expect him to ease your burden.

Find out if paying for a tax return simply means getting the paperwork completed or whether you get paperwork for the coming year (making it particularly easy to pay estimated taxes), whether you can call throughout the year when you have a tax question, and whether the meter will be running during those phone calls.

What other costs might I incur?

Some tax preparers charge for filing a tax return electronically, others charge you copying costs for the copies you take home. Today, a big fee for electronic filing makes no sense, since it's easier for the preparer to do your work on a computer; that doesn't stop some services from charging a $20-plus fee, outrageously high when a basic return costs $115 to $215.

It's a miserable feeling to get the bill for services and feel like you have been squeezed for every extra penny, so ask ahead of time what you could pay for besides the time spent meeting with you or preparing a return. For example, if the advisor needs to do research to properly prepare your return, will she bill you for that time? If so, make sure the research is specific to you, and that she isn't double-billing, putting the research time needed to check out a fairly common issue on the bills of several clients.

Smart Investor Tip

Ask ahead of time what you could pay for besides the time spent meeting with you or preparing a return

---

How can I reduce my costs?

Many advisors won't agree to go through your shoebox of receipts, particularly if you are hiring them well into tax season. Others will do it, but for a fee that you can avoid by doing some basic preparation on your own.

Even if you think you have done all of the math yourself, you may be coming to them with material that requires more preparation time than you might have expected. Find out what you can do to make the process more efficient without reducing the accuracy of the return. Most advisors will be happy to give you this information, because even though it cuts into their take on your return, it makes the filing process a whole lot easier.

If an advisor has a certain way she likes material organized and wants particular details in place before she works on your return, chances are you will cut your bill significantly if you can become the preparer's ideal client.

If you do not have the expertise to handle my return—or to advise me about the tax implications of financial moves that I may someday consider—where do you turn for help? Do you ever allow those other experts to take over a client?

You may never expect to be in this situation, but tax issues can get sticky in a hurry. Inheritances, investment losses, and changes in career, family, or your health, for example, can take a simple tax return and make it a complicated mess overnight. Find out where an advisor turns when situations get murky.

What Kind of Tax Preparer Should I Hire?

Anyone, literally, is qualified to call him- or herself a "tax preparer." Even you—looking for help on your own return—could sell your assistance to others right now. There are a lot of steps from that low level of help to the top of the scale.

The first step may actually be free help. If your income is under $60,000 roughly, you may qualify for "Free File," a partnership between the IRS and a group called the Free File Alliance, which lets you file your taxes electronically for free. Essentially, the service matches you with a preparation service, which does your return pro bono (though there may be a charge for filing a state return on your behalf).

The lowest rung of paid tax preparer is the "tax preparation specialist," which can mean a real expert or some guy looking to make a few bucks during tax season. Unless this prospective advisor has credentials, you have little to go on in making your decision. Worse yet, the most attractive thing many plain-vanilla preparers have to offer is the promise of a refund, a promise that is often kept by playing fast and loose with IRS rules.

Then there are the tax-preparation mills, the name-brand chains. These firms—the H&R Blocks of the tax-prep world—have many locations and ramp up their staff to handle the spring rush. Their obvious benefit is that they process so many returns that they can do instant estimates on what yours is likely to cost, and they offer refund-anticipation loans for people looking to get their overpayment back in a hurry.

These chain preparation services require their preparers to pass an annual course, which covers the bulk of what they'll see filing typical returns. They also sometimes hire advisors with more advanced credentials. Each year, for example, the woman who does my taxes—who is an enrolled agent, a credential we will get to in a moment—fills her tax-prep calendar by working at a regional storefront return service. If you happen to walk into that shop during tax season and she is the next available preparer, you luck out and get a highly qualified, expert tax professional doing your work on the cheap. Of course, if she is tied up, you might get the person at the next desk who, on any given winter's day, is a high school dropout who slept through the class work and has a stick-it-to-the-man complex.

Just as important, if you use a prep mill, there's a good chance your preparer will be gone by summer, unable to help you if there's a follow-up question or something you want to know before making a move that could affect your taxes the following year. The odds are extremely low the same person will still be at the tax mill if the IRS audits you; if the firm promises representation in an audit, it will probably send someone other than your actual preparer.

If you need more than tax-mill basics, inquire about their "executive tax services," which typically function more like a traditional accountant's office than a walk-in center. You make appointments and develop an ongoing relationship with a full-time, year-round advisor, and you pay about three times the going rate charged to walk-in clients. In other words, if you went to the national firm looking for a bargain but need to hire the executive-level preparers, you're not getting the sale price.

Your next stop on the selection trail would be either an Accredited Tax Preparer (ATP) or Accredited Tax Advisor (ATA), credentials that signify that the advisor has completed a tax preparation course offered by the College of Financial Planning, has five or more years of experience, and has passed an exam offered by the Accreditation Council for Accountancy and Taxation. These are often independent providers, not that much different from the "tax preparation specialist" except for the work needed to earn the ATP or ATA designation.

You should also consider "enrolled agents," possibly the most under-recognized specialist in any of the advisory fields. Enrolled agents are former IRS workers, people with extensive dealings with the agency, or folks who have passed a comprehensive exam entitling them to represent clients before Uncle Sam. Most spent at least five years working for the IRS, then passed a two-day exam; in order to retain the designation, an enrolled agent must complete a required number of hours of college-level continuing education each year; many fulfill this requirement by pursuing a master's degree in taxation or accounting.

You can find enrolled agents, like mine, who work independently, but you will also find them working with accounting firms and law practices. Like certified public accountants, enrolled agents are trained to be expert in all areas of tax preparation; the difference is that they are not certified, which often translates into lower-cost services. Enrolled agents don't sound as glamorous as certified public accountants, but they are no less qualified as tax advisors. While anyone can be a paid tax preparer, you can only be represented in an audit by an enrolled agent, certified public accountant, or tax attorney.

Certified public accountants (CPAs) must earn at least a bachelor's degree and pass a strict national exam, in addition to meeting several requirements for continuing education. CPAs may specialize in areas besides tax preparation—plenty of them don't work on returns for their clients, but focus on big-picture tax planning and leave the tax prep for underlings—so the credential itself does not make someone right for you. (You should be aware that someone can be an "accountant" without being a CPA; in some states, a licensed public accountant is considered the equivalent of a CPA, in others, only someone with the CPA designation can even claim to provide "accounting services." If an advisor mentions accounting without saying he or she is a CPA licensee, ask enough questions to be sure you are getting the expertise you expect.)

CPAs should be a member of their state society of certified public accountants as well as the American Institute of Certified Public

Accountants. As such, they are governed by a strict code of ethics, and their firm must undergo regular quality reviews conducted by peers. They also should be licensed to practice in your state.

Tax attorneys generally do not prepare returns themselves. In fact, some tax attorneys don't even have anyone on staff who handles that chore. Instead, the role of a tax attorney is to provide counsel in tricky areas of tax law, notably divorce, estate planning, and business issues. If you get into those arenas, or are embroiled in any dispute that puts you at the mercy of the Tax Court, you may at least want to consult with a tax attorney (preferably with a master's degree in taxation or some other advanced credential) to have the most competent representation.

The more complex your needs, the higher up the scale you may need to go to ensure qualified counsel. Be realistic in assessing your needs; don't pay for a Rolls Royce if all you need is a go-cart to get the job done.

Learn about Clientele and Scope of Practice

Below are some questions you should ask to learn about the advisor's clientele and scope of his or her practice so that you can make an informed decision of whether you fit within his or her niche.

How many clients do you work with?

This question is about what happens at crunch time (because you can reach a tax advisor pretty easily the rest of the year). There are about 600 working hours in a tax season, and a busy firm with an office staff may do 600 or more returns. A small practitioner with little or no office support may handle a few dozen.

Make sure the advisor is not too busy to give you his full attention. If he has a big clientele, ask how that affects your return, whether that changes when you must have paperwork ready and so on.

Are you open for business all year?

It's not just the storefronts or the local preparers out to make an extra buck who may be gone when your audit notice arrives. There are some enrolled agents and accredited tax preparers who shut down when it's not tax time.

As a result, this is a smart question. If you want more information on a return—say to challenge an IRS ruling on your deductions—or if you want tax planning and have ongoing questions, you will want someone who is in the business for the long haul.

What percentage of your clients file for an extension?

Some advisors file extensions for everyone, others make a habit of having all clients polished off by April 15. An extension does not put off paying any taxes due, it simply gives you more time in which to file the paperwork.

If you expect a refund, it slows the process dramatically.

If an advisor has a lot of clients and files extensions as a matter of course, rather than need, you should question if she has adequate time available to serve you.

Danger Signs

When it comes to your taxes, surprise is the biggest bugaboo. You may owe a monster tax bill, for example, but it shouldn't be a surprise. If you liquidated a retirement account and are facing major penalties, that should not come as a shock; your advisor should have forewarned you about these things and even helped with the math.

Obviously, if a tax planner suggests moves that generate these bills without warning you of the consequences, there's a problem.

Poor communication is costly in other ways too. Tax advisors should develop a strategy for the tough situations, and they should then work on implementing the plan; they should consider all options and likely tax outcomes. If they can't explain everything necessary at your level—if they lose you in the tax code—there's trouble ahead. You should be able to explain any decision you make in plain English to your spouse, your parents or children, and the IRS.

Failure to meet deadlines is another trouble spot. If you wind up filing for an extension that you were not prepared for, or which should not have been necessary because you have a simple return, it's fair to question whether the advisor has taken on more work than he or she can handle.

Recurring annual problems can be another sign of trouble. A tax refund is not a bonus, it's a sign that you withheld too much money throughout the year. It represents an interest-free loan to Uncle Sam; unless you use it as a form of forced savings, your advisor should work to improve your withholdings. Conversely, paying a big tax bill every April could be a strategy or a sign that your advisor hasn't got you adequately prepared to avoid trouble. If an advisor can't get you on an even keel, either she doesn't have enough information from you, one (or both) of you is pursuing a particular (and odd) tax strategy, or the advisor isn't working hard enough.

Will anyone else work on my return?

This also falls under the realm of "What do I get for my money?" You may get your answer when you ask about the size and breadth of the accounting/tax-preparation practice. If an accountant uses junior partners or enrolled agents to do tax returns, you want to know. Not only will you want to be able to check out the subordinate's credentials, you will also want to ask about the return-review process and find out whether the big shots double-check all work before asking you to sign it.

It's dumb to pay for a figurehead. Find out what, if anything, the involvement of others does to your projected costs; you should pay less if an accountant merely oversees your return than if he or she does the math and the work.

Smart Investor Tip

You should pay less if an underling does your return and the accountant merely oversees the process.

Could I get the names of a few recent clients you have worked with?

Ideally, references will be folks whose cases are similar to yours and who use the advisor for the same reasons, whether they want long-term counsel or a quick fix.

What to Ask References

Aside from the standard list of questions you ask about any advisor (see Chapter 14), there are some specific questions about tax advisors where a client's perspective is important, such as:

- Did the advisor seek deductions that might otherwise have been missed?
- Did the advisor suggest ways to lower taxes due?
- What kind of tax planning do you receive in mid-year reviews?
- Does the preparer work to keep bills down by listing in advance everything you must put together? How does he or she deal with you if there is information you can't find, or if you need help putting details together for the return?

- Has the advisor, in general, avoided nasty surprises so that even if the news was bad, you were prepared for all possible outcomes?
- If you have ever paid tax penalties because of something the advisor failed to do, did the advisor correct—and pay for—the mistake at no cost? (Remember, the advisor is likely to pay only for penalties and, possibly, interest due; the actual tax liability always is the responsibility of the customer, even when it was the advisor who suggested, say, a deduction that was disallowed.)

Inquire about Relationship and Investment Style

With this information in hand, below are questions you should ask to learn about the advisor's relationship and investment style.

What can I do to lower my taxes, both for this year and in the future?

Don't expect detailed advice in an initial interview, but get a feel for whether the advisor is content to stay the course or whether he or she believes that actively managing your tax situation could save you some dough. If all he wants is to crunch numbers you give him, he might not be the right kind of advisor to be a lifetime helper.

What is your approach to deductions?

Find out just how aggressive a tax preparer intends to be. I once interviewed an enrolled agent, for example, who told me he would not file an office-at-home deduction because "those things wind up as a red flag that makes you more likely to be audited."

That would be great logic if I were worried about facing an audit and losing.

My office is a legitimate, meets-the-IRS-standard deduction, and a big one at that. Not taking it to avoid a potential audit would cost me thousands of dollars over the years; moreover, the deduction would not be a problem during an audit because it's a legitimate, real, allowed expense.

Clearly, that tax advisor was too conservative for me.

The late American jurist Learned Hand said, "There is nothing sinister in so arranging one's affairs as to keep taxes as low as possible." Your tax advisor should be as conservative or aggressive as you are in dealing with the IRS. Is she unafraid of incurring questions from the IRS or does she take a conservative approach that is less risky but possibly more costly?

Ask how the preparer deals with the gray areas of the tax code. If the preparer wants to push the envelope of legality and you don't—or vice versa—it's a bad match. Remember, you pay the extra tax if the preparer is too conservative, and you are responsible for taxes and penalties if the preparer plays fast and loose with the rules.

Smart Investor Tip

An advisor who promises to "always" get money back from Uncle Sam is prepared to bend the rules.

Will you guarantee me a tax refund?

The answer you want is "No." An advisor who says that he can always get you money back from Uncle Sam is prepared to bend the rules—particularly if he hasn't had a chance to dig into your files and see whether you or your previous advisors have done well filing your return—or he will have you withhold too much (giving Uncle Sam an interest-free loan) so that he can look like a hero by getting your own money back.

Don't Be Lured by Refund-Anticipation Loans

One reason why some consumers first go to a tax preparer is to speed up their tax refund or to borrow money against it, effectively getting their cash now while their tax return is being processed.

But those refund-anticipation loans—and they go by a lot of different names, but are mostly know as "rapid refunds"—are a bad reason to pick a tax advisor and a terrible financial practice. No advisor truly worried about giving you the best financial deal would seriously offer you these kinds of loans.

First, to qualify for a rapid-refund loan, you already made the questionable financial decision to give Uncle Sam an interest-free loan by overpaying the taxes due, thereby creating the chance for a refund. While some consumers use a refund as a form of "forced savings," that only works if you save the dough when you get it back.

Quick-refund loans are nearly identical to payday-advance loans, except they attach to the tax refund rather than a paycheck, which also sometimes makes the terms and conditions even worse. The key difference is that the payday-advance loan business feels a bit sleazy and creepy—because it operates out of everything from spam e-mails to dive storefronts to loud websites—but the refund-loan business emanates from a trusted source, the tax preparer, which gives it the air of legitimacy.

It's a short-term loan, where your refund check guarantees repayment; that guarantee means these deals are available to people whose credit is bad and who might not qualify for other forms of financing. Despite the short loan period and the locked-in repayment, lenders charge fees as if the consumer is a horrible risk. Fees range from $34 to $130, according to the Consumer Federation of America, with some tax-preparation firms adding surcharges that run anywhere from $25 to several hundred dollars. One popular feature is the "instant" loan, which makes the money available on the same day you process your tax return, for a charge of $25 or $50 just to get the money a day or two faster than normal.

More than 8.5 million taxpayers took refund-anticipation loans in 2007, according to the latest IRS figures. The cost of getting their money a week or two early amounted to $900 million in loan fees and other charges, according to the National Consumer Law Center.

Translate the fees into dollars, and the bad deals become obvious. Say you pay between $60 and $120 to get a refund-loan of $2,500. Taken as interest, it means the loan is carrying a rate of 2.4 to 4.8 percent, which is not bad on a long-term deal, but which is huge when charged by the fortnight. If that loan was stretched out over a full year, the annual percentage rate would be 50 percent or more. And that's before any delay in repayment or any other problem that might create additional charges.

Ironically, the less you borrow, the worse the situation gets. If your refund is small, the fees eat a greater percentage, making the deal that much uglier. And if there's a problem with your tax return, and it comes in at a number less than expected, you're still on the hook for the full amount borrowed. Your tax preparer's mistake could make you look good for a big loan, but could cost you big down the line.

Short of having to come up with bail money or paying off the loan shark threatening to break your legs, rapid-refund loans are a bad idea. If the bills are pressing, financial experts suggest that you call the lenders, promise to turn over the tax refund, and get the relief—provided you follow through when Uncle Sam's check actually arrives—without the big charges involved in these short-term, high-risk loans.

What are the potential outcomes of my return?

You want a realistic assessment of where you stand now. Even if you don't have the expertise to do your own taxes, you have enough knowledge to know the shape you are in. You know whether your earnings have shot up, if you have withheld more of your salary, if you sold investments and realized capital gains, if you gained or lost deductions based on your marital status and circumstances surrounding your children and more.

After a few questions, an advisor should have an idea of what to expect, and should give it to you straight, even if they know your tax circumstances are every bit as ugly as you fear.

Are you familiar with the laws of the states in which I am subject to tax?

Presumably, every advisor knows the rules of the state in which they live. But if you have financial interests in more than one state, you will want someone familiar with the rules in both places. This is particularly important for people who live in one state and work in another, who receive income from a partnership based in another state, or who have moved and owe taxes to two state governments.

In two different years, my current employer erroneously paid at least a portion of my withholdings to Minnesota, rather than to my home state of Massachusetts. Getting the situation straightened out—including the refund of monies paid to the wrong state—would have been a real hassle were it not for my preparer's ability to zero in on the right answers.

Ask about History with Audits

As your relationship starts—and perhaps for the life of the relationship, depending on how certain questions are answered—you will want the advisor to answer the following follow-up questions:

What percentage of the returns you filed last year were audited? What percentage of returns have been audited over the course of your career?

IRS statistics suggest that less than 1.5 percent of returns are examined in an audit. If an advisor's experience shows an abnormally high number of audits— I know many preparers of all stripes who've never had a client audited—it warrants some explanation.

Periodically, the IRS focuses on certain occupations and industries and niches; specializing in returns on this hit list—a clientele composed primarily of doctors when the IRS takes a closer look at that profession, for example— can dramatically inflate a preparer's audit numbers. Without those special circumstances, ask why clients have been audited and the outcome of those examinations. Too many audits can be a sign that the IRS and the preparer don't see eye-to-eye in how certain rules are interpreted; the IRS generally wins those arguments.

Who will represent me in an audit?

Only enrolled agents, CPAs, and tax attorneys can actually represent you if the IRS comes calling. That said, even some of those advisors do not handle audits themselves, leaving the work to partners or others with more audit experience. In the case of storefront preparation services, you want to know who the firm will send with you and how you will contact the firm in the event of an audit (some storefront services set up locations that are open only during tax season; these temporary offices will be gone when the audit notice arrives).

You've already asked about the advisor's audit experience; some past audit experience is good, even if too much is a red flag.

Be sure also to ask about the cost of being represented in an audit. Just because an advisor can do it doesn't mean he or she will not charge you for it. Find out the costs involved, just in case; it may help you decide exactly how aggressive you want to be with those deductions.

If I am audited or notified of a problem with my return, who pays penalties and interest on the amount I owe?

You'll pay what Uncle Sam determines you owe, as well as for any preparation blunders you sign off on. That means that if you do not withhold enough money from your paycheck and owe Uncle Sam taxes and penalties on April 15, it's your responsibility. But say your advisor whiffs on a portion of the tax code and a deduction is disallowed; you'll be notified months after filing that you owe taxes on the income that was not deemed tax-deductible.

Find out what the advisor does if her errors result in penalties. Don't expect her to pay the actual taxes owed, but many preparers and accountants may make good on financial punishments that you incur due to their mistakes.

When will I hear from you, and why?

If you're looking for someone to get you through the current tax season, this question is unimportant. The advisor could be out of business in six months—and many are—and it wouldn't matter to you. If, however, you want to integrate a tax advisor into your financial team and work with someone you trust for many years, you will want an advisor who is interested in dealing with you all year long. Just as importantly, you will want to know what to expect from the relationship after the paperwork is filed.

There are four basic functions that you should expect from a tax advisor: suggesting tax strategies, preparing returns, minimizing tax exposure, and, if necessary, preparing you to meet tax authorities. To cover those bases, a tax advisor will have to contact you periodically; collecting your paperwork and calling you when it's over is insufficient.

Smart Investor Tip

A tax advisor should be in touch every now and then; collecting your paperwork and calling you when it's over is inadequate.

A relationship-oriented advisor will want to handle all of the four major functions plus review your estate planning and help in managing investment and insurance decisions. That may mean regular visits, phone calls when you plan to sell investments, end-of-the-year tax-reduction brainstorming, or more. Find out how involved the advisor gets in helping clients prepare for the future. That information will go a long way to deciding whether this advisor is one you can work with for a lifetime.

Have you ever been subject to any practitioner penalties? If so, for what?

Tax advisors do not have to tell you if they have been subject to practitioner penalties, and there may not be a way for you to track down that information.

Ask anyway. If a preparer reacts funny, use your intuition.

(This is one reason why you might want to go with someone who is accredited, or who has a credential like an ATA, EA, or CPA, because you can go to the sanctioning body to see if there have been problems.)

Prepare for Trouble, Just in Case

Conclude your interview with an advisor by asking about problems.

How will we resolve complaints if I am dissatisfied?

There is no standard procedure for solving problems in the preparation of a tax return. If you are dealing with a sole practitioner, for example, there is no boss to go to.

Still, you should discuss what happens if you are not satisfied with the work done on your behalf (and that means that you are displeased with the quality of the advice, not with the fact that you owe Uncle Sam some money). A tax advisor may not have a great answer to this question; that tells you that your recourse may have to be some type of malpractice action.

Where to Complain if Things Aren't Working Out

Where you seek relief depends on the kind of advisor you are hiring. If you are working with a national tax preparation service, start with the office or regional manager. With an accountant or enrolled agent from a large firm, your first step will be a complaint with the managing partner.

If you work with a CPA, your next step will be to approach the state society, to see if it can offer you any relief. Responsibility for disciplinary actions is shared by the state groups and the American Institute of Certified Public Accountants. You can reach the AICPA—which can, in turn, point you to the appropriate state authority if necessary—at 888-777-7077, or online at www.aicpa.org.

For an Accredited Tax Preparer or Accredited Tax Advisor, complain to the Accreditation Council for Accountancy and Taxation at 888-289-7763 or online at www.acatcredentials.org.

If you can't work out some relief, contact an attorney. Accountants can be guilty of malpractice as much as lawyers, brokers, or doctors.

How can I terminate this relationship if I am not satisfied?

Until you get to the level where you are hiring an accountant, there may be no formal agreement to sign. Termination may be as simple as walking away, although you may need to make sure you get all of your paperwork back. Most accountants ask you to sign a "letter of engagement." Never enter any financial arrangement without knowing how to get out of it.

Smart Investor Tip

Never enter any financial arrangement without knowing how to get out of it.

Building the Relationship

No one gets true "tax planning" in March or April. You get it the rest of the year, when there is still time to make moves that save money based on your personal circumstances.

Once you have hired a tax advisor, the best way to build a relationship starts when tax season ends, and you can sit down for a chat about positioning yourself and your family for the future. Make it a point to call for advice whenever taxes play a role in your other money-management decisions. By seeking out a tax preparer's counsel at other times of year and involving him or her in decisions you make with your other financial advisors, you turn a "tax preparer" into a "tax planner."

Because taxes play a role in almost every financial move you make, get your advisor involved, even if it's just a precautionary phone call just to make sure you understand the rules, or that you set aside the information that, because of trading or strategy shifts, will be necessary next year at tax time. Knowing what the advisor will want to see come tax season will help you prepare and reduce the frustration level when you need to work on your return.

Over time, you may want to introduce your tax advisor to your broker, financial planner, or estate planner; the more involved your tax preparer is during the decision-making process, the more he or she can help you plan, rather than just cleaning up mistakes come tax time.

Chapter

12

Interviewing a Lawyer

Insurance salesmen profit on fear.
Stockbrokers profit on greed.
Lawyers profit on everyone.

—Anonymous

You may agree with William Shakespeare's assessment in *Henry VI* that "First thing we do, let's kill all the lawyers," but the plain truth is that there will come a day when you need a lawyer on your side. In fact, over your lifetime, you may need several lawyers, each covering different specialties, so no matter how many lawyer jokes you swap with friends, you should at least know how to contact and select an attorney when your time of need comes.

Lawyers, of course, come in all shapes, sizes, and specialties, but for the purposes of this book, we will limit the discussion to attorneys who work with financial specialties, most notably taxes, estate planning, elder care, and real estate. That's not to say that the questions and concerns raised in this chapter could not apply to divorce attorneys, bankruptcy lawyers, or specialists in consumer issues, worker's compensation, intellectual property, or personal-injury cases, but rather that hiring advisors for those specialties might require additional questions that won't be raised here.

There was a time when lawyers were almost a one-size-fits-all group. The same guy who wrote your will also went to court with your cousin to defend against reckless driving charges. It's the country-lawyer image portrayed in old movies, and it's about as current as those black-and-white films; today, law is highly specialized and most attorneys concentrate in just a few areas.

Can I Do This Myself?

The oldest axiom in law is that any man who acts as his own lawyer has a fool for a client. It was, of course, lawyers who were behind that saying, and they only make money when they have clients to represent.

There are many situations when you may not need or want a lawyer. You can buy software, like Quicken's Willmaker, for less than $50 that will walk you through the process of doing a simple will and financial powers of attorney and the alike. There are packages that will enable a do-it-yourself bankruptcy, trust, and divorce, too.

That said, these generic services may be insufficient for your needs. At the very least, you may want to have a lawyer review any documents you develop through the software programs; the consultation will add to your costs, but your efforts will dramatically reduce your legal bills compared to what would have happened if the lawyer had done all of the paperwork from scratch.

In consumer cases, almost every community has some form of small claims court, where you can resolve disputes valued up to a few thousand dollars by representing yourself in informal proceedings (and with minimal court costs).

Many financial disputes contractually agree to settle disputes through arbitration, where an impartial observer—generally former judges, current and former lawyers, and business people—settles your dispute in a binding situation. The ground rules, including maximum allowable monetary damages, are set when you agree to arbitration; the process is quick and results are private, unlike court hearings. While many people suggest having an attorney with you, one is not necessary. The mediation process is similar, except that the neutral mediator only offers suggestions to resolve the dispute. There is no settlement unless you and your opponent come to terms.

With that in mind, recognize the stakes of the game you're playing. If you can represent yourself well, and your needs are straightforward and don't stretch the limits of the software or generic documents you rely on, you may be satisfied representing yourself. But if you make mistakes that wind up creating trouble with the Internal Revenue Service, forcing your heirs to pay estate taxes that they might have avoided, or more, the price tag is steep.

That doesn't mean a lawyer won't take up almost any request that comes his or her way, but it puts the onus on you to gauge whether the lawyer has the skill to handle your specific needs.

There are three factors that typically drive people to hire an attorney to help with their various financial matters:

1. *How complicated is the situation?* Complications can be caused by technicalities of the law, the type of assets involved, the number of parties to a case (and the fact that some of them live out of state), or the general complexities of the situation. An estate plan is a lot easier to draw up when a couple has an only child who will inherit everything than when it's the second marriage for each spouse, with several kids from each prior marriage and two together, and then countless nieces and nephews whom the couple wants to make gifts to. If the situation could turn adversarial, think of it this way: If the other side, for any reason, has an attorney, chances are that you should, too.

2. *How much is at stake?* That's not just a monetary question, since your home, assets, or life estate may be involved. You may be struggling with money, but that doesn't mean you'd want to face a foreclosure proceeding —with your house on the line—without an attorney on your side.

3. *Do I need someone to speak for me?* This is a personal decision, but whether it is in a courtroom or in legal documents, you need to be represented in a way that complies with the law and that gets the job done. If you can't get that done, or if the situation is emotional and could provoke anger or just make you look bad, you may want to get representation in order to keep everything calm and moving.

What Kind of Legal Specialist Do You Need?

Some lawyers cover a wide range of issues and areas, while others focus in on a single type of law or on a few closely related specialties. In alphabetical order, here are the major areas of legal practice, including those outside of the financial realm, and what each type of lawyer provides:

- *Business lawyers* give advice on general corporate matters, from startups to mergers and acquisitions, business taxation, contract and partnership issues.
- *Consumer lawyers* represent clients in disputes with stores and consumer products companies.
- *Criminal lawyers* do the obvious, defending or prosecuting cases of criminal wrongdoing.
- *Estate planning lawyers* write wills, set up trusts, establish powers of attorney, and counsel clients on property management, inheritance,

tax, and probate issues. Some also act as executor on the client's estate. Many estate-planning specialists also work on elder-care and senior law issues.

- *Family lawyers*—more widely known as *divorce attorneys* or *domestic-relations lawyers*—handle cases of divorce, separation, annulment, child custody, and support. Many family lawyers also specialize in "elder law issues," the rules and regulations and rights of seniors and the infirm.

- *Governmental lawyers* are generally considered an extension on business lawyers, helping clients comply with (or dispute) local, state and federal rulings, regulations, and statutes.

- *Immigration lawyers* represent people in immigration and naturalization proceedings, helping them to become citizens or to avoid deportation.

- *Intellectual property lawyers,* commonly called "patent attorneys," advise clients on issues involving copyrights, trademarks, and patents.

- *Labor lawyers* cover a wide range of issues. They can represent employers, unions, or individuals in cases involving workplace safety, compliance with government regulations, and questions of allowable union activity, but also get involved workplace discrimination cases.

- *Personal injury lawyers* take on cases of people hurt through the intentional or negligent actions of a person or company. Many also specialize in worker's compensation claims for people injured on the job.

- *Real estate lawyers* help clients analyze real estate contracts, mortgage paperwork, disputes with brokers or agents and contractors, and process the paperwork involved in a closing. They can also get involved in neighbor disputes and other property-ownership issues.

- *Tax lawyers* counsel individuals and businesses in federal, state, and local tax matters, interpreting the tax code when sticky situations arise. While a tax attorney can represent you in an audit, most will not work directly on completing your annual tax return, although some will be affiliated with accountants—or will have tax preparers on their staff—to handle the paperwork.

Financier J. Pierpont Morgan once described what he wanted from an attorney, saying, "I don't want a lawyer to tell me what I cannot do, I hire him to tell me how to do what I want to do."

You may not have Morgan's enormous fortune, but you want his kind of lawyers, ones who can help you achieve your goals.

Unfortunately, that may mean involve telling you what you can't do. Good lawyers know better than to waste time. They should argue on your behalf, but also be ready to fight with you in order to keep you out of trouble. You need someone who knows and pays attention to details and who does not let the little things slide.

Finding Candidates for the Job

When you need a lawyer, ask relatives and trusted friends who have been in a similar situation. Their reference will go a long way, although you must remember that each case is different.

Go beyond friends and family, however, to consider the legal referral services in many communities, many of which will recommend a lawyer to evaluate your situation—often at a reduced cost. Many of the referral organizations have minimum competency or experience requirements. Even that is no guarantee that you will find the right lawyer, however. Some referral services are more advertising than substance, with lawyers paying to get a spot on the referral list. In those situations, there is no attention paid to a lawyer's skill.

Lawyers also can advertise now on television, in newspapers, on the radio, and in the phone book. This may help you remember their name, but it does not make them the best lawyer for your case. Moreover, be careful of pricing issues; the advertising may talk about specific types of services and fees, but your case may not fall into the simple-and-straightforward category and you may not be able to get the advertised special.

The simplest places to start are with the American Bar Association, which features a referral service prominently on its website, www.abanet.org, and with

A Lawyer's Job

Once you decide not to represent yourself, only a lawyer can represent you in legal proceedings. All lawyers must pass a state bar exam and a character review in order to receive a license to practice law. Because practicing law without a license is a crime in most states, lawyers are the only ones who can be your advocates, although paralegals, bankers, and others may help draw up papers. (In some states, paralegals—working under the direct supervision of lawyers—can handle minor matters and even offer direct consultation in limited areas.)

You're hiring someone for his or her informed judgment and knowledge of legal procedures. A good lawyer listens to your problem and searches for the best, most prudent course of action.

Martindale-Hubbell, which has a definitive database of lawyers and firms and a search service on its website, www.martindale.com. The American Bar Association site also includes contact details for your state bar association, where the database of lawyers may include more options that are convenient to your home; your state association may can also tell you which counselors are part of its regional committees, which can be particularly helpful if you have a special need.

Checking Them Out

While getting a referral from the bar association or referral service, you should have asked if there was any record of the lawyer's disciplinary history. But since many of those listings are actually supplied and paid for by the lawyer, there may not be any negatives to speak of, so you may want to treat this the same way you deal with a referral made by a friend or neighbor, and dig deeper.

The Martindale-Hubbell Law Directory is a complete listing of domestic and international lawyers by state and specialty. It is available in most public libraries and provides background information on how long a lawyer has been in practice, where and when he or she got degrees, and more. You can access it, along with the search feature, at the company's website, www.martindale.com.

Unfortunately, it's still just a surface measure of an attorney's background; you will not find out whether an advisor has had complaints and malpractice suits filed against him or her.

In fact, that kind of crucial information about lawyers is lacking almost everywhere you turn. Few states make all complaints available to the public from the time allegations were filed. Most states will reveal grievance filings, but only around the time when the state bar association's grievance committee has decided to issue charges against the attorney. Those committees can take ages to make a decision, and those charges can end in "admonitions" or "private reprimands," where only the lawyer and the aggrieved client know what happened.

Regardless of those shortcomings, call your state or local bar association's grievance committee for any records it can provide pertaining to your prospective attorney. In addition, check with your local Better Business Bureau—you can get the contact details at www.bbb.org—to see if there are complaints filed there.

Interview Questions to Ask a Lawyer

Many lawyers offer a free initial consultation, although some charge a nominal fee for their time; find this out before you set up the interview. If you plan to interview several candidates, anyone who charges for that first consultation should be scheduled last.

As with every other type of financial advisor, you are shopping for trust, integrity, and ability, all of which will are hard to judge in an initial interview.

Your First Meeting

Here are the questions that will help you get a sense of the lawyers you interview:

How long have you been practicing and in what areas of the law do you specialize?

In all financial relationships, you don't want to be a guinea pig. That's particularly true of law, where one misstep could put you on the wrong side of a judgment. Find out the scope of the practice, whether your current needs are a good fit either for the individual lawyer or the firm. It's not that a patent attorney can't write up a good will, but you might have regrets when someday you discover what years of practicing intellectual property law have done to his skills as an estate-planning attorney.

If a lawyer has several specialties, ask how her workload is divided between those areas of the law. A lawyer might do real estate contracts and estate planning, for example, but her business may be heavily weighted toward the former; if you come in with a complex estate situation, she may not have the depth of experience you want, even though estate planning is supposed to be one of her specialties.

This actually happened in my own case. After moving to Massachusetts, my wife and I worked hard to find an attorney to rework our wills and protect our children. We then kept the will up to date by redoing it after several life changes. At the last of those upgrades, our attorney told us that what we needed next was some high-grade estate planning, and that his practice had become so focused on real estate—with simple estate-planning matters thrown in—that he didn't feel he was the right guy. Our wills would serve us for years, but when we took the next step, he figured it might be best without him. (I knew I picked the guy for a reason; his integrity stood out.)

Be sure to find out how long a lawyer has had each specialty. He may have 10 years of practice experience as an estate planner, for example, but might only have branched into elder law a year ago. Make sure he passes muster in your area of need.

Smart Investor Tip
Be sure to find out how long a lawyer has had each specialty. Make sure he passes muster in your area of need.

Beyond a law degree, what professional credentials do you have?

Law is not an area where you must see specific credentials to feel comfortable with a practitioner. The law degree and license speak volumes about someone having achieved the minimum standards for competency.

Still, there are some legal specialties, such as a "certified tax lawyer" or "certified civil trial lawyer." While there are major trade groups like the American Trial Lawyers Association that have developed credentials, most national specialty law groups are membership organizations, rather than education/credentialing institutions.

Thus, you may need to distinguish between whether the lawyer is a member or a certificant.

Credentials can be valuable when looking for an attorney with a particular expertise, since maintaining these designations requires continuing education and some level of field experience. Still, they are hardly a necessity because they are not uniformly administered. (Traditionally, most lawyers were prohibited from calling themselves "specialists," even if they limited their practices; some state governments continue to adhere to this outdated custom, which could put the burden on you to find someone whose practice meets your needs.)

You are looking for someone who is experienced in the kind of matters you have; if you are presented with a credential, find out the educational and experience requirements and ask to see a code of ethics, if there is one.

The one time you will want to be picky about credentials is if your lawyer is going to wear two hats on your financial team. Some attorneys, for example, also are certified public accountants or financial planners. If you intend to hire an attorney-CPA, for example, make sure she has the appropriate accounting designations; if a lawyer doubles as a financial planner, look for an advisory credential (because, unlike law, there is no minimum standard of acumen to becoming a financial planner, and a lawyers can expand into that arena without being truly qualified).

The Price You'll Pay, and How You'll Pay It

Now that you know the questions you need to ask when selecting your advisors, here's what you'll need to ask to figure out how much you should pay.

How are fees charged? How much are your fees and for what are they paid?

With all of the ways lawyers bill clients, you want to know specifically what is involved. You are always entitled to an itemized bill for the lawyer's services, but you would prefer to know in advance how fees are calculated.

Some lawyers are always on the clock, meaning that your call to check with a lawyer on your case sets the clock in motion, as do your few minutes of small talk with the attorney. You do not want to be racking up charges while talking to your attorney about his family. Find out the ground rules for being charged. Will a five-minute phone call show up on your bill, or is that a free part of the lawyer's service? If you are charged, what's the rate going to be? Will you pay to have copies of important papers mailed to you?

Smart Investor Tip

You do not want to have the meter running while you're talking to your attorney about the youth sports team he coaches. Find out the ground rules for being charged; it will affect how—and how often—you interact with an attorney.

What other costs might I incur?

Just because a lawyer gives you a great hourly rate doesn't mean you will get off cheaply. You might pay $1 per photocopy, $5 to receive a fax, or pay inflated tabs for secretarial work.

Lawyers really aren't supposed to profit on costs, but many do. They build depreciation, secretarial time, and anything they can think of into charges for using the copier, for instance; you could pay a lot more than the two-cents-per-page charge from the corner office supply store.

Again, there is nothing illegal about this, although the American Bar Association says that lawyers should only charge for "actual costs." Still, it's hard to complain about after the fact, because you agreed to pay the lawyer's costs.

Most lawyers do not want to sound like they are squeezing clients dry. They may waive some charges if you press them for details in advance. If you don't ask about these charges up front, however, don't be shocked if your bill comes back padded with extra fees.

Be sure this discussion also covers court costs that you might have to pay, plus any filing fees and the like. You may agree to the flat fee for preparation of a will or trust, and then be surprised to see charges for filing with the court, retitling assets to put them in the newly minted trust, and more.

How can I reduce my costs?

Find out if there are ways for you to minimize costs. In some situations, it may involve your doing the legwork to find certain documents or to drive documents around yourself, rather than relying on a courier service. The smaller a lawyer's practice, the more he or she will value your ability to do some of the menial chores on your own, and the savings will be very real.

Learn about Clientele and Scope of Practice

Below are some questions you should ask to learn about the advisor's clientele and scope of practice so that you can make an informed decision of whether you fit within that niche.

Who is your typical client?

You don't want actual names, so this question does not violate attorney-client privilege. What you want to find out is whether the average client is an individual or a business and whether the average job resembles what you need done, both in terms of the legal matters being covered and, when applicable, the dollars involved. If you have a big estate and fear lawsuits, so that you want to set up an asset-protection trust, you don't want to be working with an advisor whose idea of asset-protection is an ordinary estate plan and protecting life savings from Uncle Sam. You're looking for someone who can make you virtually "suit-proof," and the difference is huge.

While you want to be in the "sweet spot" for the lawyer's practice, understand that things change, as was just shown in the story of my own attorney. If you are not a good fit for a lawyer's practice today, you may be even further out of sync in the future, as the practice gravitates toward whatever specialty most pays the bills.

How many active cases/clients do you work with at one time?

This is another good indicator of how likely the advisor is to work on your case. If he has a heavy workload, your run-of-the-mill situation may not get the attention it deserves. Your will may be an everyday document to an attorney, but it is protection for your family, not something you want the lawyer to squeeze between 20 clients with needs he perceives as more pressing. If the attorney overpromises—saying you will get your documents quickly when you know there's a big caseload—you should be nervous.

There is one more major concern when it comes to a lawyer's caseload, namely "double billing," which happens when a lawyer goes to court for you and several other clients at the same time. While traveling, the lawyer catches up on other cases or reading and sends bills for that time to every client whose file is in the briefcase. You're paying for the lawyer's attention to your case, but it's not full attention; while the American Bar Association has long condemned this practice, it can't punish members for it.

If the caseload seems heavy, ask about double-billing and whether you get a reduction in the hourly pay rate if you are sharing time or don't have their full attention.

If you do not have the expertise to handle my case on your own, do you work with other lawyers? Under what circumstances would you allow them to take over the case?

Determine what makes a lawyer nervous enough to seek help or back away from a case.

Ideally, you hire a lawyer who is as aggressive or conservative in his or her approach to work as you are in your approach to life. If you are the conservative type who likes everything buttoned down before proceeding, you might be concerned about a lawyer who never consults with others before making new maneuvers for clients.

Under what circumstances would you simply refer me to another lawyer?

There are good and bad answers to this question.

Good answers involve a lawyer passing you on to a partner—or even an outsider—who is better suited for the job or when she is too busy to give your case the attention it deserves. Bad answers are that your case is not interesting enough or not likely to generate enough in fees.

If you go to a firm to interview a senior partner and find a fresh-out-of-school rookie handling your case, that's not good. You should meet and interview any lawyer who will handle your case before signing up for the firm's services.

Under all circumstances, find out if the lawyer charges a referral fee, which means they get a fee—or a piece of the action—for passing you along. In most states, the ethical rules governing lawyers say that a referral fee cannot be charged unless the client is aware of the situation and each attorney works on the case and splits the fee proportionately to the work they performed. Equally important, the referral fee cannot make the total bill unreasonably high.

Smart Investor Tip

Find out if the lawyer charges a referral fee, and if he or she will get a piece of the action simply for passing you along to someone who is better suited to help you.

Will anyone else from the firm be working with me?

You're the one paying the bill, and you want to get what you pay for. If the lawyer uses paralegals or junior partners to do the work, you should find out just how involved your attorney intends to be. It's dumb to pay for a figurehead. You also want to find out what, if anything, the involvement of others does to your projected costs; it can push costs up or keep them reasonable, depending on circumstances.

Could I get contact details for some recent clients to use as references?

Attorney-client privilege can make this sticky sometimes, but someone who can act as a reference and say how the lawyer deals with clients will help cement your decision.

    If the lawyer won't give you the names of clients, ask for professional references, perhaps the names of lawyers to whom he makes referrals. When you call those colleagues, do not identify the person who gave you his name at first, saying, "I was told you could be a reference for my attorney. I was wondering who you consider to be the best attorneys in town." If your lawyer's name comes up, then ask why the reference feels that way. If it's not on the list, ask why not.

Inquire about Relationship Style

With this information in hand, below are questions you should ask to learn about the advisor's relationship and investment style.

What are the potential outcomes of my case?

This applies mostly to adversarial situations, where the final decision could be a win, a loss, or a settlement. Before engaging an attorney—particularly if you are paying on an hourly rate instead of contingency—you want to an honest assessment of the strength of your case. This includes knowing whether the lawyer expects to settle the case or go to court—and the plusses and minuses to each of those resolutions—as well as whether a loss can be appealed and under what circumstances the lawyer would recommend it.

    If the lawyer expects the case to go to court, ask about trial experience, as there are plenty of attorneys who almost never set foot in a courtroom.

How do you work with clients?

You want contact when it's necessary, so ask when the advisor typically finds it important to call or meet with a client, and what circumstances drive those meetings. By establishing how often and under what circumstances you will hear from the lawyer, you can decide whether that contact is sufficient for you to be satisfied.

In addition, find out what paperwork, if any, the lawyer will give you copies of. A file of these papers is good to have, in case you decide to change lawyers mid-stream.

How Lawyers Are Compensated

Lord Henry Peter Brougham, a 19th-century British statesman, once noted that a lawyer is "a learned gentleman who rescues your estate from your enemies and keeps it for himself." Indeed, one reason many people fear hiring a lawyer is the cost, thinking that the only way to get good legal representation is to pay a lot of money for it. (Sometimes, those fears turn out to be true.)

Lawyers earn their keep in several different ways; more than one could apply to your situation.

Flat fees or *fee-for-service payments* are common when the procedure is straightforward and generally requires a routine amount of time. Many lawyers quote a flat rate on simple wills, title searches, reviewing a real estate contract, and other common practices.

Routine procedures also are perfect opportunities to use prepaid legal plans and legal clinics. The prepaid plans—sometimes offered as an employee benefit—function as a kind of legal health-maintenance organization (HMO), where you pay an annual fee and are entitled to a specified amount of service from lawyers who take part in the network. Legal clinics tend to offer low-cost representation, often with less-experienced attorneys than those in private practices; simple procedures such as those that generally are billed at a flat rate generally can be handled cheaply by this kind of law office.

Once you get past routine work and into cases where the amount of work involved is less predictable, chances are you will pay *hourly rates* for your services. This is the most common form of billing; depending on your location in the country, and the specialty of the lawyer involved, expect to pay anywhere from $40 to $500 per hour, and it could go up depending on the expertise of the lawyer, the complexity of the case, the size of the firm, and if there is other work that must be turned down to accept and adequately prepare your case. Most lawyers keep a detailed log of hours worked on your behalf, often breaking the time down into as much as tenths of hours. They may charge a higher rate for courtroom time than office or telephone minutes. Some lawyers quote a maximum, basically saying that once hourly charges pass a certain point, they will turn off the clock.

It is important for you to understand exactly when and why your lawyer is charging you. If the meter is running every time the lawyer picks up the phone, even if it is just to tell you there is no progress on your case, that might wear your pocketbook thin. Remember, too, that the lawyer's out-of-pocket expenses—from court fees to messenger services, faxes, copying, and more—will show up on your bill too, added to the hourly tab.

Asset-based or *percentage fees* are a sliver of the assets being managed or distributed. For example, a lawyer may earn a percentage of the assets in a will that goes through probate. The problem with percentage fees is that they aren't always commensurate with the work involved to earn them. If there are major assets involved but only routine legal work—say you are selling a $1 million home in a straightforward transaction—you might be overpaying for the service you get. In those situations, press the lawyer to use an hourly or flat rate for the service or ask for a cut in the percentage fee so that your bill is fair given the amount of work involved.

Lawyers accept *contingent fees* on cases they believe they can win, usually for a client who cannot afford to pay the other types of fee. Contingency fees only apply in situations where money is being claimed, notably personal injury and worker's compensation cases; some states forbid criminal and domestic-relations attorneys from accepting cases on a contingency basis.

If you win the case, the lawyer takes home a big cut, generally between 25 and 50 percent. Generally, the lawyer gets one-third of your winnings (many states limit the maximum allowable fee), although "sliding scale arrangements" can increase the attorney's cut if the case drags on or is appealed, or drop the percentage as the dollar value of the settlement rises.

If you lose the case, there are no winnings to split up and the lawyer gets nothing. Win or lose, however, you will owe court costs. I recently saw a television ad for a lawyer who promised that clients would "never pay a single cent out-of-pocket" to try their case. Unless the lawyer agrees to pick up filing fees and assorted court costs in the event of a loss, that statement most likely was false.

Court costs are a key consideration in hiring lawyers on contingency. You want expenses deducted from the monetary award *before* the lawyer's cut. Say you win a $15,000 judgment; court costs are $3,000. If the lawyer's cut comes first, they take one-third of $15,000 ($5,000);

you then pay court costs and are left with $7,000 for your win. By comparison, if court costs are paid first, your net award after expenses is $12,000. The lawyer gets one-third, or $4,000, leaving you $8,000. Many contingency lawyers prefer to be paid before expenses are taken from the award, but the point often is negotiable. Be sure to negotiate it.

Retainers are monies paid to lawyers on a regular basis to make sure an attorney is available when needed. Retainers are paid mostly by individuals and companies with a regular need for service. (Many lawyers agree to take work from individuals in exchange for an up-front payment for part or all of their services; they may call this a retainer but it typically amounts to a nonrefundable advance.)

Retainers are merely a method of payment, and not a charge for service; as a result, you still must find out how you are being charged for the actual work being done. If a lawyer asks for a retainer, consider this a down payment; if you have a big need for legal services, you could outspend the retainer and face a bill down the line. Make sure you have an idea how much service—hours of the lawyer's time—the retainer actually covers.

Just how tough are you?

Many legal issues come down to a test of will and nerves. You may want an aggressive lawyer, but you also must be able to live with the outcome.

For example, some lawyers are particularly tough in negotiating insurance settlements. If they can't get the desired amount from the insurer, they may walk away from a settlement and risk getting the money in court. That could tie the case up for years.

While you want someone who fights tooth-and-nail on your side, you may not want to pay the price such an aggressive lawyer exacts. Some particularly tough real estate lawyers, for example, will walk away from a house rather than giving up on the concessions they demand from buyers or sellers. Their desire to do the best deal is wonderful, but not if it costs you the dream house you had been looking for.

Hire a lawyer who is as tough as you are and who will demand nothing less than you would expect from yourself.

Smart Investor Tip

Your lawyer should be as determined as you are and should fight for you as much as you'd fight for yourself.

How often will I hear from you?

You want to make sure that the lawyer's idea of the appropriate amount of time to spend with you is similar to your own. If you need hand-holding and a call from your attorney every day, then a lawyer who calls only when there is action on the case may not be active enough. This question forges your expectations for the relationship, helping to set a standard that the lawyer will have to meet for you to feel he is living up to his promises.

Prepare for Trouble, Just in Case

Conclude your interview with an advisor by asking about problems.

How can I terminate this relationship if I am not satisfied?

Never enter any financial arrangement without knowing how to get out of it. Depending on why you need a lawyer and what kind of agreements you signed, you may just be able to walk away. If, however, a lawyer has invested hours on you and you then pull the plug, expect some charges—and possibly some unpleasantness—as you head for the door.

Signs of Trouble

Your relationship with a lawyer may be going sour if:

- *He appears to have lost interest or stopped working on a case.* Unhappy clients often complain that a lawyer is not devoting sufficient time to the case. In fact, the client might not be completely aware of the progress being made or of delays beyond the lawyer's control. Generally, this boils down to a communications issue. If the problem is more than miscommunication, write your lawyer a letter. This generally serves as a wake-up call because lawyers know it is a prelude to building a case against them for not doing their work. In addition, every case has a time limit, called a statute of limitations, within which it must be filed. And some paperwork must be filed immediately given the health and welfare concerns of the people involved. If your lawyer is in jeopardy of missing these kinds of deadlines, you must either apply pressure to get the ball rolling or simply find someone else to tackle your case now.

- *Your instructions are not being followed.* With the exception of doing something illegal, the lawyer's job is to advise a client of possible actions and outcomes and then take the path chosen by the client, even if that is not the direction the lawyer wants to go. If your lawyer is doing things in accordance with her own feelings, or pushing you hard to do things her way without explaining the situation so that you come to the same conclusions, question whether she respects you.

- *The bill is much more than you expected or was not properly explained.* You have a right to an itemized bill. You should have discussed the items ahead of time to avoid unpleasant surprises in the end. If issues arise, contact the lawyer and ask about the unexpected charges; if the situation cannot be resolved that way, contact the local or state bar association to ask about the fee arbitration process.

- *You become aware of potential conflicts of interest.* If a lawyer has a problem representing you because of other, existing relationships, you should have been made aware up front. He also can't work both sides of the same case without the permission of both parties; if you find out that your lawyer has breached this ethical standard, seek new counsel immediately. (Last word on conflicts: A lawyer should not represent you if your interests conflict with his own. In other words, a lawyer should not write your will if you plan to leave the lawyer property or money in that will.)

- *You have not received your complete share of a settlement.* If you believe that a lawyer has improperly taken or kept money owed you, it's a big problem. Contact the state and local bar association—specifically its disciplinary board—if your money is not returned in short order. (Ask bar association reps about their funds for "client assistance" or "client security." These are funds put together by lawyers that may reimburse you if a court decides that your lawyer is guilty of fraud.)

How will we resolve complaints if I am dissatisfied?

You're not expecting problems, just being realistic. And just because you know how to get out of the arrangement doesn't mean there won't be complaints to settle. That being the case, find out how potential disputes will be settled.

Most state bar associations offer arbitration committees that, for a fee, settle disputes between clients and lawyers (usually over expenses). At the same time, you could resolve those matters in small claims court.

Fees represent the biggest area of dispute between lawyers and their clients; find out whether the lawyer has had this kind of problem in the past and how it has been resolved. Then determine how it will be resolved if it happens in your case, preferably settling upon fee arbitration as the most fair solution to potential problems.

Have complaints against you been filed with the bar association? Have you been sued for malpractice?

This is the kind of cross-examination that can make a lawyer uncomfortable. But lawyers know better than anyone that, well, suits happen.

I know many outstanding lawyers who have had to defend themselves from clients whose expectations were not met and who pursued the lawyer because they did not like the outcome or resolution. If your lawyer has been sued, ask what happened and how the case was resolved.

Smart Investor Tip

You will have to use your intuition to determine whether past problems should send you off to visit someone else.

Remember, too, that the lawyer is not obligated to provide details of problem cases. You will have to use your intuition to determine whether past problems should send you off to visit someone else. If your background check shows cases that the lawyer did not own up to, hit the road and search elsewhere.

Where to Complain if Things Aren't Working Out

If something appears to be going wrong, start at the source and talk to your lawyer. If you don't get satisfaction there, you have several options:

- If the lawyer is in a firm, go to the managing partner. If you are in a prepaid legal plan, contact the plan administrator. In either case, the boss should try to resolve the complaint and get you the kind of representation you seek (although that still does not mean you will come away satisfied).

- Your state or local bar association can help in several ways. The disciplinary committee can answer questions about whether your complaint is legitimate. The fee-arbitration committee can help you if fees really are out of line, and may be able to help settle any disputes. And if you believe the lawyer has stolen money from you, you may pursue restitution from the bar's client security fund. (You will also want to contact the police or your local district attorney.)

- You can sue for malpractice. If the lawyer has been negligent and you have been damaged as a result, you can pursue reimbursement. (Of course, suing for malpractice involves hiring another attorney, this one involved in handling professional liability cases.)

What's Next?

Once you have engaged a lawyer and taken care of your current needs, contact could be sporadic. That said, if you want her acting as "my lawyer"—as in "Well, my lawyer says . . ."—you actually want an ongoing relationship.

Find out how often you will have contact with her. Will she call periodically to see if your will needs updating, for example, or if you need a new health-care proxy? When something else comes up in your life, will you be able to call her with a question—just to get a sense of the direction you want to go—and not be billed for it?

Lawyers know how they want a relationship to work; they know the circumstances under which they want to hear from clients. They also know that some of those phone calls will turn into billable hours; you want to know when they drop the flag on the meter.

By defining what you want and describing the kind of ongoing relationship you desire with a lawyer, you lay the foundation for a long-lasting, recurring business relationship.

Building the Relationship

If you want to have a lawyer as part of your financial team, you need to plan regular visits, at least as often as you have major life changes—children, buying a house, moving, etc.—and as infrequently as once every other year.

Ask the lawyer how often they feel your paperwork needs to be revisited and possibly updated; even if all you have is a simple will—and grown children so that your circumstances appear static—you may want to get your lawyer involved in estate-planning discussions that you have with your financial advisor. Moreover, if your estate-planning attorney establishes trusts on your behalf, your financial planner or broker may have to re-title assets and move them into the trusts, so they may need to work together. There is nothing worse than spending the money to establish a trust, and then to ruin the effort and waste the money because nothing was properly moved into the trust.

And, if you like your lawyer, consult with them on other legal matters, if only to get a referral to another specialist who is likely to help you in areas outside of their specialty. All of these conversations help to ensure that you will feel comfortable with your attorney, regardless of when you actually need their services.

Chapter 13

Interviewing a Real Estate Agent

In a real estate man's eye, the most expensive part of the city is where he has a house to sell.

—Will Rogers

In 2009, in the middle of a horrible real estate market and a terrible economic downturn, my parents put their home of 40 years up for sale. They had said for years that they knew who their real estate agent would be when the time came; in fact, the woman was a family friend whom they even invited to a big birthday bash for Mom as my parents started to think that the time to sell was approaching.

Within days of calling her to say it was time to list the house, however, my parents recognized that they were making a mistake. It wasn't just in hiring a friend—one of the seven big mistakes discussed in Chapter 3—it was that they were struggling to agree on anything with the agent. They were even counting the bedrooms differently, which seems hard thing to do when you're looking at the same house with the same number of bedrooms today as it had when it was purchased in 1969.

My parents quickly arranged to change real estate agents midstream, and gave the listing to someone who was more in sync with the way my parents viewed their home and the real estate market. Thankfully, the story has a happy ending, as a quick sale followed the change in agents, and my parents were pleased by the outcome.

Yet, in the middle of it all, at the most stressful time, there was my father saying, "I've come to realize that if we had talked to a few real estate agents earlier, we might have avoided the drama."

"Don't be so hard on yourself, Dad," I said, putting my tongue firmly in my cheek. "I mean, how could you have known there would have been trouble? It's not like you have a close relative who is an expert at selecting financial advisors of all stripes who had been telling you to meet with real estate agents for years, before you had a need for one. I mean, if you had *that* kind of guidance, then doing it wrong would be unforgivable, but lacking that kind of resource you will make the same mistakes everyone else does."

Honestly, I am thrilled with the way things turned out for my folks, and I doubt the end result could have turned out better if my parents had gone through the process exactly as espoused in this book. That's the vagary of the market, to some extent. I am certain, however, that they had a much bigger hassle factor—and that the outcome could have been *much* worse—because they took the common approach to finding a real estate agent, rather than engaging in a proactive search long before the house was due to hit the market.

Smart Investor Tip

You should find an excuse to "work" with a real estate agent before you ever need them. The more you learn about them without a pressing need, the more comfortable you will feel with them when the time comes to make a move.

The problem is that most people work with a real estate agent only when they are buying or selling a home. It's not surprising, really. Real estate agents get paid on commission for doing a deal, so the idea of continuing the relationship past the point of a sale—when there is no commission to be made—is foreign to many people.

But a home is the single biggest investment most people ever make, and it makes sense to periodically consult with a specialist who can help determine the appropriate steps to take to get the most from that holding. You might think that the $25,000 in renovations you plan to make will come back to you in sales price someday, but an agent familiar with the local market may know better. You might have a particular type of house—say a townhome—where there seems to be an upper limit as to what local buyers will pay; if you bought near that upper limit, you may not get the $25,000 in improvements back out of the home because prospective buyers may not be willing to pay that much for a townhome in your neighborhood.

Real estate agents are a valuable member of your financial team, precisely because they can help you determine the monetary impact of your otherwise unsupervised moves affecting the biggest piece of your investment portfolio. Just as many people wouldn't invest $10,000 in their stock portfolio without consulting a broker, it is prudent not to make a big change in your real estate portfolio without consulting an expert.

While most people work with real estate agents when there is an imminent transaction, part of hiring the right one to make a transaction is looking at what happens after the sale.

By only working with a real estate agent during sale periods—the way my parents did—you treat your home entirely as a "use asset," akin to a car, using and repairing it and getting whatever value possible from it when it's time to sell. Unlike a car, however, you probably expect your home to appreciate in value. The pre–baby boom generation and the front edge of the boomers lived through tremendous home-price appreciation. In the late 1980s, however, real estate price growth slowed dramatically and even turned negative in some parts of the country. Prices began appreciating sharply again in the late 1990s, but only in certain popular locations. Then the 2000s brought the bursting of the housing bubble and the mortgage crisis, which sent home prices plummeting in many areas.

If location alone won't make your house appreciate, it puts a premium on managing your property. It's not that every quart of paint trickles down to the bottom line, or that you might not want to spend money for your own comfort, even if you will not be rewarded with a better sales price, but it does make it smart to consult with an expert every now and again.

"You should treat real estate as part of your portfolio and treat it the same way as any other asset, and your market perception is best formed by checking with a realtor, not by sitting at home coming up with your own opinion of what everything is worth," says John Tuccillo of John Tuccillo and Associates in Arlington, Virginia, the former chief economist for the National Association of Realtors. "Given all the ins and outs of the market and financing, you can own more or less of your house every day, depending on leverage. And that's before you get into issues like the value of repairs and additions and more.

"You may not be ready to buy or sell, but it's a good idea to have a real estate agent you can talk to every now and again."

Presumably, that agent will be the one who served you when you bought or sold a home in the community where you live, or the one you are likely to work with years from now when it comes time to move. Had my parents actually had serious discussions with the agent they first worked with during the years they were certain she was "the one," the issues almost certainly would have surfaced long before there was a real problem.

Advice given over time can be a precursor to doing business down the road, which is precisely why agents will take the time now to have informal meetings and to create a comfortable working relationship before the time comes to sign an actual listing contract.

Can I Do This Myself?

The law doesn't require that an agent be involved in the purchase or sale of a home, and there is good reason to believe you can do just fine on your own if you have the right home in the right location and under the right market conditions. But unless all of those things are aligned—and you should disqualify yourself as a judge of whether you have "the right home" since you are emotionally attached—then the standard pitch of an agent selling his or her services is probably true.

Real estate agents typically say that they can get you a better price and sell your home more quickly and with less hassle. Barring all of those "right" circumstances, they're probably correct.

The main reason to represent yourself is to save money, generally a commission of 6 percent, although it sometimes varies by a point or two in either direction, of the sale price that gets paid to the agents involved in the deal. On a $200,000 house, that's $12,000; depending on individual circumstances, that can be the difference between making a profit on the home or bringing a checkbook to the closing to settle up your losses.

But that assumes you can actually get to a closing on your own. Selling without representation is not a go-to-closing-free card. You must do your own market analysis—in order to price your house reasonably (but not too cheaply)—pay all marketing costs, organize any and all open houses, and you must find buyers without free use of the Multiple Listing Service (MLS), a computerized system where member real estate brokers and agents advertise and swap information on available homes. (In the Internet era, ordinary folk can access the MLS for a fee, typically ranging from $150 to $500; pay enough fees and costs—to listing services, firms that help stage the home for an open house, for advertising, to put a sign in your yard, and more—and your commission savings start to shrink noticeably.)

And unless you have the cash to do a seller-financed deal, you probably lack the kind of financing muscle that a good agent can produce for a prospective homebuyer.

In other words, there's a reason why estimates suggest that "independent sellers" represent anywhere from 12 to 20 percent of all home transactions, but anyone who goes it alone will have to earn every penny of the commission savings by properly setting the asking price, marketing the home, showing the home, enlisting an attorney to handle the documents, negotiating with buyers, and much more.

It's Different for Homebuyers

For homebuyers, the issue of going it alone is a bit different. There is no drawback to scouring the newspaper, finding the right home, and making appointments on your own. You can get online access to most listings—even those in the MLS—and you get to see the for-sale-by-owner homes (which an agent might not show you, unless the owner has said he or she will pay a commission to a buyer's agent).

If you simply walk into an open house and work with the agent who is handling the listing—the seller's agent—the transaction may go smoothly, but you are dealing with a "conventional agent," and conventional agents always work for the seller. In fact, if you simply call a real estate agent whose name you see on a lot of houses in town, and you tell that person you want to buy a home, that agent will represent the *seller*—and not you—unless you specifically sign him or her up to act as a "buyer broker." (In real estate terms, the conventional agent who brings the buyer to the bargaining table is a "subagent"; don't be fooled by the jargon.)

> ### Smart Investor Tip
>
> A real estate agent may work with you as a buyer, and you may think they are on your side, but they have a legal obligation to always represent the seller unless they sign a contract to work with you as a "buyer's agent."

Say, for example, you found an agent who showed you available listings in town. You find a home on which you bid, say, $175,000, but tell the agent you would be willing to go as high as $200,000. Because the agent works for the seller, he has a responsibility to look out for the seller's best interest—even if he has met you and doesn't know the seller at all—which means that your willingness to go higher also must be communicated, along with your bid.

Chances are, the sellers are not going to settle for the $175,000 once they know you'd pay $200,000.

The fact that an agent works for the seller should not discourage you. For years, conventional agents were the only game in town, and it didn't stop people from buying homes at a fair market price. Indeed, most conventional agents do everything in their power to represent buyers well; it is in their best interest for you to be happy, to find a home you love, to refer other people to them and, perhaps, to someday sell your home through them.

What you should remember if you choose to work with a conventional agent is that he cannot tell you which home to buy (if you are looking at more than one home in the area, he represents both sellers and is not allowed to favor one), how much to offer (his job is to get the seller the listing price) and—with the exception of hidden defects that, because they are invisible, must be pointed out—cannot tell you what is wrong with the property (he is not allowed to influence you not to buy). In addition, a conventional agent is not required to provide you with a comparative market analysis—although many do—unless you ask for it.

The conflict of a buyer's contact point actually working for the seller is as old as the business itself; if the potential biases worry you, consider a buyer broker.

Working with a Buyer Broker

With a buyer broker, you sign a contract that says you will not look for a house with any other agent for a specific period of time. The buyer broker comes to you with appropriate listings and handles every part of the negotiation, including bidding strategy. Many also help clients search for the best available financing and insurance and set up all inspections.

Shrewd buyer brokers also watch the for-sale-by-owner market, meaning they may find homes a conventional agent would ignore. (They do this because you pay for their service, rather than the seller, so they get paid even if the house is sold by its owner.)

When buyer-brokers were first coming into vogue in the late 1980s and early 1990s, they often found themselves discriminated against by conventional agents, who either refused to share commissions, who would not work with buyer's agents and more. While that eased in time, it is a reason why there are some parts of the country where virtually no one attempts to work on behalf of buyers. What's more, a few bastions of those days sometimes come up in contracts, which can affect how (and how much) you pay for using the services of a buyer broker.

For anyone who has worked with conventional agents and jumped from one to the next based on the open houses or areas you are looking at, the exclusivity of a buyer-broker arrangement will seem a bit limiting. In addition, one frequent complaint from people who have gone to buyer brokers and not been satisfied is that the broker got pushy as the exclusivity period neared its end.

Most buyer brokers also work as seller's agents; in other words, they are conventional agents except when hired to be otherwise. It is possible, therefore, to have an agent who is doing both sides of the deal, selling you one of her own listings; in that case, she acts as a "dual agent," which she must disclose to you. She is supposed to represent both you and the seller, which I think is impossible since she probably has too much information from each side to cut an honest deal, and since she is basically negotiating the deal with herself. Think of "dual agency" as "no agency"—the agent is going to try so hard to close the deal to capture both sides of the commission that she won't act in either party's best interest—and ask your agent to appoint a colleague to work with you if this conflict arises.

Full-Service, Discount, or "For Sale by Owner"?

Between doing it yourself and paying full freight for an agent, there are discount real estate brokerages where, effectively, an agent puts you into the Multi-List and you do virtually everything else.

That may be a bit harsh, but you get limited services, most revolving around the marketing of the house, and then you do the open houses, the showings, the price negotiations, and the rest. The agent then gives back up to half of his share of the commission when the sale is completed.

Let's go back to that $200,000 example. The listing agent normally would get half of the $12,000 or so commission on the property (assuming there is a subagent or buyer broker for the bidder). That would make your take about $3,000.

That said, you might consider a discount situation a bit like looking at an a la carte menu at a restaurant. If you purchase a full meal, it is typically cheaper than buying everything piecemeal. But if all you want is the pieces, then a la carte works fine. The issue in real estate is simple; plenty of people like the idea of a discount, but they wind up needing—and ultimately paying for—the full service.

For buyers, the system works roughly the same way. The agent gives you a listing of the available homes in the area, and the comparative data and other information to help you bid effectively, but you set up appointments, negotiate the contracts, and all of the rest. If you do all of the work, you get to split the commission.

In both cases, however, what you really are working on is a pay-as-you-go system. You get the full split of the commission if you do all the work; if you want the agent to step in and arrange for inspections, for example, that'll cost you. Talk to your banker? Fee for that, too.

That's not necessarily bad. You might be able to save money doing a lot of legwork and leaving the tasks you dislike to someone else. Just find out up front how much those "extras" will cost you and what, exactly, you are being charged for.

The Difference between Brokers and Agents

In terms of handling the purchase or sale of a piece of property, there is no real difference between a broker and an agent. A real estate broker, however, had to first qualify as an agent, taking the requisite classes and passing a licensing exam; moving up to broker requires additional class work, a certain amount of experience in the business and another test.

By earning a broker's license, an individual earns the right to work independently and to open or operate a real estate office. An agent, meanwhile, must work for a broker.

Just because the broker is the Big Kahuna at the office does not make him a better advisor than one of his agents; plenty of agents have no desire to run an office, and plenty of brokers become office-bound and lose some of their feel for the community. You should worry more about an advisor's knowledge of the community than about the hierarchy in the real estate office.

That said, an agent can also be a person who simply handles property on the side, who does this job part-time, and who barely keeps up his standing. Either way, worry less about the credential and more about the person's experience, know-how, and understanding of the area.

Finding Candidates to Interview

With real estate agents, very little works better than word of mouth, or driving around and seeing who handles a lot of listings in the areas that appeal to you.

But there is also nothing wrong with going to the national organizations, or their local or regional chapters, to find a referral, particularly if you are looking for a buyer's agent. Contact:

- The National Association of Real Estate Brokers, which oversees the Realtist designation, has a find-a-Realtist page at its website, www.nareb.com.
- The National Association of Realtors' website, www.realtor.com, has a search feature, plus contacts for state and local associations, which will come in handy for checking credentials of any agent you are interested in.
- The Real Estate Buyer's Agent Council, which is part of the National Association of Realtors, oversees the "Accredited Buyer's Representative" credential and can help you find a buyer broker at www.rebac.net.

If you go to the local arm of any of these groups, try this trick: Ask which firms in the area do the most business, then schedule appointments with the top-selling agents in those firms. It won't guarantee that you find the right personality match, but it does ensure that your candidates will all be very active members of the local real estate community. The big plus to this method for a buyer is that the most active agencies are likely to have the most listings and give you the chance to see the most houses before they go out to the rest of the world.

Smart Investor Tip

If you want to see how an agent will represent your house, show up at an open house they're doing for someone else. You'll get an idea pretty quick of how they come across to potential buyers.

One other plus when looking for a real estate agent is that it's easy to see them in action. While you can't see an estate-planning lawyer write up a will, you can go to open houses in your neighborhood and check out the broker in action. As a seller, this helps you see how the agent represents a home and helps the owners get it ready for a showing. In addition, going to open houses and looking at homes through the eyes of a buyer is a good "reality check."

After you have done a walk-through of a house—preferably something similar in price range to your own—talk to the agent. Chat about the local market and some of the broad home ownership issues in the area. The agent will invariably ask what you are looking for—she thinks you are a buyer and wants your business, even if it is not to buy the house you are visiting. Then you can tell her that you are shopping for an agent or that you want advice on prioritizing your improvements so that you get the most for your home-ownership dollar. This informal time will tell you a lot about chemistry. Coupled with the interview and market evaluation, it can be a good way to begin a relationship.

Credentials Are Less Important in Real Estate, but Still Worth Checking

In real estate, your hiring decision will be based more upon what you perceive the agent can do for you than on what plaques hang on the wall. Credentials and memberships are important mostly if they mean that the advisor is living up to a code of ethics.

Still, be sure your agent or broker is properly licensed by the state. Most states require brokers and agents to post their license in plain sight, but don't be afraid to ask for it (especially if you do the initial interview in your own home and don't ever get to their office to see it). And if your agent claims membership in an organization—like the Realtors or Realtists groups—make sure she is in good standing and has no troublesome disciplinary actions filed with the group. Check for her record as an individual as well as seeing if there has been case action against the firm she works for.

If a credential check raises red flags—and you might want to run an agent's name past the local Better Business Bureau, too—ask about them during your interview. You want to know what happened, how it was resolved, and what can be done to make sure these problems never happen to you.

How Agents Are Paid (and if It's Negotiable)

By now, you know that a real estate agent gets paid in commission, but that does not mean there is no room to negotiate.

A small segment of real estate agents will make flat-fee arrangements—essentially a different form of discount brokerage—where they'll provide certain services for a prearranged fee. There still may be commission to pay for the broker who brings in the buyer, and there may be some work to do on your own behalf. Sometimes, with these arrangements, half of the flat fee must be paid up front and is kept by the agent regardless of whether the home sells during the time of the listing agreement.

When it comes to buyer brokers, the commission issue also can get sticky. Technically, you sign a contract that specifies what the broker is to be paid either as a percentage of the purchase price or on an hourly or flat rate. In practice, however, the seller's agent agrees to split the commission with the buyer broker, just as he would do with a conventional subagent.

But you can't bet on the fact that you won't have to come up with money to pay a buyer broker. Sellers can structure a listing so that any buyer's agent gets less than an equal share of the commission, or even no commission at all. (There would also be no commission for a buyer broker if you buy a home sold by its owner, although this, too, can be negotiated.) If the commission offered in the MLS is less than what you promise to pay a buyer-broker, you will owe her the rest or have to negotiate something out with the seller.

As for negotiating commissions, that's a sticky issue with many real estate advisors. The problem with reducing the commission is that you may not get the same level of service or traffic; I have had a scary number of real estate agents say they don't work as hard when the commission is reduced, and that they are reluctant to show buyers homes where a less-than-normal commission is being paid.

Still, if you have a seller's market for homes—where it is easy to make properties move and where there are not many homes to be listed—there may be the leverage necessary to get agents competing for the business. That kind of condition ebbs and flows. In Massachusetts, for example, the housing market was poor in the mid-1990s, and agents would not cut commission deals; then things heated up and the market went crazy, and commission cuts became much more common, only to see the real estate bubble burst and the agents go back to a hard line about their pay structure.

There are a lot of ways to play with commissions without necessarily insulting an agent. Find out if commissions can be shaved if the firm handles both sides of the deal; if the firm lines up the buyer, it doesn't have to share the seller's commission, so it might be willing to take a bit off to entice you to sign up.

If you have an expensive home, ask for a commission that is staggered. For example, the commission could be structured to equal 6 percent of the first $300,000 in sale price, 5 percent on the next $200,000, and 4 percent thereafter. If the house is worth enough to generate a big commission—particularly in a seller's market where there are few available houses—this kind of structure may be appealing. In addition, many brokers and agents won't negotiate commission because they don't like the principle of taking less money for their services; this may be a fair compromise, since it is not necessarily harder to sell a $400,000 home than a $250,000 home.

Last, if you have a home that is hard to sell—you live next to a toxic waste dump or, hopefully, some lesser evil—you might actually consider raising the commission. It is not out of line to pay a 10 percent commission for a home that is particularly tough to unload. Raising commissions, to a lesser degree, also helps generate traffic if you have a short time to move the house; just as brokers and agents don't like to work in situations where their rates are cut, they love situations that bring home extra money.

Smart Investor Tip

There are times when desperate sellers pay commissions of up to 5 percent to a buyer's agent or pay bonuses of thousands of dollars. While some buyer agents put a provision into their contract that they will refund the buyer any commission greater than 3 percent, others simply keep whatever cut they get from the seller for themselves. If that refund clause is not in your agreement with a buyer broker, ask for it.

Interview Questions for Real Estate Agents

If you are picking an agent to sell your home, the interview should occur at home, or at least after the agent has seen the property. Invite several agents to do a comparative market analysis. Even if you have no intention of moving and simply want advice and the chance to start a relationship, a market evaluation—where an agent sizes up what your house is worth in its current state, based on current market conditions—is the place to start. It's a service most agents gladly provide because they know it can lead to future business and referrals. Essentially, you want the agent to evaluate your home's plusses and minuses and to look for what you can do to both improve your quality of life and your resale value.

It will generally take the agent a few days to put together a market evaluation, which includes checking the prices of similar properties currently on the market, as well as prices of like homes that have sold in recent months.

You can interview a real estate counselor either when he or she does the walk-through or when he or she delivers the analysis; I prefer the latter because the evaluation always brings up more questions.

The First Meeting

Here are some things you will want to go over with any agent. Some apply only to seller or buyer agents, others to both; some must be altered slightly to fit both types of agents.

How long have you been in the business? Is this your full-time job?

Full-time, experienced people generally are the way to go, although there may be nothing wrong with folks who have less experience but know the area very well.

Part-time agents are the best option only if you are looking to buy a home and don't want your search to be too active, the kind of thing where you are moving slowly, happy to see the occasional home that might spur you to act. The problem with part-timers is that they are not always going to be available when you need them. Remember, too, that a real estate agent's life heats up when a sale is pending; if she squeezes in business between a lot of other activities, she may not have sufficient time to handle the demands of the deal at its most delicate time.

Are you a broker or a sales agent?

This is a minor concern, but you want to know the answer so that you can make sure a broker has sufficient time to represent you effectively. If he is too busy managing the office or keeping tabs on associates, he might be too much of an administrator to meet your day-to-day demands.

Do Name-Brand Firms Matter?

All member agents have access to the Multiple Listing Service, so bigger does not necessarily mean better when it comes to your agent's firm. Supply and demand in your market, the property itself, and the initiative and energy of the agent will determine how quickly your home sells more than whether an agent runs a one-person shop or is affiliated with the local office of a giant national chain.

At the same time, one key factor for any agent is his contacts. If you are a buyer and you hire someone from the firm that has the most listings in the area, you are likely to get a chance to see those houses before they appear in the Multi-List. In a tight market, that can be an advantage.

There is no guarantee that the bigger firm does more business in your area than the mom-and-pop shop, so the agents there don't necessarily have more pull with local bankers. They may have more pull with the local media, however, if they have a big advertising budget; that can lead to better display in the paper, access to television shows spotlighting area homes, and more. And although no one at a big firm would ever admit this, it's no secret that some big firms encourage agents to show prospective buyers the firm's listings first, meaning that a pool of prospects may see your property only after all of the alternatives have been reviewed.

The brand-name shops establish their reputation in your region not because of what happens at the national office, but because of what happens right there in your town. In the area where I live, for example, Century 21 seemed to handle half the listings when I moved to town, right up until its primary agent hung out her own shingle with a different firm. Now that firm—which had no local presence when I moved to town—is a big deal. The moral of the story? It's about the people more than the firm.

What continuing education classes have you taken?

Real estate sales practices keep changing. So do the laws governing many specific aspects of land ownership. You are always best off working with someone who keeps her education current and is trying to make herself a better representative for you. As long as you are asking about education and background in the business, don't be shy about asking for a resume. There is no reason for a real estate agent to withhold that information.

How far afield do you go to get clients?

If you're a buyer and want to look in a region—like the suburbs of a big city—you want someone who knows more than one community. If, however, you want to live in a specific town or neighborhood, you may want someone who really specializes in local real estate and has superior knowledge of the community you want to call home.

As a seller, your concern when someone gets spread out is time. Since an agent can't be two places at once, having listings that are spread over a 25-mile radius can be a problem, particularly if you want your advisor to attend all showings of your home.

How many listings do you work with at one time?

I know agents who say they can handle eight listings at once; I know others who claim to comfortably handle twice that many. There is no right number, but the amount of business an agent has right now does affect your service, ranging from how much time an agent might have to communicate with you to how often she will be able to show your home.

If you are working with a buyer's agent, those other clients could actually be your competition for a home. If a terrific property comes on the market, you'd like to know you will get first crack at it, and that may not happen if the buyer broker has a lot of customers and you're second—or sixth or eighth—on his list of people to call.

As with all advisory relationships, a lot of your decision will be based on instinct and who you feel you can trust. If you hear about a workload that sounds unreasonable, ask about it.

How many homes have you listed and sold in the last year? (How many buyers have you represented in the last year?)

Ask for a list of the homes the agent has sold in the last year, with the asking and final sales prices. Real estate is not unlike financial planning or insurance in that you want to be a lot like an advisor's average client.

If you have a $200,000 home (or that amount to spend on a new home) and the agent's sales sheet includes mostly homes valued at three times that much, you may not be getting a great match. After all, the agent will be better compensated by the commissions on the other properties, which may mean you get less attention.

Similarly, you want to make sure that the agent handles your kinds of properties. If their sales in the last year have been mostly single-family homes and you have a condo (or want to buy a condo), she may not be expert at dealing with the issues you're facing.

Have any of your showings or sales included homes in my neighborhood?

Just because someone is the top agent at his firm does not make him the best for you. If he is not familiar with your neighborhood, if he can't describe it knowledgeably to a seller, you may be better off with someone else.

What is your standard commission?

You MUST ask. Enough said.

Do you accompany all would-be buyers through my home?

This is a personal preference issue, but one that you want settled in advance. Many real estate agents use a "lock box," essentially a special key holder with a combination that is given to a buyer's agent. The buyer's agent brings clients to your home, opens the box, and uses the key to show people around your empty home.

It's convenient, particularly if you live a busy life and can't always be around the house to open the door for a showing. Still, many selling agents prefer to be present—or to send their associates—for walk-throughs, hanging around to answer questions about the home.

You can consider it either a service or a privacy issue, but consider it in advance so that you can let the agent know your preferences. Remember, you want the agent to hire you as a client; if trekking to your house for each showing is more work than she cares to do—but you think their presence is important—neither you nor the agent is going to be happy with the relationship.

What are you going to do to help the house sell?

The Multiple Listing Service is a no-brainer. You want to find out if the rest of the advertising will consist of newspaper ads, exposure on a local television show, glossy advertising giveaways or, maybe, a radio transmitter that lets passers-by get a description of the house 24 hours a day.

Agents are paid to market your house; if they don't have a marketing plan, you'd be better off doing this yourself.

You also want to know if they will help you "stage" the home for sale, either themselves or by bringing in an expert, possibly for an additional fee. There are plenty of things you may love about your house that a professional seller will tell you are turn-offs for would-be buyers. Will your agent give you suggestions, or will she get in the trenches with you and help you dress things up to put the best foot forward in an open house?

Are you going to hold a broker's open house?

A broker's open house shows your home to other agents in town. Your agent sends a notice to every firm in the area, inviting interested agents to come for lunch and a look-see.

Don't kid yourself; there are plenty of agents who just come to eat, especially if your broker is known for putting out a good spread. Still, for a few hours on a weekday afternoon, you will get some agents in your home who could decide it is perfect for someone they are working with.

Many agents choose not to do a "broker's open," particularly if the customer doesn't request it; their reasons vary, but I have heard agents say they dislike a broker's event because there is no direct possibility of making a sale. If you think it will help your house move, ask for it.

How often will you have weekend open houses?

This is both a marketing and lifestyle decision. For most busy people, there are only so many weekends in a month that they can disappear from home for five hours without falling behind on housework, yard work, or homework. You need to get people in the door and looking at the property, but too many open houses—opening the doors every week or two—smacks of desperation; too few, by contrast, may mean that you aren't bringing potential buyers through your doors. Find a happy medium; if you know the advisor's strategy on open houses in advance, you'll either be prepared to live with it later, or you will turn to an agent who is willing to follow the schedule you want to use.

What are the positives and negatives of this house?

Few of us have a perfect house, no matter how much we love it. Ask an agent to tell you the home's best selling points and biggest drawbacks; you want to make sure the two of you perceive the house in the same way; otherwise, you could be in for a big disagreement on pricing.

This was the key issue in my parent's situation. My parents' house in New Jersey had one very small bedroom, with an attached bathroom, in the lowest floor of a split-level house. It was my big brother's room, then it became my grandmother's room, then it became my father's office.

It was a bit cluttered with a bed, his big desk, and a dresser. The first agent suggested removing the bed and basically calling it an office. My parents disagreed (they could have removed the desk or the dresser to open up the space); they felt that someone who might want an in-law apartment or a space for a nanny or au pair would look at the small bedroom and reconditioned bath next to it—downstairs and away from the main bedrooms—and feel like he or she had found a house that served the purpose. Moreover, they could better justify the asking price with four bedrooms.

It turned out that my parents were right, and the first agent's ideas were wrong; had any of the discussion happened in advance—perhaps when my mother was planning at the bathroom remodeling project and wondering if she'd get the money back from the upgrade—they could have avoided the trouble that came up when they were anxious to get the house on the market.

What can I do to improve the house and make it easier to sell?

No one likes dumping money into a home she is about to move out of, but a coat of paint can do a lot to refresh an older home. And while prospective buyers generally don't purchase your furniture, they do notice the way you live; cluttered closets, for example, look small and make people wonder if they will run out of space.

Ask what can be done to get your house in the best condition to be shown. Plan to do the work early, so you don't have to rush around at the last minute before a prospective buyer shows up.

The earlier you meet with an agent, the more valuable her input can be, and the more you can enjoy some changes that may have to be made. Again using my parents as an example, the agent who handled the sale told my folks when she first saw the home that there were certain issues that would have to be resolved, such as changing an old glass sliding door. My parents might have enjoyed the family room for the last few years they lived in the house with the upgraded door that they put in to meet the buyer's demand for an upgrade. Instead, they spent the money to make the fix, but never really got to enjoy it.

What price range would you suggest for my home and why? If the house stays on the market, when and by how much will we lower the asking price?

This is where the agent details the comparative market analysis and tells you what he thinks you can get for your house. Obviously, some level of agreement between you and the advisor is necessary.

What you are listening for is a fair market price based upon current market conditions and the urgency of your need to sell, as well as a strategy that makes sense if the house doesn't attract buyers and you need to cut your price to get more interest.

Don't be impressed by big numbers; some agents price everything high in order to impress potential clients. After the contract is signed, the house goes on the market at an inflated price before dropping to the more reasonable price suggested by less-aggressive (or, perhaps, more scrupulous) agents.

If the projected price is below your expectations, find out whether the agent's calculations or your impressions of the home are what is askew.

Make sure you know the agent's feelings about how long a home should sit on the market before dropping a price because you do not want the relationship with the agent to deteriorate later if there are pricing surprises. Many homeowner-broker relationships sour when the parties disagree on the next pricing move; since you both make money on the sale of the home, you are teammates, and you'll function best if you agree on strategies before the game begins.

Who are the best agents in town—besides yourself—and why?

Unlike virtually every other form of financial advisor, real estate agents are in a cooperative situation. A lawyer can sit in a corner office and write and file paperwork for you, an accountant can crunch numbers, and a financial planner can develop a strategy all without consulting anyone.

But real estate agents can't close the deal without working with their peers. Real estate is a small community where most of the local players know of each other (at least by reputation). If your agent can't say a nice thing about anyone else in the field, then chances are that he doesn't work well with those people. That is not good.

Asking this question lets you see what an agent admires in his peers. It's also a pretty good list of professional references, because the names you get represent the competition. If you call, say, a lawyer whom the agent works with, there is a potential bias because the agent may routinely refer clients and the lawyer doesn't want to lose that business. The competition has no reason to say something nice, especially if they might be interested in your business for themselves.

Could I get the names of a few recent sellers (or buyers) who you have worked with?

Unlike many other financial advisory relationships, where confidentiality and privacy are major concerns, you should have little trouble getting the names of references from a real estate agent. Property transactions are public record, so the confidentiality issue is moot.

Don't just accept the names of friends or relatives who referred you in the first place, as in "Why don't you just talk to your Uncle Morty about that? You know how he feels about me." This is your biggest investment and a bad advisor can cost you a lot of money, so make sure you talk to more than one reference. In fact, try to find references who had to deal with this agent in different circumstances, possibly one whose home sold quickly and another whose house sat on the market for months.

What to Ask References

Aside from the standard list of questions you ask about any advisor (see Chapter 14), there are some specific questions about real estate agents where a client's perspective is important, such as:

- Did you feel the same about the agent after the sale was done as you did after you signed the agreement to work together? What, if anything, changed?
- Did the advisor's suggestions pay off?
- If there were troubles with the buyer (or seller), how do you feel they were handled?
- Were there any times during the process that you were frustrated? If so, what set you off?
- To professional references—especially other real estate agents in your area who might also be on your list of candidates—ask, "If you were selling (or buying) a home and couldn't do the deal yourself, would this agent be one of the three top candidates to get the job?" You can't expect him to say that this person is "the one," because he has many professional ties to maintain. If he says your candidate would be one of, say, a half dozen candidates, as why he'd have so many people; listen for whether the answer is trying not to break wide-ranging ties, or if he is hemming and hawing, trying not to say that your prospective agent does not have his full faith and confidence.

What can I do to make myself a better buyer?

If you are buying a home, there are ways to make bids more attractive, such as being preapproved for a mortgage so that the deal can be written without a mortgage contingency. This question will give you insight into the kinds of strategies a buyer broker thinks will work, both with lenders and sellers.

Can you assist with financing?

Real estate agents often track interest rates and have contacts with favorite lenders who can speed the application process. That not only comes in handy when you buy a home but, years later, when your agent may be able to say who can help you pursue refinancing, home equity lines of credit, reverse mortgages, and other options. (A good real estate agent knows which bankers bend the rules, flexing standard industry formulas to improve your chances of getting, say, a home-equity loan.)

Do I need a "reality check"?

A reality check is where an agent puts you in the car and drives you around to look at other properties. As a seller, she is showing you that your expectations are unreasonable compared to similar homes in similar neighborhoods. For buyers, a reality check may be to prove that you have too little money to afford the neighborhood and that perhaps you need to adjust your hopes and dreams down to the size of your wallet.

How often will I hear from you?

Obviously, the agent should contact you the moment she has an offer (or a home she thinks might be right for you). The question is what happens when nothing is happening.

You should hear from your agent enough to quell your fears and to strategize about the price and marketing strategy (or whether to widen your search area because no homes are available in neighborhoods you desire). Generally, those conversations take place weekly, but you should know what to expect because lack of communication is where real estate relationships falter.

Are you planning a vacation soon?

Yes, it's a personal question. Brokers and agents are entitled to vacations like everyone else, but the hot time for activity on a home is when the listing is new, generally in the first three to four weeks after it is listed. That's when every buyer in your price range and interested in your community—and every broker working with a prospective client in your area—will want to see the house. If you are putting your house on the market and need it to sell quickly, you may not be comfortable having your agent on the road during the first few weeks.

Does a vacation automatically disqualify an agent? Absolutely not. There is an adage in the real estate business that when brokers go on vacation, all of their listings sell.

If I sign a contract, how long is the listing agreement good for? Can I change agents without paying a double commission (or would you get a piece of the deal no matter what)? How can I terminate the listing, and for how long after that are you entitled to payment?

The listing agreement is fraught with terms that are to the agent's advantage. Ask about them and read the agreement carefully. Picking the wrong agent is bad enough, but signing a restrictive contract can actually make the situation worse.

Some contracts force you to list with the agent for six months—try to get that cut to no more than three—and have no termination clause. Before signing a contract, you should know exactly how you get out of it if you change your mind or dislike the service.

Paying a double commission can occur when you switch brokers. Brokers know that lost listings mean lost commissions, and they want to cash in on their work even if you didn't think it was so great. Say someone sees the house today and comes back to see it again in six months, when you have a new agent. If this person buys the home, the first agent may try to get paid for having "brought you the buyer." This is the kind of language you do not want in your listing agreement.

Similarly, say you decide to test the waters—hoping, perhaps, to move to a better place in town—and put your home on the market. A few people come through, but no one makes a worthy offer, and you decide to terminate the listing. Five months later, one of the prospective buyers knocks on your door, wondering if you are still interested in selling, and you like her improved offer. If your listing agreement specifies that the agent gets a commission for six months after termination, you are going to pay that fee on this deal.

There are even listing agreements who can force you to pay a commission without selling the home, rewarding the agent for landing a "ready, willing, and able buyer." If that buyer backs out—say he gets a job offer or transfer or just cold feet—you could be on the hook for the commission. Make sure the agreement language does not force you to pay if the deal collapses.

If you go over a standard agreement line by line, you can find at least the potential for unfavorable terms.

In general, listing agreements are designed to discourage you from taking advantage of an agent's time, then bolting to stiff the agent and do the deal on your own. That's fair and reasonable, up to a point; there's a fine line between the planning to stiff a broker—which presumably you will not do—and protecting yourself and your options.

What happens when there is an offer? What's the drill when we find a house to bid on?

For sellers, you want to be walked through the process of will happen once a bid comes in, how the agent feels about counter-offers and pricing strategy, and what he does to get the deal from start—the first contract with an acceptable offer—to closing.

Buyers, too, want to go over the way a bid works and what the broker's responsibility is when it comes to helping push the deal through.

Describe your nightmare client/house.

This is a good opportunity to hear some funny stories about the agent's worst client, the house that had the ugly shag carpeting that was badly soiled by pets, and so on. In between cringing and laughing, however, listen carefully to hear if the agent is describing you and/or your house.

If you might fit the description of her worst nightmare, find someone else to work with.

Danger Signs

Big problems in real estate relationships often involve personality, communication, and interest. Don't sign on with an agent—no matter how highly recommended—if you don't click. Chemistry is important, because it is hard to build a trusting relationship when the person across the table from you creeps you out.

While personality clashes account for the major problems, they are not the only warning signs to consider. Others include:

- **Loss of interest.** Almost every broker is excited about your business after first getting you as a client. But he may not be so excited when there is no movement. If your house isn't selling (or you, as a buyer, are extremely picky and not willing to bid on any number of houses that meet your own definition of what you're looking for), keep an eye on whether your broker or agent is doing everything possible to make things work.

- **Lack of communication.** During your interview, you set a standard for how often you should hear from the agent. Even if nothing is happening, there should be contact on the schedule you agreed to. Even if infrequent calls are acceptable, there could be a communication problem—and a loss of interest, for that matter—if your agent does not return phone calls within six hours. And, obviously, you do not want any surprises. If you call and find out that your broker has gone on vacation without telling you, that's a problem.

- **Failure to follow instructions**. If you are buying a home and the first few houses the agent shows you are out of your price range or not even close to the description of what you want, the agent is trying to make you more like her average client and fit you into her own comfort zone. Don't go there; you control the relationship.

  In Pennsylvania, Susan and I once worked with an agent—very briefly—when we were just starting to search for a home. We had little time, a very specific price range, no need to rush into a purchase, finite resources, and definite tastes; when the agent wanted to show us four homes a week—all slightly above our price range—and kept trying to convince us that we could find a way to finance these homes, we felt pressured. The agent had stopped listening to what we wanted and was trying to bring us around to what she wanted, which was to sell a house in her favored price range.

- **Maximum commission at your expense**. It's understandable that agents hate the idea of reducing commissions, but it's shameful the way some unscrupulous agents nickel-and-dime buyers and sellers. Say you have agreed on a deal, but the home inspection brings up a few issues. The buyer wants the price reduced, the seller agrees to make up the difference, but the real estate agent pushes to keep the original selling price and to have the seller "credit back" money at the closing. That keeps the agent's commission the same, but benefits neither the buyer nor seller. The buyer is not only taking a bigger mortgage to meet the higher price, but could face higher property taxes, since many communities use sales price as part of their valuation of the home. The seller faces a larger capital gain on the home, plus the higher commission. If you have problems like this one, contact the managing broker and complain.

- **Incomplete disclosure or conflicts of interest.** This chapter has covered several potential conflicts of interest. If those problems show up, and you were unaware or unprepared, that's a problem. An advisor has a responsibility to remind you that he works for the seller—unless you have contracted with him as a buyer broker—and also must tell you if he is acting as a dual agent, representing you as a buyer and the seller as a conventional agent. Failing to disclose these kinds of conflicts is an enormous breach of both your trust and professional ethics.

Building the Relationship

My parents could have started working with an agent long before they were ready to sell the home. Over the years, they had heard from several agents offering them a free market analysis, and they had talked with their friend about how they looked forward to working with her someday (now that it didn't work out, the friendship is rocky, highlighting why friends should never let friends become their advisors, one of the biggest mistakes described in Chapter 3).

While an agent's time is valuable, so is the time she spends with you, even if no sale is on the horizon. You have friends in town, people who might someday chat with you about their plans to move. Now you have a real estate agent whom you met and who impressed you, and whose name you pass along.

What happens after the sale?

The final question of your interview gets back to the concept of developing a relationship so that your real estate advisor is with you long after you have moved in.

When my wife Susan—the most patient and understanding woman in America—and I bought our first home in Pennsylvania, it had a roomy, windowed attic that was perfect for a master bedroom suite. The previous owners had started the work; we just needed to finish the job.

Before hiring a contractor, however, we went back to the agent who helped us buy the house (the same agent we planned on using to sell it when the time came), and she advised against fixing up the room, warning that we would never get the money out. She provided a very compelling comparative analysis that saved us thousands of dollars, because we wound up selling during a down time in the market; the extra room would not have generated enough additional revenue to cover its own costs.

Find out if an agent is willing to consult with you periodically, to "come see what I've done to the place" and to advise you as to the value of adding a fill-in-the-blank (fireplace, new kitchen, addition, swimming pool, etc.). Her knowledge of the market can be a major asset to you, provided she is interested in you for more than your current transaction.

You are not talking about getting her tips for decorating or asking her to pick the color of your new shutters, so you won't see her often. It may be a once-a-year cup of coffee or lunch.

Most agents like doing this because they are always curious to see what happens to a house after the sale. It's good for you as a homeowner because it helps you set your priorities, particularly as you near a selling period. If you expect to stay in a house for only a few years but have the choice of which repairs to make next—say replacement windows versus a replacement kitchen—the agent would probably advise you to make the repairs that will make the most difference in selling price (the kitchen). If you plan to live in the house for 20 more years, the windows might be the better investment now, because they will save money on the heating bill.

Last, one reason to keep in touch with an agent is that it never hurts to have representation. You may not be in the market to sell your home, but few people would turn away an offer without at least reviewing it. If an agent knows your house and meets someone tomorrow who wants to move to your town and describes your house as his dream home, the agent may just pick up the phone and call with an unsolicited offer. If it's good enough, you might decide that it's a good time to move to something bigger or to downsize. At the very least, it never hurts to listen, and you will never have a shot at an unsolicited offer if a broker or agent is not familiar with your home.

Get What You Need from References and Referrals

The only source of knowledge is experience.

—Albert Einstein

In 1988, I was named business editor at *The Morning Call* in Allentown, Pennsylvania, and I needed to make as many contacts as possible quickly in the business community. So I started networking, meeting with the top executives in the Lehigh Valley area and, at those meetings, asking for introductions and ideas on who else to meet.

Because of my strong interest in investing and personal finance, I asked everyone to recommend a stockbroker or financial planner. Quickly, a few names stood out, because they seemed to be the advisors of choice for the community's elite business leaders.

There was Al, from the big-name firm, who was recommended for reasons ranging from "he's so nice" to "everyone who is anyone uses him" to "he has the biggest minimum investment requirements in town" to "he's well connected."

There was Sean, who was "the funniest guy in town," "really sharp on picking stocks," and "who seemed to have the right attitudes about money." Stan "ran the show" at the second-largest brokerage house in town, and was "a whiz with the market." Ed was the head of the local stockbrokers club, had written articles for the newspaper, was "reasonably priced" and "just a guy who you meet and are sure you can trust."

And there was Matt, who apparently was nice, conservative, and "the right religion for some people in town."

I'm not kidding. I kept notes and built files. (Eventually, I invited these men to participate in a stock-picking competition run by the newspaper. It turned out particularly badly for Al, because his performance was not only worse than the others but so much less than cracked up to be.)

Each person had something different to say about the advisors; if you had just moved to town and were looking for an advisor, one or more of those attributes—bestowed on the brokers and planners by leading business minds in the area—would stand out. Someone would jump to the top of your prospect list because of who he works with—"If he's good enough for the chairman of a Fortune 500 company (or the rising executive star from another big multinational firm), he's good enough for me"—or because he prices his services reasonably or because he's the same religion as you.

What's interesting about the list of advisors and their personal attributes is that it came from a group of executives who had a lot in common with each other. Money and work was a focal point of their lives, they were all successful, they had big aspirations and dreams, and they wanted to believe they could trust whomever they hired to oversee their financial life. Moreover, they were happy with their advisor and glad to discuss what made their guy so great; none of these people had any sort of horror story in finding or working with a broker or planner.

If you had been there, looking for a financial advisor and didn't know any better, you would have felt reasonably comfortable that any and all of these counselors could meet your needs. You also might have felt that the general impressions of the people providing you with a reference—saying they would hire this guy or that—was enough to tell you that an advisor was good.

That's where you'd be sadly mistaken. Each of the people I talked to made his or her referral by citing the one thing that stuck out about his or her particular advisor. In many ways, that referral was an attempt to justify each person's own decision, to say he had picked the right man because he was hard working, successful, diligent, well-connected, or reasonable. If I decided I liked a particular advisor—and each person knew I was looking for sources, and not for a financial planner myself—it would validate his or her opinion.

Therein lies one of the inherent problems with referrals, the potential for conflict of interest. With referrals, you always have to wonder whether the advice—even when you go out of your way to seek it—truly is in your best interest.

In this situation, the referrals were personal, rather than professional. When a financial planner recommends an accountant, however, there is reason to question the motives of the advisors involved. There can be referral fees or other incentives involved, either monetary or in the form of returned favors. (This almost always is the case in full-service firms, in which a financial planner wants to keep you in the house when you need, say, an insurance agent.)

Many trade groups are happy to provide you with the names and numbers of counselors in your area. Obviously, the groups have a bias toward their own membership, meaning anyone who is not a member or who has not achieved a certain credential won't be included. Your state society of certified public accountants, for instance, will not give you referrals to enrolled agents, a different status of tax preparer that may be better suited and less expensive to the tax preparation needs of many individuals.

Many advisors actually pay for a spot in a referral service, meaning their names go out only if they pony up some dough; there is no qualitative standard applied to these referrals, only a monetary one. What's more, the fact that an advisor needs to pay the freight to advertise on a service for more clients is not necessarily an endorsement for the advisor's business.

Good Referrals Can Go Bad

Even if the referral is honest and true, it still may not deliver the right person for you. Think of it in terms of interior decorators. Your mother may have a lovely home, but it might not be your style and taste; when she refers you to her decorator, it's entirely possible that you wind up with someone who does lovely work, as long as it's for your mother.

When it comes to financial advisors, a referral should be a starting point, not a selling point.

Reference versus Referral

A reference is someone who is in a position to recommend someone or vouch for his or her fitness for a job, because the reference knows the person well enough to comment on qualifications, character, and dependability.

A referral is a direction to a source for help or information.

The difference, for the purposes of hiring financial advisors, is that most references come from customers, while referrals come from other service providers. Referrals can be paid, or given in trade—where an advisor suggests a friend who covers a different specialty—or they can simply be "Here's someone I know who can handle that."

With a reference, you will want to know the tenor of the relationship. With a referral, you will want to know how one professional selected and qualified another, whether it was from a working relationship, a personal friendship, or through any form of rigorous selection process.

Referrals tend to come early in the selection process—when you are finding candidates for the job—while references provide context after you have met with an advisor and are trying to decide if she is the one for you.

Let's go back to the story of Al, one of those stockbrokers I was referred to during my early days in Allentown. When the newspaper held the stock-picking competition, everyone in the area was surprised that Al decided to participate; he was already THE broker in town, the one who handled the local money elite, the name routinely kicked around as the biggest big shot in the neighborhood. He was efficacious and personable, handsome, and well connected. He had the highest minimum in the area for establishing an account and the highest profile clientele.

The rules of our year-long contest were a bit stilted—most money managers do not shoot for big short-term results, and we were running a competition to see who could achieve the most growth in 12 months—but all of the brokers accepted the situation, the same way you would hope they would handle the special needs of an individual client.

By the time the year was gone, so were most of Al's clients. He lost nearly 40 percent, while three of his peers—Stan, Sean, and Ed, actually—earned 40 percent and a fourth (yes, it was Matt) was up 20 percent.

Worse yet, Al lost the money with the exact same strategy he used for his real-life clients, a particularly dumb move since the vagaries of a one-year competition are a lot different than the long-term investment concerns of a wide-ranging clientele. Those customers started to realize over the course of the year that Al pigeonholed all of his customers into the same investments, regardless of their specific needs. Investment choices that were inappropriate for the contest's imaginary client were mistakes for some of his real clients, too.

His one-strategy-fits-all style had never been apparent to customers until it was in the paper, and, by then, Al couldn't sweet talk his clients into walking around wearing his poorly fitted portfolio. Al's performance was so wretched that his firm—one of the national giants—hasn't allowed brokers to take part in similar contests since then without written consent from headquarters.

When the whole episode was finished, Al told me his greatest mistake was not his strategy so much as participating in the first place. As he put it, "A whale only gets harpooned when it comes to the surface."

But what stuck with me was not just that line or the losses, but rather a comment made to me over breakfast by a prominent local executive, one of the clients who left Al about nine months into the game. "What the game made me realize," the executive said, "is that he's been losing my money with a smile on his face for a long, long time."

The last time I checked, Al was selling a lot of insurance and annuity products, mostly to the long-time customers who at least left some of their money with him.

The point of the story: Here was the guy with the best word of mouth in town, but everyone who kicked his name around was, essentially, justifying his or her own decision. The recommendation raised his good points, and reconfirmed the people's decision, allowing them to brag about working with the "best broker around." Al's business had survived for years more on his ability to generate referrals than on his ability to generate profits.

Get Beyond a Simple Referral

The late Dr. Harry Clark Noyes, a psychologist who examined consumer behavior for his New York firm Psychological Motivations, said there are plenty of people who generate good references from customers despite mediocre results. "Some people re-sell themselves when they give a referral," Noyes said, "They list the attributes of someone to you, and they are also re-examining the decision on their own. They may want you to choose the same person because it confirms their decision and because if you choose someone else it could raise more doubt in their mind.

"It's not that everyone who makes a referral does this, but it certainly happens."

This is precisely why consumers should not take referrals at face value and why they should want to turn a "referral"—where someone gives you a name and minimal information—into a "reference," where you delve into the experience someone has had with an advisor.

Smart Investor Tip

Don't take referrals at face value. Instead, try to turn a "referral"—where someone gives you a name and minimal information—into a "reference," where you delve into the experience someone has had with an advisor.

Getting a name from someone who answers the question "Who is your insurance agent?" is insufficient. You want to know why he recommended that agent, if his work with the agent covered the same ground you now need help with, and more.

Even when there is an obvious conflict of interest, referrals can have some value. I have bought my cars for the last 15 years from an establishment where every time you refer someone who buys a car, you get $100 off your next purchase or repair job. The incentive is there for me to make the referral, but I wouldn't do it if I expected someone to be dissatisfied with the dealer. Such disappointment could, potentially, erode a friendship.

And so while the people who first told me about stockbrokers in Allentown may have had their own biases or conflicts of interest, chances are they would have told me to avoid anyone with whom they had a bad experience.

One key factor to guard against with referrals is the "instant trust" factor, where you put so much faith in someone that you let your guard down. It is too easy to use a referral as the sole basis for hiring a financial advisor. You trust your friend, who got a big fat tax refund check, so you believe he must have a good tax preparer. Or you get a referral from your financial planner for a tax preparer. You trust the planner (or already should have dumped him), creating instant trust in the referral.

That trust may be well founded, and the referral may be perfect, but the basic rule holds true: No one gets a position on your financial team until you have checked him out and feel comfortable that he belongs.

Referrals are a great way to make a short list of candidates for any position on your team. Asking your financial planner and banker for the names of estate planning attorneys can yield you very good choices (particularly if they name the same person), and the word of a trustworthy friend should generate your confidence in an advisor. But the crucial thing is to compile a short list and not stray from the process of selecting a financial helper just because one candidate was built up by friends and colleagues as the "right" choice.

Smart Investor Tip
Don't stray from the full process of selecting a financial helper just because one candidate was built up by friends and colleagues as the "right" choice.

You may not take the same approach to financial relationships as your friends or need the same kind of assistance. Your neighbor may drive a fancy car and be a "wealthy doctor," but that may also make him self-employed and dealing with a completely different kind of retirement savings situation than you have working for a big, public company or the local school system.

Your other neighbor might be satisfied getting an update on his portfolio every six months, while you want a report every time the market burps.

What you think of the person making the referral also colors how you feel about the advisor; that's why it's important to dig deep. Like your mother's decorator, the advisor you have been referred to may be competent and skilled but not your style.

In essence, once you have the referral, you need to treat your friend like a reference—asking all the same questions—so that you can use that information in making your own decision.

Some Advisors Refuse to Give References

Some advisors will throw up a major roadblock in your quest to get good information; they don't give references. Oh, they will pass you to another professional they have worked with, but they'll say that giving you the name of a client is an invasion of the client's privacy. They'll cite confidentiality agreements, where they are not supposed to discuss their customers, and you're asking them to give you a name and contact details.

They may also say that references are silly, since your circumstances are your own, and since anyone they pass you to, obviously, will be on their side.

Explain the kinds of questions you will ask a reference, and tell them to take any client or two with whom they have a reason to talk today and to ask that client if he or she is willing to function as a reference. Yes, you will get someone who is on their side, but you are asking tenor-of-the-relationship questions, not "How much money did he make for you?" and the advisor cannot necessarily give you a true picture of how he interacted with a customer at all times.

If the advisor still refuses to give a reference, think long and hard about whether you want to do business with him. This refusal to do something that you consider important raises a significant question—one you should raise with the advisor—which is, "If you are not willing to work with me on something I consider important *before* you have my money, how should I expect you to treat me if I become a client and you no longer need to impress me to work with my money?"

Getting Blood from a Stone

When you ask for references, don't expect to be given the names of the last five clients who walked through the door—a measure that might provide some objectivity—but rather the names of good customers or volunteer praise-singers.

Assume you are about to talk with people who are in the advisor's corner.

Some advisors include that assumption in their reasons for not offering references. They argue that a prospective client won't gain much insight from what amounts to an endorsement, while the existing client loses both confidentiality and time.

If you check references by asking the typical questions, the advisor would be right, there would not be any blood in this stone, this rock-solid reference.

There are ways to extract a pint or two of blood—information—if you know how. Start with the premise that every counselor will tell you during an initial interview precisely how he expects to work with you, but only another client can give you an idea of how the process feels from the other end. The advisor is giving you the picture from his side of the desk; you need to walk the proverbial mile in the shoes of another customer to see how they'd fit you. (This is also why you want clients, and not professionals, as references; another advisor has worked side-by-side with the pro you are interviewing, she hasn't been on your side of the desk.)

Finally, assure the advisor that you intend to call references only as a final check, as the last piece in your decision-making process, so that you will not bother anyone with questions until you are close to making your selection. What's more, point out that you do not expect answers to personal questions like "How much money do you have with this advisor?" or "How much money has he made you?" That information is none of your business and not relevant to your personal situation.

Questions to Ask References

In the chapters on interviewing each advisor, there are questions that may be specific to a particular specialty. But no matter which kind of advisor you are hiring, here is the general information that you want to get from references and why the responses will help you make a decision about the advisor:

How did you come to work with the advisor? How long have you been working together?

Just because you picked up this book and learned to pick an advisor the right way doesn't mean the advisor's other clients did. Get the story on how this person found out about the advisor and what kind of work he put into qualifying the person before hiring, as it will go a long way to coloring the rest of what you hear from this person and whether he is someone who is detail-oriented or who leaves things to chance.

The more you determine about the reference's background, the more easily you can evaluate whether his standard of a good relationship measures up to yours. Obviously, you want to know how long the reference and advisor have worked together and whether the relationship is ongoing. (Many references for real estate agents and lawyers are people who have no continuing tie to the advisor because they do not have a current need for services.) If there is no current relationship, find out how long ago the person worked with the advisor; you would prefer a recent client to one from years ago, when the practice presumably was smaller.

Smart Investor Tip

The more you learn about the reference's background, the more easily you can evaluate whether his standard for a good relationship measures up to yours.

How often do you hear from the advisor? Who initiates contact and what are most of those calls about?

A big part of every successful advisory relationship is communication. That doesn't necessarily mean a phone call every week, but it does mean an advisor should show appropriate concern.

For an insurance agent, for example, it may be when policies are up for renewal. In the case of real estate agents and lawyers working on a case, it may be at regular weekly intervals or whenever there is any action you need to know about. For brokers and financial planners, the amount of contact will vary depending on the scope of the relationship.

The general rule is simple: The bigger percentage of your assets you entrust to someone, the more often you want to hear from her.

If the advisor initiates all contact, but only when there is a sale to be made—a hot stock tip, a change in the recommended mutual fund portfolio, or a new insurance product that might generate a commission—that would be a sign the advisor is more interested in doing transactions than building a relationship, even if his happy client/reference hasn't figured it out yet.

Does the advisor always return your calls promptly? Does he or she give you the time necessary to answer questions?

You can't overemphasize communication. While you can't expect an advisor to take an hour in the middle of his day to take an unsolicited phone call that rambles over various points of your financial situation (and maybe on to how the kids are doing, etc.), you have a right to expect that each call will be taken seriously.

Find out, too, how the advisor reacts to what might be considered dumb questions. Even if you never ask one, you want to feel like you can without being made to feel stupid. (There are no dumb questions, only things that people would be embarrassed to ask; you should never be embarrassed if you have a good working relationship with your advisor.)

Does the advisor include your spouse—or parents or children—in discussions and meetings?

Good advisors get to know the family, at least in the beginning. After that, however, many deal exclusively with the decision maker. There's nothing terrible about that. In my household, for example, my broker, insurance agent, and tax preparer all deal with me. Susan is included in important meetings and has enough of a relationship with each advisor to feel comfortable if anything should happen to me.

But if you and your partner make all decisions jointly, you want to make sure the advisor is happy explaining things to you as a couple and has the patience to do that, rather than pressing for instant decisions.

How does the advisor react when you raise questions or come in with suggestions?

Many advisors try to make all clients fit into the same basic circle of reference. Accountants, for example, decide which types of deductions they like to pursue and may focus on those; insurance agents and financial planners have their favorite products.

If you ask questions, rather than immediately accepting the advice as gospel, or if you bring suggestions to the table ("I read about a [mutual fund, tax deduction, home-selling strategy] that I think might work for me . . ."), you want to know the advisor won't give you the brush-off. The advisor would never acknowledge giving short shrift to a client issue, but only an existing client would know for sure.

Have you ever decided not to take your counselor's advice? If so, how did she react?

Just because the reference is happy with the advisor's service does not mean he has taken all advice blindly. You want to find out what suggestions the advisor may have made that the client didn't like—why did the client decide they were not appropriate?—and how the advisor responded when her recommended course of action was not taken.

Have you ever had any pricing/billing problems? (If so, how were they resolved?)

You always ask an advisor about how he charges for his work. You should ask the reference to make sure there never have been any problems with the advisor's charges. If there have been issues, find out how things were settled (and you may want to rehash billing procedures with the advisor before finalizing your hiring decision).

Has anything about the relationship—or the financial outcomes from it—surprised you?

This is a good way to find out if the relationship has lived up to, or exceeded, expectations.

Has the advisor's service ever disappointed you and, if so, what did you do about it?

Many times, a client working with an advisor does not recognize problems or disappointments until he is asked to think about them. Issues then come into sharper focus.

A reference's disappointments may not bother you—perhaps he wanted more face-to-face contact and you don't care about that—but it's important to ask about shortcomings.

Smart Investor Tip

A reference's disappointments in working with a counselor may not be items that bother you, but it's important to ask about perceived shortcomings.

Have you ever worked with other advisors? If so, why did you make a change—and what does this advisor do better than the last one?

Many people bounce from one advisor to the next, rather than picking one advisor with whom they can work comfortably for a lifetime. If the reference has worked with other advisors, that experience may be valuable. Presumably, the old relationship was lacking in some way, and the new one doesn't have the same problem.

Again, this helps qualify what the reference wants from the relationship and how it compares with your desires as well as how well those needs are being met.

What do you think the advisor does the best?

Hopefully, what an advisor does best is something you value as a prospective client.

Remember Al, the would-be best broker in town who wound up losing the stock-picking contest using the same miserable advice he gave clients? What he did best was schmooze customers and make them feel important.

No one knows better than you what you want out of an advisory relationship, whether it is hand-holding, financial acumen, the emotional discipline to stay the course, or whatever. You are looking for an advisor whose strong points fit your needs.

Is there any area in which you wish the advisor would give you even more attention?

This is a logical follow-up to the previous question. Again, it helps you determine whether your expectations for the relationship are in line with the reference's and helps you decide if the advisor can meet your specific needs.

How long do you anticipate working with this advisor? (Or, if the advisor is hired on a need-now basis, such as a real estate agent: Do you anticipate working with the advisor again?)

This is a substitute for the standard hiring question asked of a reference: "Would you hire the candidate again?"

You're looking for financial relationships that can last a lifetime, or close to it. Yes, a reference is going to be biased and say nice things. But if she can't see working with that advisor for a lifetime (or again), then you need to know why she might hire someone else. Indeed, you might want to hire someone else, too.

Would you recommend this advisor for your mother, your brother, best friend, or your (adult) children? Is there anyone you would NOT recommend this advisor to?

If my parents had ever asked me to recommend a financial planner, I would have recommended one person for my dad, a different person for my mom, and a third person to handle them together (and they have been happily married for well over 50 years). It's about personalities working together.

If the reference recognizes that the advisor would not be right for "everybody," then you want to know who he would say is the wrong client for the advisor, and why. If the reference gives a description that sounds like an assessment you might make of yourself, then he has just told you that he doesn't think this advisor would be right for you.

Key Points

- Don't take referrals or references at face value. They're not worth anything until you get the information you want.

- Keep your questions to the tenor of the relationship and the demeanor of the advisor. These are the things that the advisor can never give you a clear picture of.

- An advisor who won't give you references to check now may not give you the service you want later.

- References and referrals may try to sell you on the advisor, but you didn't call for a sales pitch. Keep the criteria you consider important at the forefront of your mind, and remember that no one but you will live with the consequences of your selection.

Chapter 15

Breaking Up Is Hard to Do

If you don't like something, change it. If you can't change it, change your attitude.

—Maya Angelou

Years ago, there was a television show called *Caroline in the City,* where the lead character was never any good at ending relationships. In one episode, she couldn't bring herself to change dry cleaners—no matter how many valuable pieces of clothing were ruined—until he died (and, at that, she gave the eulogy at his funeral).

And rather than tell her hairdresser she was seeking a new look from someone else, Caroline said she was moving to Norway, which the hairdresser bought until bumping into her at a party (and, at that, she hastily agreed to go rushing back to him).

Of course, Caroline was a fictitious character. The difference between her and real people like us is that we could never pull off that Norway thing in the first place.

Ending relationships is never easy. The mere thought smacks of confrontation, hardship, betrayal, and a whole range of emotions most of us would rather avoid.

Still, the more you let a bad financial relationship linger, the more it costs you, literally.

When managing your affairs, remember one rule: Business is business. No matter your personal feelings for someone, he's gone if he can't do the job to your satisfaction. The fictional Caroline got lucky with the lousy dry cleaner because he died; you might not be so lucky if you pick a nice-but-incompetent financial planner.

Smart Investor Tip

Business is business. Your personal feelings for an advisor don't matter; if he can't do the job to your satisfaction, he's gone.

Typically, financial relationships end when expectations aren't met. If a real estate agent doesn't sell the house, your decision not to renew the listing is easy because the contract you signed was finite; in most investment, banking, accounting, and legal relationships, there's an unwritten stick-with-the-guy-for-life mentality. As this book noted in Chapter 1, the ideal relationship with an advisor ends when you die or he retires.

Firing an advisor is easy if you suspect fraud, wrongdoing, or any sort of problem. You don't just dismiss the counselor in those cases, you file complaints and pursue legal remedies to get your money back.

But short of those extremes, there are plenty of times when advisory relationships just don't work out, when you feel let down by the goods and services offered, and you believe you would be better off working with someone else. If a relationship sours for any reason, the dismissal process is simple and straightforward. You may allow a final chance at redemption, but here are the steps to follow:

Step 1: Talk to Your Advisor

At the first sign of trouble when service does not jibe with your expectations tell the advisor your concerns.

If the advisor pooh-poohs them, remind him that "It's my money." For that money, you deserve, at the very least, an explanation of why your expectations are not being met. If no explanation is forthcoming, you know the advisor isn't taking you seriously.

If that's the case, skip Steps 2 and 3 and go directly to Step 4.

Signs of an Advisory Relationship Gone Wrong

Your advisors work for you, and they should be responsive to your inquiries, needs, and issues. The following are all service-related reasons that show a problem in the relationship; if you have experienced even one of them, you should consider whether it was a "firing offense."

- There is unexplained/unexpected account activity.

- You don't completely understand the advisor's actions.
- Promised services are not delivered.
- Charges and fees are higher than anticipated, or there are hidden costs you were unaware of.
- Key information is only revealed when questioned or when trouble is evident.
- The advisor expresses disappointment or anger over your decision NOT to follow some piece of advice.
- There are disagreements over core strategies/beliefs.
- There are unpleasant surprises.
- The advisor shows a lack of time and interest, as if he was more anxious to get you as a client than to serve you now.
- Your spouse or partner distrusts the advisor (especially if you picked the advisor, and the mistrust from your significant other has increased over time).
- Your advisor is thinking only "inside the box," so that your service is more one-size-fits-all than personalized for you.
- The advisor treats you more like an account number than a client or friend.
- The advisor fails to meet the expectations you set out during the hiring process.

Step 2: Redefine the Relationship

You have explained what the trouble is. Now set out to fix it.

Don't change your expectations, but make sure your hopes for the relationship are reasonable. It would be *unreasonable* to expect an investment advisor to deliver above-average market returns when you don't allow her to buy securities that take sufficient risk to deliver those gains; it would be *reasonable* for the planner or broker to suggest ways of diversifying risks and goosing yields without putting your financial future in jeopardy.

Smart Investor Tip

Your expectations, to this point, have not been met, but don't change them. Simply make sure your hopes for the relationship are reasonable.

It is unreasonable to expect a tax preparer to cut your taxes by taking deductions he isn't comfortable claiming, but it is desirable to discuss all manner of deductions for which you qualify, even if a particular credit or benefit is worth just a few bucks. After all, it's your money.

You can even re-examine the basic levels of service being provided. If your insurance company raises premiums when they should be falling due to a clean driving record, consistently sends incorrect bills, and is just plain sloppy, you have a right to ask the agent to clear up the problems. You never would have anticipated these problems when buying coverage, and they are not the agent's fault, but if the agent won't go to bat for you and save you the hassle, you need to redefine the relationship.

Return on investment is the hardest area to judge. Presumably, you and your broker or financial planner set targets based on your investment profile. But many advisors are chastised by customers not for missing return targets but for not "beating the market." The Standard & Poor's 500 Index has no way of knowing when you are retiring or the kids are off to college, and a diversified portfolio—built to stay afloat when the market is imploding—will inherently lag the market during bullish runs. If you hired a planner or broker to help you retire or put the kids through school, and to manage your money in good times and bad, don't whack him because he did his job but you hate lagging the market during its hottest times.

If you no longer believe the advisor has the acumen to reach the investment targets you set together—and your unhappiness stems from the advisor's actions, and not from a downturn in the market that brings everyone down—then a change is in order. But when the stock market was imploding in 2008, I heard from a lot of consumers upset that their advisor hadn't completely sidestepped the carnage; they were down 10 percent in a year when the market was off more than 30 percent, yet they were still upset with the advisor's inability to make money in all market conditions. That's unreasonable and irrational.

Revisit what you sought out when you first signed on as a client and review how your needs have changed and how you see things differently now that you have had time to get used to having an advisor.

Make a list of what you want from the advisor, including the services you currently receive and the areas in which he or she falls short. Prioritize your wants, giving the advisor a chance to see how the service being provided is not meeting your key needs.

Realize, too, that the advisor may opt to drop you as a client, because she handles everyone the same way and you want services that are outside of that box. That's not necessarily a bad thing, particularly if some of your payment is refunded to salve your dissatisfaction.

If the advisor is willing to refocus his or her efforts to keep you as a client, set a specific trial period. During that period, say six months or a year, you should . . .

Step 3: Sharpen the Ax

There's a bit of advance preparation before you fire an advisor. You may need to have records transferred or to take possession of some securities; you will want a place for those records and securities.

You may also need to be prepared to move some money around. Quit your brokerage firm, for example, and you may need to pull money out of mutual funds run by the house; even if you can keep the money in place while you search for a new advisor, you may not want to (since those investments may have been part of your problem with the broker). Transferring assets is a pain; make sure you know the rules and can avoid screw-ups that could cost you at tax time. Learn the rules involved before making a change; get the necessary information so your new advisor—whenever he is hired—can help you move your money.

Once you are prepared and you don't see the situation getting better, it's time to . . .

Did You Get a "Happiness Letter"?

If you work with an advisor from a big, name-brand firm and the company sends you a letter, out of the blue, to make sure you are happy with your counselor, check your pockets to see if your wallet is missing.

As mentioned in Chapter 8, a "happiness letter" sounds like a good thing, but in reality when a financial services firm wants you to acknowledge in writing that you are happy and satisfied with its services, it's a red flag.

The firm expects its customers to be pleased with the service they get, so its reason for sending a "happiness letter" is because someone at the firm fears that activity patterns in your account are awry, that you are trading, investing, or acting—with the advisor's help—in a fashion that might not be best suited for you. Sign and return the letter indicating your happiness and that testimony can and will be used against you in court; if you subsequently have a problem, allege that the broker was churning your account, or that the planner was selling you investments you did not fully understand, the firm will show that it asked you if everything was all right and that you said you were pleased with the service you received.

It is possible that the firm is simply doing quality control, but any sudden request for your feelings should be viewed as a danger sign, not a welcome mat. Review your account immediately to make sure everything is in keeping with the action plan you established with the advisor. If you see actions or investments you do not completely understand, you should immediately call the firm to arrange a meeting with the advisor and a supervisor; if the firm feared a problem in your account—which is why it sent you the letter in the first place—it will want to resolve any dispute before formal filings are made.

And even if you love the advisor's service today, you might want to consider whether you truly want that signed, dated note in your file, because it can only be used against you. You can always praise your advisor privately, or chat with their boss in passing, without putting anything in writing in response to a more formal inquiry.

Step 4: Drop the Ax

The moment you are not satisfied with an advisor's performance, start preparing for this action. For an advisory relationship to work, you must trust and have confidence in the advisor and her abilities; if either of those elements is gone, so too is the advisor.

You can't get out of your obligations—the listing contract with a real estate agent, the management fee with a planner, surrender charges on an annuity or the unexpired term of a bank certificate of deposit—but you can be out the door the moment it can be opened. Moreover, if you believe the situation is desperate, examine the cost of an early escape, such as paying early withdrawal fees, surrender penalties, or simply foregoing services that you paid for but no longer want; in some rare cases, it is worth making your changes at all costs immediately, rather than letting time compound mistakes.

The actual dismissal should be clean and concise. If you need to notify the firm in writing, make the note short and say only that you no longer intend to use the advisor's services after a specific date, by which time you want possession of all monies, pertinent records, and paperwork. Even if you expect to file an arbitration case or a lawsuit, keep that out of your note; handle the business at hand and be as bloodless as possible.

If the advisor or a supervisor wants to discuss your decision, be brief and firm. This is when the situation can get ugly and emotional, and you don't need that. Worse yet would be to wind up like Caroline and the hairdresser, rushing right back into a situation that you already have deemed untenable. You should not be badgered, pestered, or otherwise bothered about making a decision that is clearly in your own best interest.

Having dispatched with the advisor, you are ready to:

Step 5: Hire a Replacement

If you did not go through the full-blown process described in this book while picking the departed advisor, change your interview and preparation style.

If you picked the departed helper by the book, you need to start over again and try to figure out how to avoid making the same mistake twice. Ask yourself what went wrong with the relationship and what impressed you during the interviews that failed to materialize later.

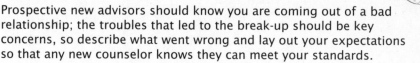

Smart Investor Tip

Prospective new advisors should know you are coming out of a bad relationship; the troubles that led to the break-up should be key concerns, so describe what went wrong and lay out your expectations so that any new counselor knows they can meet your standards.

Make sure prospective new advisors know you are coming out of a bad relationship; express your concerns and describe what went wrong and what you expect from a new counselor. Ask how they would react in a situation like the one that ruined your last advisory relationship and whether they consider your expectations unreasonable. Be honest about the circumstances so an advisor can pull out of the running if you sound like her nightmare client.

Your new advisor should review the work of the departed player, keeping whatever is worthwhile. It's especially important to justify investment changes, as such decisions have tax consequences and may be motivated by self-interest (the new broker gets commissions when you sell the old stocks and purchase new ones, creating an incentive to say stocks purchased under your previous brokerage relationship were dogs).

The new relationship comes with no guarantees that it will be better than the old one, but if you learn from experience and hire by the book, you should not have to go through many advisors to find one you can keep for a lifetime.

Key Points

- Leave the emotions and personal feelings out of your evaluations—if your advisor isn't doing the job and can't change her ways to make you happy, she has to go. Make a clean break and move on.

- If the advisor deserves a second chance, give him a plan of action that, if followed, would make you satisfied or, even, happy with his services. If he can't follow the plan, give him the boot.

- Don't let a bad experience turn you off completely to hiring advisors. If you need help—if your personal circumstances and knowledge have not changed and don't seem likely to make you a good self-advisor—then you still need help. Don't be bashful about getting it, just be careful.

The Last Word

If you do not change direction, you may end up where you are heading.
—Lao Tzu

You bought this book for a reason; now it's time to put it to work. The secret my publisher is glad you did not know before picking this book out to help you is that virtually every professional group of advisors has some sort of "interview questionnaire" that they suggest will help you pick someone good. Typically, you're asking eight to ten questions, using those lists.

What you got out of this book was a lot more questions—including many that make the advisory groups wince—and a guide on what to expect in the answers, but you will only get your money's worth if you ask them of advisors and references. By not just asking the common questions, by delving much deeper, you raise the bar for the advisor and the relationship. Some advisors hate that, because it makes them work a lot harder to get your money in house; they don't deserve your money at all.

Good advisors not only like a thorough discussion of the issues, they relish it. They'll take your good questions and put them into a list of FAQs (frequently asked questions) to make sure everyone gets his or her answer.

Where you go from here depends on you. It can be as simple as "get some names, interview one, and go forward," but I hope it will be much more than that, that you will do things "by the book."

In some respects, that method is overkill. Presumably, people who found the free 10-question interview forms online have had some measure of success. I just like to go beyond "some measure" and get to a "reasonable degree of certainty." I can't guarantee that the process will deliver good relationships, fabulous investment results, and complete avoidance of scoundrels, but I can say that the odds of achieving those outcomes go up once you weed out the personality mismatches, the boobs, the incompetents, and the rogues. If nothing else, following the methodology should make you more comfortable with the advisors you hire, and your increased comfort will go a long way to feeling good about how things turn out.

At the same time, you do not need to follow every suggestion or ask every last question in order to determine an advisor's qualifications and establish a reasonable comfort level. Just as you may have skipped around in the book to seek out specific bits of information, so can you pick and choose the type of data you get from an advisor. Know the shortcuts you are taking in the process and take them only if they ultimately lead you to the same place.

In journalism, there's an old saying about what you take for granted and what you research. It goes like this: "If your mother says she loves you, check it out."

That's the approach I hope you will take with advisors. Be thorough, and don't take the important stuff for granted.

Whether you use just a few suggestions from this book or carry your copy into an interview and make an advisor answer every last question, remember one thing: As the client, you are entitled to overkill. You are allowed to worry, fret, and sweat the small stuff.

It's your money. No one will ever be more interested in protecting it and managing it properly than you are. Use your knowledge to make the most of it; hire advisors who help you protect it and make more of it.

Good luck on that journey.

Index